ECSTASY AND E

The Institute of Ismaili Studies
Ismaili Heritage Series, 6
General Editor: Farhad Daftary

Previously published titles:

1. Paul E. Walker, *Abū Ya'qūb al-Sijistānī: Intellectual Missionary* (1996)
2. Heinz Halm, *The Fatimids and their Traditions of Learning* (1997)
3. Paul E. Walker, *Ḥamīd al-Dīn al-Kirmānī: Ismaili Thought in the Age of al-Ḥākim* (1999)
4. Alice C. Hunsberger, *Nasir Khusraw, The Ruby of Badakhshan: A Portrait of the Persian Poet, Traveller and Philosopher* (2000)
5. Farouk Mitha, *Al-Ghazālī and the Ismailis: A Debate on Reason and Authority in Medieval Islam* (2001)

Ecstasy and Enlightenment

The Ismaili Devotional Literature of South Asia

ALI S. ASANI

I.B.Tauris *Publishers*
LONDON • NEW YORK
in association with
The Institute of Ismaili Studies
LONDON

Published in 2002 by I.B.Tauris & Co Ltd
6 Salem Rd, London W2 4BU
175 Fifth Avenue, New York NY 10010
www.ibtauris.com

in association with The Institute of Ismaili Studies
42–44 Grosvenor Gardens, London SW1W 0EB
www.iis.ac.uk

In the United States of America and in Canada distributed by
St Martin's Press, 175 Fifth Avenue, New York NY 10010

ISBN 1 86064 758 8 HB
1 86064 828 2 PB

A full CIP record for this book is available from the British Library
A full CIP record for this book is available from the Library of Congress

Library of Congress catalog card: available

Typeset in ITC New Baskerville by Hepton Books, Oxford
Printed and bound in Great Britain by MPG Books Ltd, Bodmin

The Institute of Ismaili Studies

The Institute of Ismaili Studies was established in 1977 with the object of promoting scholarship and learning on Islam, in the historical as well as contemporary contexts, and a better understanding of its relationship with other societies and faiths.

The Institute's programmes encourage a perspective which is not confined to the theological and religious heritage of Islam, but seek to explore the relationship of religious ideas to broader dimensions of society and culture. The programmes thus encourage an interdisciplinary approach to the materials of Islamic history and thought. Particular attention is also given to issues of modernity that arise as Muslims seek to relate their heritage to the contemporary situation.

Within the Islamic tradition, the Institute's programmes seek to promote research on those areas which have, to date, received relatively little attention from scholars. These include the intellectual and literary expressions of Shiʿism in general, and Ismailism in particular.

In the context of Islamic societies, the Institute's programmes are informed by the full range and diversity of cultures in which Islam is practised today, from the Middle East, South and Central Asia and Africa to the industrialized societies of the West, thus taking into consideration the variety of contexts which shape the ideals, beliefs and practices of the faith.

These objectives are realized through concrete programmes and activities organized and implemented by various departments of the Institute. The Institute also collaborates periodically, on a programme-specific basis, with other institutions of learning in the United Kingdom and abroad.

The Institute's academic publications fall into several distinct and interrelated categories:

1. Occasional papers or essays addressing broad themes of the relationship between religion and society, with special reference to Islam.
2. Monographs exploring specific aspects of Islamic faith and culture, or the contributions of individual Muslim figures or writers.
3. Editions or translations of significant primary or secondary texts.
4. Translations of poetic or literary texts which illustrate the rich heritage of spiritual, devotional and symbolic expressions in Muslim history.
5. Works on Ismaili history and thought, and the relationship of the Ismailis to other traditions, communities and schools of thought in Islam.
6. Proceedings of conferences and seminars sponsored by the Institute.
7. Bibliographical works and catalogues which document manuscripts, printed texts and other source materials.

This book falls into category five listed above.

In facilitating these and other publications, the Institute's sole aim is to encourage original research and analysis of relevant issues. While every effort is made to ensure that the publications are of a high academic standard, there is naturally bound to be a diversity of views, ideas and interpretations. As such, the opinions expressed in these publications are to be understood as belonging to their authors alone.

Ismaili Heritage Series

A major Shiʿi Muslim community, the Ismailis have had a long and eventful history. Scattered in many regions of the world, in Asia, Africa, Europe and North America, the Ismailis have elaborated diverse intellectual and literary traditions in different languages. On two occasions they had states of their own, the Fatimid caliphate and the Nizari State of Iran and Syria during the Alamut period. While pursuing particular religio-political aims, the leaders of these Ismaili states also variously encouraged intellectual, scientific, artistic and commercial activities.

Until recently, the Ismailis were studied and judged almost exclusively on the basis of the evidence collected or fabricated by their enemies, including the bulk of the medieval heresiographers and polemicists who were hostile towards the Shiʿa in general and the Ismailis among them in particular. These authors in fact treated the Shiʿi interpretations of Islam as expressions of heterodoxy or even heresy. As a result, a 'black legend' was gradually developed and put into circulation in the Muslim world to discredit the Ismailis and their interpretation of Islam. The Christian Crusaders and their occidental chroniclers, who remained almost completely ignorant of Islam and its internal divisions, disseminated their own myths of the Ismailis, which came to be accepted in Europe as true descriptions of Ismaili teachings and practices. Modern Orientalists, too, have studied the Ismailis on the basis of these hostile sources and fanciful accounts of medieval times. Thus, legends and misconceptions have continued to surround the Ismailis through the twentieth century.

In more recent decades, however, the field of Ismaili studies has been revolutionized due to the recovery and study of genuine Ismaili sources on a large scale – manuscript materials which in different ways survived the destruction of the Fatimid and Nizari Ismaili libraries. These sources, representing diverse literary traditions produced in Arabic, Persian and Indic languages, had hitherto been secretly preserved in private collections in India, Central Asia, Iran, Afghanistan, Syria and the Yemen.

Modern progress in Ismaili studies has already necessitated a complete re-writing of the history of the Ismailis and their contributions to Islamic civilization. It has now become clear that the Ismailis founded important libraries and institutions of learning such as al-Azhar and the Dar al-ʿIlm in Cairo, while some of their learned *daʿis* or missionaries developed unique intellectual traditions amalgamating their theological doctrine with a diversity of philosophical traditions in complex metaphysical systems. The Ismaili patronage of learning and extension of hospitality to non-Ismaili scholars was maintained even in such difficult times as the Alamut period, when the community was preoccupied with its survival in an extremely hostile milieu.

The Ismaili Heritage Series, published under the auspices of the Department of Academic Research and Publications of The Institute of Ismaili Studies, aims to make available to wide audiences the results of modern scholarship on the Ismailis and their rich intellectual and cultural heritage, as well as certain aspects of their more recent history and achievements.

For my mother,
Shirinkhanu Asani,
and in loving memory of my father,
Sultaan Ali Asani.

Table of Contents

Illustrations and Tables xii
Foreword by Professor Annemarie Schimmel xv
Acknowledgements xix
Editorial Note xxi

1. Introduction: The Nizari Ismaili Tradition in South Asia 1
2. The *Ginān*s as Devotional Literature: Their Origins, Characteristics and Themes 25
3. Bridal Symbolism in the *Ginān*s 54
4. The *Gīt* Tradition: A Testimony of Love 71
5. Reflections on Authority and Authorship of the *Ginān*s 82
6. The Khojkī Script: A Legacy of Ismaili Islam in the Subcontinent 100
7. The Khojkī Script and its Manuscript Tradition 124

Appendix: Translations of Selected Devotional and Mystical *Ginān*s 153
Bibliography 169
General Index 177
*Index of Ginān*s 184

Illustrations and Tables

The illustrations in this book are from the Khojkī manuscripts collection in the library of The Institute of Ismaili Studies and are identified below by the references given in brackets.

Illustrations

I. From *Kalām-i Mawlā*, a Hindustani translation written in Khojkī script of an Arabic-Persian poem attributed to Imam ʿAlī (KH 42, p. 22, dated 1851, copied by Khoja Alarākhiā Kurjī of Bombay).

II. From *Būjh Niranjan*, a *ginān* attributed to Pīr Ṣadr al-Dīn, from a Khojkī manuscript (KM 117, folio 173a, copied in late 19th/early 20th century).

III. From *Hun re pīasī tere darshan kī*, a *ginān* attributed to Sayyid Khān, from a Khojkī manuscript (KH 84, p. 259, dated 1867, copied by Khoja Jāfar Dhālānī).

IV. Arabic text written in Khojkī script of the 'Throne-verse' (*ayāt al-kursī*) from the Qur'an (2:255), followed by invocatory prayers (KH 101, pp. 90–1, copied in late 19th century).

V. Persian text written in Khojkī script of *Pandiyāt-i jawānmardī*, attributed to the Imam Mustanṣir-bi'llāh II (d. 885/1480), (KH 48, vol. 3, dated 1802–1830, in Shah Bandar, Sindh).

vi. On the left: the *Shahāda* inscribed in Arabic within a circle, surrounded by invocations to Allāh, Muḥammad, ʿAlī, Fāṭima, Ḥasan and Ḥusayn. On the right: text of *Nāde ʿAlī*, an invocatory prayer addressed to Imam ʿAlī, with the representation of his sword *dhu'l-fiqār* (from a Khojkī manuscript, KH 21, pp. 308–9, dated 1817–1823, copied in Surat, Gujarat, by multiple scribes including the daughter of Pīr Ghulām ʿAlī Shāh).

Tables

1. Khojkī script: Vowel system (early 20th century) 146
2. Khojkī script: Consonants (early 20th century) 147

Foreword

Who among the orientalists can tell you what *ginān*s are? How many scholars of Islam who specialise in the classical fields of Arabic, Persian and Turkish know of the rites and customs current in the Ismaili community and its devotional literature? Scholars of Islamic literature are certainly aware of the great medieval poet Nāṣir-i Khusraw, who excelled in philosophical thought and whose poetry was considered by a leading expert like E.G. Browne as ranking among the finest expressions of Persian literature, worthy of being rendered into a European language. And Nāṣir's thoughts even impressed a modern Muslim poet-philosopher, Muḥammad Iqbal, who introduced him in his *Jāvīdnāma* (1932) in the 'Sphere of Paradise.' Perhaps some linguists may have heard of the Ismaili literature in Burushaski, the difficult language spoken in the mountainous region of Hunza in northern Pakistan – but *ginān*s? What are they?

I was lucky to encounter the *ginān* literature during my early years teaching at Harvard where my first Ismaili student, Gulshan Khakee, wrote her doctoral dissertation about the *Dasa Avātara*, a long poem in which Muslim and Hindu traditions seem to merge as the poet represents Ismaili Islam as the culmination and fulfilment of the Hindu religious tradition. From that time onwards the topic of the *ginān*s never ceased to fascinate me although it was difficult to decipher and properly understand many of these poems. Yet, in some of the *ginān*s which I came to know, thanks to Ali S. Asani, the similarity of expression with Sindhi mystical folksongs struck me immediately. Indeed, Sindhi, in its earliest known form seems to be one of the most important vehicles for the preservation of the *ginān*s. It has been claimed that some of the earliest known *ginān*s, ascribed to Pīr Shams and his circle, may be the oldest specimens of the Sindhi language. Gujarati as well was to play a major role in their formation. Many of the *ginān*s are sung in a mixed idiom, for as they were in the first place oral literature, words could be changed in the course of time – a singer might explain an unfamiliar word by something better known to his audience, or change the rhyme – exactly as it has happened in every early culture. This process is called in German *Zersingen*, that is, to sing a verse so often and under different circumstances that it becomes 'threadbare' and changes colour to a certain extent. Such changes reflect the living presence in the community of certain beloved songs.

Ali Asani's scholarship has focused on the development of the *ginān*s from the viewpoint of strict philology; but after carefully dealing with the formal aspects of this literature he shows the particular role of the *ginān*s in the piety of the Ismaili *jamāʿat* (community) of South Asian origin. They reflect a warm, loving feeling for their *Hazir Imam*, the current Imam of the Ismailis, and it is touching to see how even modern forms of devotional literature never cease to express this deep love and the longing for his *darshan* (vision). Likewise the didactic *ginān*s and the more theologically important *ginān*s are highly interesting and reflect the community's ideals as well as the perhaps unconscious attempt to participate in the overall Indian tradition, exactly as Sufi poetry in Sind and in the Punjab is replete with words and images reminiscent of the songs of the Hindu *bhakta*s (hence the aversion of shariʿa-minded theologians to mystical poetry despite the warm, tender feelings that permeate it).

The *ginān*s have been the precious possession of the Ismaili community for centuries, but, as Ali Asani shows, changes in their form and function are also visible. Thus, the standardisation of the texts in Gujarati script in the early 20th century produced some changes which were barely noticed by those who did not know the earlier tradition. Yet, the transliteration of the *ginān*s into Gujarati script, or even in the Arabic or Latin alphabet, was unavoidable because the knowledge of Khojkī, the script traditionally used to record them, was rapidly disappearing among the Ismailis. Among the most important contributions in the present book are the chapters on the Khojkī script – a script that can be deciphered nowadays only by a handful of scholars. To draw the readers' attention to the enormous difficulties offered by this mercantile script, that resembles a kind of shorthand, is necessary as it is useful not only for those interested in the spiritual contents of the *ginān*s but for all those who deal with the general history of writing and the role of the script in different cultural traditions.

Ali Asani's book is a treasure trove for everyone who is interested in Ismaili history and thought. It offers important material not only to the members of the community but also to scholars from various branches – be they Islamicists, Indologists, sociologists or historians of religion – for the *ginān*s are placed here in the context of the general history of religion and not seen as an isolated phenomenon.

This book combines erudition with love for the tradition, a strictly scholarly approach with a deep understanding of people's religious feelings. I hope that it will help foster a better understanding of important aspects of the devotional literature of Indo-Pakistani Ismailis, their history and their unfaltering love for their Imam.

Annemarie Schimmel
Bonn, 2001

Acknowledgements

The essays in this book are the result of my long-standing interest in Ismaili devotional literature, a personal and academic involvement that began many years ago when I was a student at Harvard University. During my years of study, I was honoured and privileged to have received generous support from His Highness Prince Karīm Aga Khan. For providing this crucial support early in my career, when there was so little scholarship on the *ginān*s, I remain most grateful to His Highness.

Among the faculty at Harvard who were crucial in helping me develop my ideas, Professor Annemarie Schimmel provided not only guidance but took a personal interest in much of my work on the devotional literature of the Ismaili community. Her vast knowledge and scholarship on Islamic literatures have been truly inspirational. I am also indebted to Professors William A. Graham and Diana Eck for their encouragement, support and friendship over the years. Beyond Harvard, various scholars at other institutions have also been most kind and generous with their assistance. Professor Azim Nanji, formerly of the University of Florida and currently Director of The Institute of Ismaili Studies; Dr Aziz Esmail, a Governor of the same Institute; Professor Christopher Shackle of the University of London; Professor Peter Gaeffke of University of Pennsylvania; and Professor Charlotte Vaudeville of the Sorbonne, have all helped in various ways in the development of my work. My students at Harvard and at the Institute in London, where I have for several years offered a seminar on Ismaili devotional literatures, have provided a patient forum in which to articulate many important ideas and concepts. To all of them I express my deep appreciation.

Over the years, many colleagues and friends have also played a crucial role. Here I can mention only a few: Chottu Lakhani, Zawahir Noorally (Moir), Hossein Khanmohamed, Ghulamhyder Alidina, Françoise Mallison, John Hawley, Joel Brenner, Wayne Eastman, Fariyal Ross-Sheriff, Mali and Lutaf Dhanidina, Carol Alexander, Anaar Kanji and Kamal Taj. I would like in particular to thank Michael Currier not only for the many hours he has spent editing my work, but also for his constant and loyal friendship and unending encouragement of my scholarship.

For their assistance in compiling this particular volume, I acknowledge with gratitude the hard work and editorial efforts of Kutub Kassam and Nadia Holmes in the Department of Academic Research and Publications at the Institute of Ismaili Studies.

My eternal gratitude to my parents, my brothers Muhammad and Karim, and my sister Shahenshahbanu, who have been unfailing pillars of support during my academic career. I am particularly conscious of the depth of gratitude I owe to my parents. My late father, Sultaan Ali Asani, was the first to encourage me to undertake my studies on the *ginān*s. It is to his memory and to my mother, Shirinkhanu Asani, for her love and kindness through the years, that I dedicate this book.

Editorial Note

This volume of seven essays brings together a number of key writings by Professor Ali S. Asani focusing on the Nizari Ismaili tradition of devotional literature in South Asia. With the exception of the introductory chapter on 'The Nizari Ismaili Tradition in South Asia' and the final chapter on 'The Khojkī Script of Sind and its Manuscript Tradition,' both of which appear here for the first time, the other five articles were originally published in academic journals or collective volumes. In reprinting them here, the permission of the following publishers is gratefully acknowledged:

Egbert Forsten, Gröningen, and École Française d'Extrême-Orient, Paris, for 'The *Ginān* Literature of the Ismailis of Indo-Pakistan: Its Origins, Characteristics and Themes,' in D. Eck and F. Mallison, eds, *Devotion Divine: Folk Sources of the Bhakti Tradition* (1991), pp. 1–18.

Cambridge University Press, Cambridge, for 'The Ismaili *Ginān*s as Devotional Literature,' in R.S. McGregor, ed., *Devotional Literature in South Asia: Current Research, 1985–88* (1992); and 'The Ismaili *Ginān*s: Reflections on Authority and Authorship,' in Farhad Daftary, ed., *Mediaeval Ismaʿili History and Thought* (1996), pp. 265–80.

Peter Lang, New York and Bern, for 'Bridal Symbolism in Ismāʿīlī Mystical Literature of Indo-Pakistan,' in Robert Herrera, ed., *Mystics of the Book: Themes, Topics and Typologies* (1993), pp. 389–404, and 'A Testimony of Love: The *Gīt* Tradition of the Nizari Ismailis,' in A. Giese and J.C. Bürgel, ed., *God is Beautiful and He Loves Beauty* (Festschrift in Honour of Annemarie Schimmel), (1993), pp. 39–51.

The Journal of the American Oriental Society, for 'The Khojkī Script: A Legacy of Ismaili Islam in the Indo-Pakistan Subcontinent,' 107, 3 (1987), pp. 439–49.

As most of these essays first appeared in the form of independent articles in different journals and books over several years, the author has taken the opportunity of their republication to revise and update them, where necessary. The collection of these essays in one volume has also required the reorganisation of certain material and the application of a consistent system of translation, transliteration and referencing. A few terms from Arabic, Persian or Indic languages which have become part of the English lexicon have not been transliterated. In most cases, dates are given from both the Islamic and Christian (Common Era) calendars.

The following abbreviations are used for certain periodicals and encyclopaedias cited frequently in the Notes and Bibliography.

BRIIS	*Bulletin of the Royal Institute of Inter-Faith Studies*
EI2	*Encyclopaedia of Islam (2nd edition)*
JAOS	*Journal of the American Oriental Society*
JAS	*Journal of Asian Studies*
JASB	*Journal of the Asiatic Society of Bengal*
JBBRAS	*Journal of the Bombay Branch of the Royal Asiatic Society*
JIMMA	*Journal of the Institute of Muslim Minority Affairs*
JRAS	*Journal of the Royal Asiatic Society*
SEI	*Shorter Encyclopaedia of Islam*

Remember the name of the Lord
And light will emerge within you;
Taste the nectar of love
And ecstasy will overwhelm you.

Translated from *Candrabhan*,
a *ginān* attributed to Pīr Shams

1

Introduction: The Nizari Ismaili Tradition in South Asia

This book is a compilation of essays concerning the literary tradition of the Nizari Ismailis of India and Pakistan. These essays introduce readers to various aspects of a rich and unique devotional literature that has, until recently, received little or no attention from students of Islamic or South Asian literatures. Who are the Nizari Ismailis of India and Pakistan? Among the subcontinent's Muslim communities, the Nizari Ismailis are well known for the extensive social, educational and philanthropic activities of their Imams known as the Aga Khans and the various institutions they have established to promote social, economic and cultural development in the region; as well as the community's prominence in financial and trade circles, and for the highly structured nature of its institutions and organizations. Aga Khan III Sir Sulṭan Muḥammad Shāh, the Ismaili Imam from 1885 to 1957, played a prominent leadership role among the Muslims of pre-partition India and in the Pakistan movement. He also served for a short time as the President of the League of Nations, the predecessor to the modern United Nations. Moreover, Muhammad Ali Jinnah, the founding father of Pakistan, also had his roots in this community.

In terms of religious doctrine, the Nizari Ismailis, in common with other Shiʿi Muslims, hold that upon the death of the Prophet Muḥammad guidance of the Muslim community continued in his progeny through a succession of Imams descended from his daughter Fāṭima and his cousin and son-in-law ʿAlī b. Abī Ṭālib. Over the course of time, the Shiʿi Muslims crystallized into different factions, mainly based on disputes over succession to the office of Imam and later over differing interpretations of the nature of the institution of Imamate. The Ismailis derive their name from the fact that, following the death of Imam Jaʿfar al-Ṣādiq in 148/765, they supported the cause of his eldest son Ismāʿīl, while the alternative group, who came eventually to be called the Ithnāʿasharīs (Twelvers), followed the line of his brother, Mūsā al-Kāẓim. Similarly, when in 487/1094 there was another dispute concerning succession to the Fatimid Ismaili Imam-caliph al-Mustanṣir, the Nizari Ismailis were those who supported the claims of his son Nizār (d.488/1095), while the Mustaʿlī Ismailis followed his younger brother, al-Mustaʿlī.[1] At present, the Nizari Ismailis are the only Shiʿi community with a living Imam in the person of Prince Karīm al-Ḥusaynī, Aga Khan IV (b.1936). The Ismailis believe that he is a direct descendant of the Prophet Muḥammad, being their 49th Imam through the line of the Imams ʿAlī, Ismāʿīl and Nizār. As *Ḥāẓir Imām* (Present Imam) or *Imām-i Zamān* (Imam of the Age) he has the sole right to interpret the faith and provide authoritative guidance to his followers on spiritual and worldly matters. It is on account of their allegiance to the Aga Khan that the Nizari Ismailis are sometimes called 'Aga Khanis' by other Muslims, a term that the Ismailis never use for themselves.

On the basis of differences in ethnicity, cultural traditions and historical evolution, we can, at present, distinguish two distinct groupings among the Nizari Ismailis of the subcontinent. The first, centred in northern Pakistan, particularly around Hunza, has been strongly influenced by its connections with the Central Asian world; the second has been historically and culturally associated with the western regions of the subcontinent, specifically Gujarat, Sind and Punjab. The essays in this volume focus primarily on the literary traditions of the second group. Members of this group have also been popularly known as Khojas, Shamsis, Momnas or Satpanthis.

The term *satpanth* means 'the true path,' the name under which Nizari Ismailism was preached to them in the past. Today the Nizari Ismailis of the Satpanthi group are found scattered in most parts of modern India, Pakistan and Bangladesh. They are specially concentrated in western India around Bombay, in Gujarat and Kutch, and in the Sind region of Pakistan. Many have also migrated to various areas in the Indian Ocean region, in particular East Africa, and more recently to North America and the United Kingdom.

The Satpanth Ismaili Tradition and its Contexts: Ismaili, Indo-Muslim and Indic

The development of the Nizari Ismaili Satpanth tradition in South Asia can best be understood if it is considered within three overlapping cultural contexts. The first is a transnational or global one, for it places the tradition within the broader historical context of Ismailism as it has manifested itself and evolved in many different cultural areas beyond the Indian subcontinent. Thus, through their institutions such as the *daʿwa* (mission) and the Imamate, the Ismailis of South Asia were connected as early as the 4th/10th century to historic centres of Ismaili power in Egypt and later in Iran, where their Imams once resided and from where they directed the affairs of their followers. While transnational or global influences on the development of Nizari Ismailism in the subcontinent have been important through the centuries, they have now become particularly significant as the Nizari Ismailis of the region are inextricably linked to Ismaili communities in other parts of the world through their central administrative headquarters at Aiglemont in France, the residence of the current Imam.

The second context is an Indo-Muslim one, placing the Satpanth Ismaili tradition within the overall framework of the growth of Islamic institutions and movements in the Indian subcontinent as well as the establishment of political rule in the region by various Muslim groups. From the 5th/11th century onwards, when Muslim dynasties of Central Asian or Turkish origin gained political power over parts of northern and western India, several

Sunni rulers deemed it necessary to physically eliminate Ismailis whom they considered to be heretics and political dissidents.[2] Obviously, such persecution has had significant consequences on the character and nature of the Nizari Ismailism. Unable to declare their tenets openly, adherents were forced to observe *taqiyya* (precautionary dissimulation). On the other hand, the tradition has been equally influenced by its complex and often enigmatic relations with other Muslim religious groups in the region, particularly various Sufi orders. In many instances, to circumvent possible persecution, Ismaili *pīr*s (preacher-saints) appear to have adopted the guise of Sufi teachers. Consequently, over time, non-Ismaili populations have come to regard them as holy men in the Sufi tradition rather than in the Ismaili one.[3] The blurring of Sufi and Ismaili boundaries is also evidenced by the strong mystical character of the Satpanth Ismaili literature.[4] And yet, relations between Ismailis and Sufis were not always positive, for we also have evidence of an intense rivalry. For example, in the region of Punjab, particularly around Multan and Ucch, the relationship between the *shaykh*s of the Suhrawardi order and the Ismaili *pīr*s was fraught with friction and tension as a result of competition for adherents.[5] Bahā al-Dīn Zakāriyyā (d. ca. 666/1267), a prominent Suhrawardī *shaykh*, is said to have played an active role in converting Ismaili populations to Sunni Islam.[6] In the contemporary period, Nizari Ismaili identity continues to be profoundly impacted by developments in the Indo-Muslim context, particularly by the emergence of a variety of reform and revivalist movements which promote neo-conservative interpretations of Sunni Islam and monolithic definitions of what it means to be Muslim.[7]

The third context is an Indic one within which the Satpanthi Ismaili tradition interacted at various levels with local cultures and folk traditions as well as indigenous religious groups such as *bhakta*s, *sant*s and Shaivaite ascetics, particularly the Nath *yogi*s. Moreover, the corpus of Satpanth Ismaili religious literature was composed in local Indic languages, utilizing poetic forms drawn from various folk traditions. At the level of religious ideas, symbols and concepts from the Indic context permeate the tradition, albeit in a reformulated form.[8] In some instances, the Ismaili *pīrs*, as representatives of the tradition, are even portrayed as ascetics or *yogīs*. The designation of this context as Indic, rather than Hindu, is deliberate and has a double intent. The first is to avoid the pitfall of several scholars of Satpanth Ismailism who have projected modern notions of religious identity, developed in the context of intense communalism and nationalism in colonial and post-colonial India, onto the study of the past. As Wilfred Cantwell Smith, the prominent historian of religion, has pointed out, the use of the term 'Hindu' for an adherent of a 'world religion' called 'Hinduism' is a 19th-century construct and originated in the attempt by Westerners in India, especially missionaries, to lump together everything that they found that was not 'Islamic' religiously.[9] Indeed, an examination of the use of the term 'Hindu' in the pre-modern milieu within which the Satpanth Ismaili tradition developed reveals that the term had predominantly a geographic, cultural or ethnic nuance rather than a religious one.[10] A second justification for the use of the term 'Indic' is to circumvent another fallacy that perceives the subcontinent's cultures to be intrinsically 'Hindu,' by projecting a specific religious identity onto indigenous cultural elements such as language, literature, art, music and so on. For instance, the Bengali language, widely spoken by a substantial number of Bengali Muslims, has been perceived by some as a 'Hindu' language and, therefore, a non-Islamic one. Suspicion of the vernacular, the Indic, as non-Islamic among contemporary Muslim groups has had significant consequences on the manner in which many Nizari Ismailis currently relate to the Indic context of their faith. As they assert what is perceived to be a normative Islamic base for their identity, there is also a tendency to distance themselves or to de-emphasize the Indic context.[11]

Historically, each of these three contexts has played a profound role in shaping the evolution of the Satpanth Ismaili tradition in South Asia. Their contributions are manifest in the plurality of strands within the tradition, a plurality that has become increasingly difficult to sustain in the present as these contexts are buffeted by, and respond to, the polarizing forces of religious nationalism and communalism and changing conceptions of religious identity. Approaching the study of the Satpanth Ismaili tradition within the framework of these three contexts, and appreciating the dynamic and fluid interaction between them, results in an integrated and finely nuanced understanding of the tradition and its ethos.

For instance, many scholars have remarked on the manner in which various elements of the Satpanth Ismaili tradition are acculturated or indigenized to the Indic milieu. They, however, differ widely in their perceptions of the character of the tradition. The pioneer of modern Ismaili studies, Wladimir Ivanow, conceives of the process of acculturation as one during which 'the meaning and spirit of Islam' were separated 'from its hard Arabic shell'[12] and two cultures [religions] welded together into one 'with remarkable tact and intuition.'[13] Others have judged the process to be a syncretistic phenomenon, a random and irrational combination of elements drawn from different religious traditions and have, therefore, raised questions about the identity of adherents. Hence Bernard Lewis, a historian, declared Nizari Ismailis in South Asia as 'Hindus under a light Muslim veneer.'[14] The late Aziz Ahmad, scholar of several works on Islam in South Asia, grouped them with other 'syncretic' sects of indeterminate identity, declaring that their chief interest is as 'curiosities of mushroom religious growth.'[15] Consequently, he declares that the *ginān*s, the tradition's principal literary genre, 'lack the Islamic personality.'[16] Wilferd Madelung, a prominent scholar of Shiʿi Islam, considers these hymns in which 'Islamic and Hindu beliefs, especially popular Tantric ones, are freely mixed' to be devoid of theological or credal content.[17] To be sure, there have been other scholars who have reacted against such characterizations by raising serious concerns about the nature of the assumptions that underlie them. Azim Nanji, for instance, questions the use of a vague, unilateral concept of Islam or Ismailism as an index to measure the 'Islamic' character of a movement or literature.[18] Tazim Kassam attempts to show that the syncretism in the tradition is not 'a haphazard mishmash' but an intricate weave of Hindu and Ismaili ideas that creates 'a religious and cultural synthesis that sustained the fledgling community.'[19] Dominique-Sila Khan argues that the term 'syncreticism' should be discarded altogether, for it is a convenient label employed when 'one does not have a better understanding of the various factors that led to a contemporary phenomenon' and results in 'a reductionist approach.'[20] Quoting M.I. Khan's work on Islam in Kashmir,[21] she proposes that we should not attempt to analyse a tradition such as Satpanth by 'cramping it into pigeon-holes of "cultural synthesis", "syncretism", "orthodoxy" versus "popular religion".'[22]

Although there is much to commend a critical examination of the manner in which scholars have perceived the phenomenon of acculturation and the categories they use, what most of these analyses overlook are the causes underlying the process of acculturation in the first place. For this, we need to recognize that these causes may, in fact, lie embedded in the triple contexts within which the Satpanth Ismaili tradition developed, namely the Ismaili, the Indo-Muslim and the Indic. When viewed from this perspective, we see that the acculturation of the tradition is a multifaceted phenomenon and reinforced by a set of factors, derived from diverse contexts, yet working in concurrence.

Within the Ismaili context, the impetus to acculturation can be traced to a fundamental impulse within the community wherever it has manifested itself geographically and historically. The Ismailis, in their attempt to understand the central aspect of their faith – the concept of the Imam – have called on the available tools of various philosophical and religious systems, making them highly adaptable to different political and cultural environments. According to Paul Walker, the Ismailis have:

> tolerated a surprising intellectual flexibility and leeway. That in turn has allowed men of various philosophical temperaments to enter into and promote with enthusiasm this particular kind of Islam ... This fact may explain why the Ismaili movement attracted a number of brilliant and creative thinkers and also why others of equal brilliance seem to lean in their direction.[23]

As a result of this ecumenical outlook, multiple motifs from many streams of thought manifest themselves in works by Ismaili authors from the earliest days of the community.[24] For example, the scholarship of Henry Corbin has shown that during the Fatimid period Ismaili thinkers embarked on a remarkable formulation of Islamic, Gnostic, Neoplatonic, Manichaean and Zoroastrian elements to elaborate the concept of the Imam.[25] That the tradition would react similarly to the religious environment of the Indian subcontinent by reformulating the concept of *avatāra*, for example, so that it corresponded with the Ismaili concept of Imam, is, therefore, hardly surprising. The motivation to integrate and reformulate, to acculturate to a different environment is specifically part of the Ismaili legacy.[26]

The Ismailis, however, were not the only Muslims who acculturated their traditions to the local Indian environment. From the very early periods of the development of the Islamic tradition in the subcontinent, we find individual Muslims and religious groups all over the region advocating and promoting the process of acculturation, actively fostering interpretations of Islamic concepts and ideas that could relate to the indigenous religious and cultural contexts.[27] The *shaykhs* of the Chishti Sufi order, for example, promoted the creation of devotional poetry on Islamic mystical themes in local languages which, in its attitudes, expressions and similes, was strikingly similar to that written by poets influenced by the tradition of *bhakti* devotionalism.[28] In several Hindi-speaking areas of northern India, Chishti patronage led to the development of mystical-romantic epics in various Hindi dialects in which local Indian romances were retold by poets who incorporated within them a mystical symbolism embedded in Sufi ideology.[29] Sufi poets in Sind and Punjab appropriated within an Islamic context the theme of *viraha* (love-in-separation) and the symbol of the *virahinī* (the woman longing for her beloved). Both were associated in the Indian devotional tradition with the longing of the *gopīs* (cow-maids), particularly Rādhā, for the *avatāra* Krishna. Following the Indic literary conventions, they represented the human soul as a longing wife or bride pining for her beloved who could be God or the Prophet Muḥammad.[30] Beyond developing a common poetical language, some Sufis also adapted Indian practices of *yoga* and meditation to those inherited from the classical Arabo-Persian tradition. In an identical spirit, the authors of the extensive *puthī* literature of medieval Bengal attempted to incorporate various figures of Indian mythology, particularly Krishna, an *avatāra* of the deity Vishnu, into the historical line of Islamic prophets which ends with the Prophet Muḥammad.[31]

Not all Muslims, however, were comfortable with this assimilationist strand, for it was vigorously opposed by those who espoused an exclusivist, separatistic position. Historically associated with the Muslim ruling and intellectual elite of a Turko-Persian origin, adherents of the separatistic strand desired to maintain their privileged status, as well as their ethnic and cultural difference, by disparaging and rejecting all Indian cultural manifestations. Many of the members of the religious elite, in particular, were anxious to prevent their religious identity from being absorbed and overwhelmed by 'an environment which could only be described as an anathema to their cherished ideal of monotheism.'[32] Typical of the separatistic attitude was the 8th/14th century spiritual leader Makhdūm-i Jahāniyān Jahāngasht (d. 787/1385) who prohibited his Muslim followers from using linguistically Indian terms in reference to God.[33] Similar sentiments were echoed several centuries later by Shāh Walīullāh (d. 1176/1762), an important religious reformer, who demanded that the Muslim community of South Asia substitute the customs of the Arabs for the 'foreign' customs they had adopted.[34]

Viewed within this dichotomy of mutually antagonistic stances among Muslim groups over the appropriate attitude to the local Indian environment and the plethora of Indic religious and cultural manifestations, the Satpanth Ismaili position is evident. Historically the tradition clearly belongs to the assimilationist mode, that is, among those whose vision and interpretation of Islam saw no contradiction between a person's religious identity and their full participation in indigenous culture. The fact that many Sufi groups with whom the Satpanthi Ismailis came into contact shared a similar attitude fostered the development of literary traditions with close parallels, particularly in their use of indigenous languages, symbols and motifs. This commonality was also crucial in circumstances when Satpanthi Ismailis had to conceal their identity by observing *taqiyya* (precautionary dissimulation) as Sufis. More recently, in the colonial and post-colonial periods, as notions of religious identity among the subcontinent's Muslims have undergone a radical change, elements of culture have been viewed increasingly from a purely religious perspective. Consequently, groups that were previously assimilationist have been forced to redefine their attitude vis-à-vis their acculturated forms and practices. As a result, there has been a general shift in attitudes towards the separatist pole. It is within this context that one may see significant changes within the contemporary Nizari Ismaili tradition in South Asia as acculturated modes of expression are modified in response to external changes and pressures. For instance, formulations of the faith within a Vaishnavite frame of reference, which were so central to the tradition for several centuries, have now been replaced by those that utilize universally understood Islamic concepts and emphasize the context of Islamic history.[35]

A significant aspect of the Satpanth Ismaili tradition's acculturation to the Indic milieu was vernacularization. That is to say that the bulk of the tradition's religious literature was written in various vernacular Indic languages and dialects rather than in Arabic or Persian, the traditional languages of Ismaili religious and literary discourse in the Middle East and North Africa. Beyond the use of local languages, Satpanthi literature also employed vernacular literary forms and structures, frequently incorporating imagery and symbols drawn from the Indian environment. Since much Indian devotional poetry in the vernacular is generally sung to specific melodies, the Satpanthi literary tradition also preserved this close association between poetry, music and performance, as is evident in the *ginān*s. We should not attribute the intensely vernacular character of Satpanthi literature to simply the tradition's impulse to acculturate to a local environment. Rather, when viewed from the perspective of the Indic context, we observe that the vernacularization of the Ismaili tradition carried, in fact, a much greater significance, for it mirrored trends in the broader Indian milieu.

The period between the 5th/11th and 11th/17th centuries,

during which the Ismaili tradition emerged and consolidated its identity, was a time of great religious ferment all over northern India. The ferment was a result of several popular counter-cultural movements challenging the long-established brahmanical tradition and its emphasis on the authority of the *brāhmins* (priestly class) and the Vedas. Among these movements, *bhakti* stressed love and devotion to the divine (manifested in the form of specific deities, such as Krishna) as the most efficacious mode of attaining salvation. Another, called the *sant* movement, on account of its association with *sants* (poet-saints of subordinate caste origin), rejected priestly and scriptural authority, the caste system, worship of traditional deities, and rituals and sacrifice, in favour of an interior search for the unqualified Absolute through *sādhanā* (meditation) of the divine name under the guidance of the *satguru* (true preceptor).[36] Under the older brahmanical tradition, religious life was dominated by the performance of numerous rites, rituals and strict adherence to *dharma* (correct conduct) within the caste system. Now, as a result of the *bhakti* and *sant* movements, these traditional elements were gradually abandoned in favour of a more egalitarian view that stressed the importance of personal religious experience and interiorized forms of religion over religious authority and ritual.

Integral to the challenge of the *bhakti* and the *sant* movements to the classical brahmanical tradition was the abandonment of Sanskrit, the official language of ritual worship monopolized by the priestly *brāhmins*, in favour of the vernaculars as means of religious expression. Probably inspired by the vernacular compositions of a small, though influential, group of wandering ascetics (the Nath yogis), *bhakti* and *sant* poets began writing poems in various local languages and dialects. Thus, poetry in the vernacular became the principal medium through which they attracted a great deal of mass support and effectively managed to undermine the brahmanical system. Along with newly emerging regional polities in the region which also patronized vernacular languages,[37] these religious movements contributed to the phenomenal blossoming of literatures in a wide range of vernaculars from all over the subcontinent.

Vernacular languages were preferred as vehicles of religious literature by not only the *bhakti* and *sant* movements but also, as we have seen, by the Ismailis and several Indian Sufi groups who employed local languages for composing mystical verse. This common feature among the traditions is, in fact, indicative of a deeper and more complex interrelationship. Increasingly, recent scholarship reveals that the *bhaktas*, *sants*, Sufis and Ismailis were all interconnected, although in precisely what manner is not yet clear.[38] One result of this interrelationship was a shared emphasis among traditions on certain themes: the efficacy of interiorized modes of worship over external ritual; the importance of love on the path to salvation; the power and effectiveness of remembering the divine name; and the pivotal role of the *guru* or spiritual guide. As a result, even though a tradition contained aspects that were doctrinally distinctive, it also had other aspects that resonated with kindred religious traditions. In expressing these analogous concepts, poets from different religious contexts drew from the same common pool of cultural and literary symbols and metaphors which, by not being anchored to a specific religious tradition, lent themselves to an open system of interpretation.[39] Consequently, certain symbols, such as the representation of the soul as a *virahinī* or yearning woman separated from her beloved, became pan-Indian symbols with each group interpreting them within its own frame of reference. For example, depending on the religious context, the *virahinī*'s beloved could be any one of the following: God, the Prophet Muḥammad, the Ismaili Imam, the Sufi *shaykh*, Krishna, Vishnu, the *guru* and so on.[40] The sharing of such 'open' symbols that could be interpreted in multiple, even contradictory, ways resulted in a literary phenomenon that Robin Rinehart, in her study of Punjabi poetry, has termed 'portability.'[41] A poem, hymn or song from one tradition became, in fact, 'portable' since a listener could interpret a central common core of thematic, symbolic and cultural elements within his or her particular religious framework. For our purposes, this would mean that a single poem could, in fact, be interpreted in three different contexts – Ismaili, Indo-Muslim and Indic – provided its symbols were 'open.'

Interestingly, manuscripts recording Ismaili devotional literature in Khojkī, a script unique to the subcontinent's Nizari Ismailis, show evidence of such 'portability' when they juxtapose poems originating from both the Indo-Muslim and the Indic contexts with Ismaili *ginān*s and other texts of Ismaili provenance.[42] Presumably, these poems of non-Ismaili origin, on account of their language, structure and symbolism, could be interpreted by Ismaili audiences within an Ismaili framework. Similarly we can document instances of *ginān*s being 'transported' beyond formal Ismaili settings and their message being interpreted and appreciated within entirely different theological contexts. For example, in the 1950s, Mr Aziz Tejpar, a renowned *ginān* singer in East Africa recited *ginān*s in public forums much to the acclaim of Hindu and Sikh members of the audience who were able to relate to the poems within their respective religious frameworks. In a pamphlet celebrating the activities of Mr Tejpar's *ginān*-singing group, the Chairman of the Sikh Gurudwara at Arusha in Tanzania writes: 'We have enjoyed "Ginans" so much that we invite Mr Tejpar to sing some at our temples, we shall welcome him.' Seth Maganlal Rugnath Jeram, President of the Nakuru Indian Association, who presumably was Hindu by faith, comments: 'Ismaili Ginans are rich in philosophy and music. I request Mr Aziz Tejpar to stay longer at [*sic*] Nakuru and give us the opportunity to become hosts of the Ginan Party. The Indian Association of Nakuru will be happy to arrange a large function for such event. I assure you your short stay has not satisfied us, we wish to hear many more Ginans which were wonderful.'[43] These concrete examples underscore the dynamic interplay between the triple contexts within which the Satpanth Ismaili tradition is located.

Conversion to Satpanth: Some Unanswered Questions

Although, presently, the Nizari Ismailis constitute a significant subgroup among the Muslim communities of South Asia, we are not at all certain about the actual processes by which Ismaili ideas spread in the region, or the reasons why the Satpanth tradition attracted adherents. The history of its origin and development is confused and complicated by the fact that the traditional accounts of the *pīrs*, the preacher-saints commonly believed to have been responsible for converting local inhabitants to the Ismaili cause, are embedded in layers of myth and hagiography. Furthermore, since the preaching of Ismaili ideas was carried out in an inconspicuous manner in order not to attract undue attention and possible persecution, works by non-Ismaili Muslim authors contain almost no specific references to the Satpanthi Ismaili tradition and its adherents.

It is commonly assumed that the presence of Ismailis in the region was the result of the activities of a unique Ismaili institution, the *daʿwa* (mission), a formal, highly organized and effective system to propagate the Ismaili interpretation of Islam. The contemporary Nizari Ismaili community in South Asia traces the origins of the Satpanth tradition to the *daʿwa* originating in Iran. In the 5th/11th century, after a dispute over succession to the Fatimid caliphate in Egypt, supporters of Nizār (the Nizārīs), the eldest son of the Fatimid Caliph al-Mustanṣir (d. 487/1094), broke all ties with the declining Fatimids and established an independent state centred at the fortress of Alamūt in northern Iran where the descendants of Nizār were proclaimed to be the rightful Imams. As a Shiʿi enclave in a predominantly Sunni environment, the state of Alamūt was constantly attacked by the Saljuqs who saw its presence as a threat to their suzerainty. Although Alamūt survived these attacks, it suffered a serious blow during the Mongol invasions of the 7th/13th century when it was forced to capitulate to the forces of the Mongol general, Hülegü, in 654/1256, with the Ismaili Imam, Rukn al-Dīn Khurshāh, subsequently being murdered. Notwithstanding this disaster, Nizari Ismailism in Iran continued to survive under the guise of a Sufi order with the Imam as its *shaykh* or *pīr*. In the 9th/15th century, a new Ismaili centre of Ismaili activity emerged in Anjudān, central Iran, where the Nizari Imams took up residence.

Throughout these turmoils, Ismaili tradition claims, the Imams in Iran continued the *daʿwa* in the subcontinent through *dāʿīs*, also known as *pīrs*. Unfortunately, we have little historically reliable information about these *pīrs*, especially the earlier ones who seem to have been active in the region of Gujarat and Sind from perhaps as early as the 5th/11th century. In the case of many *pīrs* we cannot be sure of even basic biographical details, such as dates of birth and death.[44] To add to the confusion, some of them seemed to have had Persian as well as one or more Indian names as a strategy for *taqiyya* and their desire to appear close to the indigenous population.[45] Significant questions relating to the organization of the *daʿwa* remain unanswered. We are not sure whether the *pīrs* worked alone or with the help of disciples. Did they receive specific instructions from Iran or did they operate more or less independently? Was there any central organization in the subcontinent or were there small isolated pockets of adherents with ties to the Imams in Iran, who were eventually consolidated into a larger community?

A great deal of ambiguity also surrounds the factors that may have attracted local populations to the Ismaili *pīrs* and their teachings. While there certainly were religious motivations, primarily of a soteriological nature, scholars have proposed a variety of additional explanations. Wladimir Ivanow attributes the success of the Ismaili *daʿwa* not only to religious zeal and enthusiasm of the preachers, but also to socio-economic circumstances such as the hard conditions of the masses, economic distress, poor administration and their acute discontent with the established order.[46] Tazim Kassam, on the other hand, based on the presence of what she refers to as 'political' allusions in the *ginān*s (such as references to kings, queens, armies and warfare), postulates that the initial impulse of the *daʿwa* was essentially political. Hence, she interprets the phrase '*pār utāro*' ('deliver to the [other] shore') a standard metaphor for religious salvation in medieval Indian devotional literatures, as also being a reference to 'political liberation' – local Hindu rulers seeking help from the Ismaili Imam in Iran to rescue them from their Sunni oppressors.[47] She therefore suggests that in its initial phases Satpanth embraced the ideals of a political liberation movement before it evolved into a pacifist and mystically-oriented form.[48] In contrast, Azim Nanji asserts that the *daʿwa* was non-political in its orientation and that references to the conversion of rulers probably 'reflect the urge to revive the ambition in symbolic terms ... .'[49] He argues that since the *ginān*s belong to the category of esoteric literature, its statements appear in 'mythical state or are couched in symbolism.'[50] Concerning the process of conversion, he suggests that the Ismaili *pīr*s may have been closely associated with pre-existing Hindu caste groups of an 'intermediate' rank.[51] These groups, he asserts, tended to be professional units such as goldsmiths, farmers, traders, and that it was the economic strength of such units that may have played a role in attracting additional converts.[52] Dominique-Sila Khan believes that the Ismaili *pīr*s were perceived as charismatic holy men, similar to Sufi *shaykh*s, with powers to aid individuals with their worldly problems, and that their appeal was to the untouchables and lower castes. Ishtiaq Hussein Qureshi agrees that the initial appeal was based not on dogma or belief but rather by impressing on the potential convert the spiritual greatness of some person, usually the Ismaili 'missionary.'[53] The varying explanations given by these scholars indicate that the matter is too complex to have a single definitive answer. Given the paucity of concrete evidence, we may never really know what combination of factors motivated individuals to become Satpanthis.

In terms of the techniques, we know that the *pīr*s presented Ismaili concepts to Indian audiences in acculturated forms that were accessible to them within their indigenous cultural and religious milieu. And yet, we are not certain of the actual mechanics by which the *pīr*s approached potential converts. A 4th/10th century Arabic treatise describing the manner in which Ismaili *dāʿī*s engaged in proselytization in a Middle Eastern context reveals that the method adopted was 'secretive and individualized, not public and mass.'[54] The incognito *dāʿī* would identify a likely candidate and then gradually lead him through various pedagogical stages to the esoteric meaning of Ismailism.[55] While this text describes the operation of a paradigmatic *dāʿī* working on his own, Wladimir Ivanow dismisses this method as being totally impractical. He asks: 'How many thousands of such extraordinarily clever, tactful and learned missionaries would be required to convert a Berber tribe, or the inhabitants of one Persian or Indian village?'[56]

The pattern of preaching described in this text does not seem relevant to the South Asian context on another count. Through descriptions in the *ginān*s, we see that prosleytization to an acculturated form of Ismailism took place at a mass level. For example, the *garbī*s attributed to Pīr Shams consistently portray him addressing large groups of people or entire villages.[57] Given the Indian social context, it is logical to assume that the *pīr*s had to preach to entire castes rather than to individuals. In this regard, Wladimir Ivanow observes that since the spirit of caste in Indian society is 'much stronger than any religious principle,' it is unlikely that any individual would act alone and risk social ostracization.[58] The fact that individuals responded to the *pīrs*' teachings *en masse*, however, raises questions about whether this process could be called 'conversion' in the usual sense of the word. The modern usage of the word implies choice – an individual consciously choosing one belief system over another. And yet, as Ivanow points out, mass conversion is rarely a question of personal initiative or even personal conviction. Under such circumstances, religious considerations, however inspiring and attractive, rarely outweigh economic, political, social and other motives.[59]

The inadequacy of the term 'conversion' is also apparent when we examine the acculturated forms in which Ismailism was presented in the Satpanth tradition. As remarked earlier, the Ismaili *pīr* introduced his teachings as a natural culmination of local belief systems without totally 'rejecting the conceptual and even social framework of the society he has penetrated.'[60] Intrinsic to this approach was the acceptance by the individual of both his original beliefs and the newer ones in an integrated manner. If the individual still retained previous beliefs and practices and did not see the new faith as something radically different from the old, could this process be called conversion, a term that usually implies complete abandonment of the old in favour of the new? To describe this complex situation, scholars have proposed using terms such as 'incomplete conversion'[61] or 'adhesion.'[62] Dominique-Sila Khan, however, points out such terms imply value-judgements based on the perspective of the scholar and ignores the perspective of the participant. She prefers looking at the religious identity of such groups as being 'liminal.'[63] At some point in their history, she argues, groups with liminal religious identity are subjected to processes of 'reIslamization' or 'reHinduization.'[64] These processes are initiated when they come into contact with external agents who have their own ideological index of religious identity by which they judge others. Under these circumstances, it is, therefore, more appropriate to view the process of conversion or acculturation as not a sudden act but rather a slow and gradual process, perhaps involving several generations, during which adherents respond to changing contexts, be they religious, socio-economic, cultural or political. Indeed, the recent history of the Nizari Ismaili community in the subcontinent bears witness to the gradual processes by which it has had to redefine its identity in the face of changing contexts.[65]

The fact that there are so many unanswered questions concerning the establishment and spread of the Ismaili Satpanth tradition no doubt indicates the extent of scholarly research that still needs to be undertaken before we fully understand the processes at work. One approach would be to examine the manner in which other Muslim groups in the subcontinent propagated their ideas and gained adherents. Unfortunately, the spread of the Islamic tradition in the subcontinent, too, is a process not fully understood. Moreover, colonial, religious, nationalist and communalist agenda have so influenced perspectives on this subject that Peter Hardy comments: 'to attempt to penetrate the field of the study of the growth of Muslim population in South Asia is to attempt to penetrate a political minefield.'[66] Traditionally, various theories have been advanced: people converted either under duress at the point of the sword, or to acquire political and economic patronage, or to escape the evils of the Indian caste system. None of these theories are adequate, for they are not supported by sufficiently convincing historical and sociological evidence.[67]

The Sufis have also been regarded as 'missionaries,' responsible for the peaceful spread of Islam in South Asia, using folk poetry in the vernacular languages as the primary medium through which they affected conversion among the masses. Recent scholarship has, however, raised important questions on the issue of conversion to Islam, particularly the role of Sufis in this process. As a result, the function of Sufi folk poetry as being explicitly composed to convert people to Islam has been questioned. Carl Ernst, on the basis of his study of the Chishti Sufis of Khuldabad, observes that their vernacular compositions are so heavily laden with Islamic material that 'it is difficult to imagine them as devices to impart a knowledge of Islam to non-Muslims.' He argues that the verses could only be directed at an audience already familiar with the Islamic tradition.[68] On the other hand, Richard Eaton, in his study of Sufi orders in the Deccan, contends that the authors of Dakkani folk songs, whose lyrics contained various Islamic teachings, primarily desired to secure for themselves the role of mediators or intermediaries between God and the people who recited these songs. If, in the process of singing these songs, he writes, local populations became familiar with or acculturated to popular forms of Islamic practice, the phenomenon should not be construed as 'conversion' in the sense of a 'self-conscious turning around in religious conviction.' Nor should the authors be considered missionaries, or 'self-conscious propagators,' even though this is the general context in which Sufis often tend to be viewed.[69] In another study on the spread of Islam in Bengal, Eaton traces the diffusion of Islamic ideas to the spread of agrarian civilization. Here, too, he feels that in the context of pre-modern Bengal, it is inappropriate to speak of 'conversion' of 'Hindus' to Islam or of specific moments of 'conversion' when peoples saw themselves as having made a dramatic break with the past.[70] Instead, he sees the process of Islamization as a gradual and imperceptible process during which a community moves through various stages: inclusion, identification and displacement.[71] He further writes:

> Viewed historically, religious systems are created, cultural artifacts, and not timeless structures lying beyond human societies. As such they are continuously reinterpreted and readapted to particular sociocultural environments.[72]

Many of these observations are pertinent to our understanding of the development and spread of Satpanth Ismailism. Perhaps the most interesting concerns the role of literature in the propagation of the faith. Although Sufi folk literatures may not have been explicitly written for conversion purposes, their role in acculturating populations to Islamic ideas is difficult to deny. Similarly, the Ismaili *ginān*s were also instrumental in spreading awareness of acculturated forms of Ismailism among populations, although we must be careful not to term this process as conversion. And yet, beyond their didactic role, the *ginān*s and the literary culture associated with them play a multifaceted role in the devotional life of the Satpanth Ismaili community. It is in consideration of this role that we now turn to the essays which follow.

Notes

1. For a detailed analysis of the historical and doctrinal development of Ismailism, see Farhad Daftary, *The Ismāʿīlīs: Their History and Doctrines* (Cambridge, 1990); and for a more synoptic view, his *A Short History of the Ismailis* (Edinburgh, 1998).

2. Azim Nanji, *The Nizārī Ismāʿīlī Tradition in the Indo-Pakistan Subcontinent* (Delmar, NY, 1978), p. 68.

3. During my various research trips to the subcontinent, I found that many of the Ismaili *pīr*s buried in Punjab and Sind are considered by the general population to have been Sunni *shaykh*s of Sufi orders.

4. See Ali S. Asani, The *Būjh Niranjan: An Ismaili Mystical Poem* (Cambridge, Mass., 1991), pp. 37–41, and Nanji, *The Nizārī Ismāʿīlī Tradition,* pp. 120–30.

5. There are several legendary accounts concerning the confrontation of the Suhrawardi shaykh Bahā al-Dīn Zakāriyyā and the Ismaili *pīr* Shams. See Nanji, *The Nizārī Ismāʿīlī Tradition,* pp. 53–4, and Dominique-Sila Khan, *Conversions and Shifting Identities: Ramdev Pir and the Ismailis of Rajasthan* (New Delhi, 1997), pp. 35–7. During a visit to the Punjab in 1982, I found that the Ismailis of the region still consider the Suhrawardī *shaykh* Rukn-i ʿĀlam (d. 735/1334) to be 'an enemy of the faith.'

6. Ishtiaq Hussein Qureshi, *The Muslim Community of the Indo-Pakistan Subcontinent (610–1947),* (Karachi, 1977), p. 50.

7. See Ali S. Asani, 'The Khojahs of South Asia: Defining a Space of their Own,' *Cultural Dynamics,* 13, no. 2 (2001), pp. 155–68.

8. See Nanji, *The Nizārī Ismāʿīlī Tradition,* pp. 110–20; Tazim Kassam, 'Syncretism on the Model of Figure-Ground: A Study of Pir Shams' Brahmā Prakāsa,' in K.K. Young, ed., *Hermeneutical Paths to the Sacred Worlds*

of India (Atlanta, 1994), pp. 231–42; and Gulshan Khakee, 'The Dasa Avatāra of the Satpanthi Ismailis and Imam Shahis of Indo-Pakistan' (Ph.D. thesis, Harvard University, 1972).

9. Wilfred C. Smith, 'The Crystallization of Religious Communities in Mughul India,' in M. Minovi and I. Afshar, ed., *Yād-Nāme-ye Irānī-ye Minorsky* (Tehran, 1969), p. 22.

10. Carl Ernst, *Eternal Garden: Mysticism, History and Politics at a South Asian Sufi Center* (Albany, NY, 1992), pp. 22–37.

11. See Ali S. Asani, 'The Khojahs of Indo-Pakistan: The Quest for an Islamic Identity,' *JIMMA*, 8, no. 1 (1987), pp. 31–41, and his 'The Khojahs of South Asia: Making a Space of their Own,' pp. 160–2.

12. Wladimir Ivanow, 'Satpanth (Indian Ismailism),' in W. Ivanow, ed., *Collectanea*, vol. 1 (Leiden, 1948), p. 21.

13. Ibid., p. 27.

14. Bernard Lewis, quoted by Jacques Duchesne-Guillemin, 'How Does Islam Stand?' in Gustav E. Grunebaum, ed., *Unity and Variety in Muslim Civilization* (Chicago, 1955), p. 8.

15. Aziz Ahmad, *Studies in Islamic Culture in the Indian Environment* (Delhi, 1964), p. 156.

16. Aziz Ahmad, *An Intellectual History of Islam in India* (Edinburgh, 1969), p. 126.

17. Wilferd Madelung, 'Shiʿism: Ismāʿīlīyah,' in Mircea Eliade, ed., *Encyclopedia of Religion* (New York, 1987), vol. 13, p. 257.

18. Nanji, *The Nizārī Ismāʿīlī Tradition*, pp. 131–5.

19. Tazim Kassam, *Songs of Wisdom and Circles of Dance: Hymns of the Satpanth Ismāʿīlī Muslim Saint, Pīr Shams* (Albany, NY, 1995), p. 119.

20. Dominique-Sila Khan, *Conversions and Shifting Identities*, p. 23.

21. Mohammad Ishaq Khan, *Kashmir's Transition to Islam: The Role of Muslim Rishis, 15th–18th Century* (New Delhi, 1994).

22. Ibid., p. 24.

23. Paul Walker, 'Abū Yaʿqub al-Sijistānī and the Development of Ismaili Neoplatonism' (Ph.D. thesis, University of Chicago, 1974), p. 8.

24. Nanji, *The Nizārī Ismāʿīlī Tradition*, p. 132.

25. Henry Corbin, 'Le Temps cyclique dans le Mazdéisme et dans l'Ismaélisme,' *Eranos-Jahrbuch* 20 (1951); 'Epiphanie Divine et naissance spirituelle dans la Gnose Ismaélienne,' *Eranos-Jahrbuch* 23 (1954); 'De la gnose antique à la gnose Ismaélienne,' in *Oriente ed Occidente nel Medio Evo* (Rome, 1957); 'Herméneutique spirituelle comparée,' *Eranos-Jahrbuch* 33 (1964). English translations of the first three articles appear

in Henry Corbin, *Cyclical Time and Ismaili Gnosis*, tr. R. Mannheim and J.W. Morris (London, 1983).

26. Nanji, *The Nizārī Ismāʿīlī Tradition*, p. 132.

27. For a discussion of varying Muslim attitudes to acculturation, see Yohannan Friedmann, 'Islamic Thought in Relation to the Indian Context,' *Puruṣārtha*, vol. 9 (1986), pp. 79–91; Imtiaz Ahmad, 'The Islamic Tradition in India,' *Islam and the Modern Age*, 12 (1981), pp. 44–62; Annemarie Schimmel, 'Reflections on Popular Muslim Poetry,' *Contributions to Asian Studies*, vol. 17 (1982), pp. 17–26; Ali. S. Asani, 'Muslims in South Asia: Defining Community and the "Other",' *BRIIS*, 2 (2001), pp. 103–13.

28. For the role of the Sufis in the development of devotional poetry in the vernacular languages of the subcontinent, see ʿAbd al-Ḥaqq, *Urdū kī ibtidā'ī nashwo numā meṅ ṣūfiyā'i kirām kā kām* (Aligarh, 1968); Annemarie Schimmel, 'The Influence of Sufism on Indo-Muslim Poetry,' in Joseph P. Strelka, ed., *Anagogic Qualities of Literature* (University Park, PA, 1971); Richard Eaton, 'Sufi Folk Literature and the Expansion of Islam,' *History of Religions*, vol. 14, no. 2 (1974–75); Ali S. Asani, 'Sufi Poetry in the Folk Tradition of Indo-Pakistan,' *Religion and Literature*, 20 (1988), pp. 81–95.

29. The Sufi romantic epic *Candāyan*, composed by Mawlānā Dā'ūd (late 8th/14th century), and the *Padmāvat*, composed by Malik Muḥammad Jāyasī in 947/1540, are two prominent examples of early Sufi mystical-romances in Hindi dialects, a literary tradition that continued until the 20th century.

30. Ali S. Asani, 'The Bridegroom Prophet in Medieval Sindhi Poetry,' in A. Entwistle and F. Mallison, ed., *Studies in South Asian Devotional Literature: Research Papers 1989–91* (Delhi-Paris, 1994), pp. 213–25.

31. See Asim Roy, *The Islamic Syncretistic Tradition in Bengal* (Princeton, NJ, 1983) and 'The Pīr Tradition: A Case Study in Islamic Syncretism in Traditional Bengal,' in Fred Clothey, ed., *Images of Man: Religion and Historical Process in South Asia* (Madras, 1982), pp. 112–41.

32. Yohannan Friedmann, 'Islamic Thought in relation to the Indian Context,' p. 79.

33. Annemarie Schimmel, 'Reflections on Popular Muslim Poetry,' p. 18.

34. Shāh Walīullāh, *Tafhīmāt al-ilāhiyya*, ed., Ghulam Mustafa al-Qasimi (Hyderabad, Sind, 1967–70), vol. 2, p. 246.

35. Asani, 'The Khojahs of South Asia: Defining a Space of their Own,' pp. 159–62.

36. For a brief description of the characteristics of the *sant* and *bhakti* movements, see Charlotte Vaudeville, 'Sant Mat: Santism as the Universal Path to Sanctity,' in Karine Schomer and W.H. McLeod, ed., *The Sants: Studies in a Devotional Tradition of India* (Berkeley, Calif., and Delhi, 1987), pp. 21–40.

37. See Sheldon Pollock, 'India in the Vernacular Millennium: Literary Culture and Polity, 1000–1500,' paper presented at the Center for International Affairs South Asia Seminar, Harvard University, 1997.

38. See, for example, Dominique-Sila Khan, *Conversions and Shifting Identities*.

39. A.K. Ramanujan identifies a similar process at work in the retelling of the *Rāmāyana* during which authors 'dipped' into a 'common pool of signifiers' but emerge with different interpretations of 'crystallizations.' See A.K. Ramanujan, 'Three Hundred *Rāmāyanas*: Five Examples and Three Thoughts on Translation,' in Paula Richman, ed., *Many Rāmāyanas: The Diversity of a Narrative Tradition in South Asia* (Delhi, 1994), p. 46.

40. Ali S. Asani, *The Ismāʿīlī Ginān Literature: Its Structure and Love Symbolism* (B.A. thesis, Harvard University, 1977), pp. 43–50.

41. Robin Rinehart, 'The Portable Bullhe Shah: Biography, Authorship, and Categorization in the Study of Punjabi Sufi Poetry,' paper presented at Seventh International Conference on Early Literature in New Indo-Aryan Languages, Venice, 1997.

42. See Ali S. Asani, *The Harvard Collection of Ismaili Literature in Indic Languages: A Descriptive Catalog and Finding Aid* (Boston, 1992), pp. 21–2.

43. *First Anniversary of the Ginan Mandal, 'A Tract on Ginan Party'* (Dar-es-Salaam, 1956,) pp. 28–9.

44. For a reconstruction of the history of the *daʿwa* in the subcontinent, see Azim Nanji, *The Nizārī Ismāʿīlī Tradition*, pp. 33–96.

45. Dominique-Sila Khan, *Conversions and Shifting Identities*, p. 48.

46. Ivanow, 'Satpanth,' p. 20.

47. Kassam, *Songs of Wisdom*, pp. 96–8.

48. Ibid., p. 122. For a critique of Tazim Kassam's theory, see Ali S. Asani's review of her *Songs of Wisdom and Circles of Dance* in *JAOS*, 119 (1999), pp. 327–8.

49. Nanji, *The Nizārī Ismāʿīlī Tradition*, p. 68.

50. Ibid., p. 101.

51. Ibid., p. 68.

52. Ibid., p. 76.

53. Qureshi, *The Muslim Community of the Indo-Pakistan Subcontinent*, p. 41.

54. Derryl Maclean, *Religion and Society in Arab Sind* (Leiden, 1989), p. 149.

55. Ibid., p. 149.

56. Ivanow, 'Satpanth,' p. 22.

57. See translations in Kassam, *Songs of Wisdom and Circles of Dance*, pp. 320–70.

58. Wladimir Ivanow, 'The Sect of Imam Shah in Gujrat,' *JBBRAS*, New Series, 14 (1936), p. 60.

59. Ivanow, 'Satpanth,' p. 22.

60. Nanji, *The Nizārī Ismāʿīlī Tradition*, p. 101.

61. Sachedina Nanjiani, *Khojā vrttant* (Ahmedabad, 1918), p. 14.

62. Maclean, *Religion and Society in Arab Sind*, p. 151, where he defines adhesion 'as the adding on of additional beliefs to the converts' original system of beliefs or rituals.'

63. Dominique-Sila Khan, *Conversions and Shifting Identities*, p. 163.

64. Ibid., pp. 164–7.

65. See Asani, 'The Khojahs of South Asia: Defining a Space of their Own.'

66. Peter Hardy, 'Modern European and Muslim Explanations of Conversion to Islam in South Asia: A Preliminary Survey of the Literature,' in Nehemia Levtzion, ed., *Conversion to Islam* (New York, London, 1979), p. 70.

67. For a detailed description and critique of these theories, see Hardy, 'Modern European and Muslim Explanations of Conversion to Islam in South Asia,' pp. 68–99 and Richard Eaton, *The Rise of Islam and the Bengal Frontier* (Berkeley, London, 1993) pp. 113–34.

68. Carl Ernst, *Eternal Garden*, pp. 166–8.

69. Richard Eaton, *Sufis of Bijapur, 1300–1700* (Princeton, NJ, 1978), pp. 172–3.

70. Eaton, *The Rise of Islam and the Bengal Frontier*, p. 310.

71. Ibid., pp. 269–303.

72. Ibid., p. 314.

2

The *Ginān*s as Devotional Literature: Their Origins, Characteristics and Themes*

Ginān bolore nit nūre bhareā;
evo haiḍe tamāre harakh na māeji.

Recite continually the *ginān*s which are filled with light;
boundless will be the joy in your heart.[1]

In this manner does a verse explain the importance of the *ginān*s, the collection of hymn-like poems belonging to the Nizari Ismaili community of the Indian subcontinent. The verse in Gujarati cited above suggests that the *ginān*s are perceived as containing 'light'– specifically, the light of knowledge that leads to enlightenment by banishing the darkness of ignorance. Indeed, the very term *ginān* is derived from the Sanskrit *jnāna* for contemplative knowledge.[2] The *ginān*s are the focus of intense veneration, being regarded as the repository of spiritual knowledge and wisdom, which transmit in the vernacular the essential teachings of the Arabic Qur'an, the primary scripture of Islam. Although popularly believed to be medieval in origin, the *ginān*s continue to play, to our day, a central role in the community's religious life. They are recited daily whenever members congregate for ritual prayers in their *jamāʿat-khāna*s (houses of congregation). And with the community's 'diaspora' within the last hundred years, these devotional poems are now also recited in many areas outside the subcontinent, such as East Africa, Europe, Australia, Canada and the United States.

The Nizari Ismailis of the subcontinent employ the term *ginān* to designate and distinguish a special type of poetic composition: specifically, a composition whose authorship is attributed to Ismaili *pīr*s or preacher-saints who, according to the community's traditions, came to the region as early as the 5th/11th century to propagate the Ismaili form of Islam. It was during their proselytizing activities that these Iranian *pīr*s are believed to have composed the several hundred poems of varying length known as the *ginān*s which have come down to us. Through the poetic medium of the *ginān*s, the *pīr*s provided guidance on a variety of doctrinal, ethical and mystical themes for the edification of their followers.[3] In common with many of their Sufi contemporaries, the Ismaili *pīr*s adopted an approach that stressed indigenization of Islam to the local Indic linguistic and cultural milieu. For this purpose, they employed not only the indigenous languages of Gujarat, Sind and Punjab where they operated – tradition claims, rather exaggeratedly, the use of thirty-six languages – together with indigenous poetic forms and metres, but also their musical modes, for like most medieval Indian vernacular poetry the *ginān*s are meant to be recited and sung. Not surprisingly, in their literary forms, symbols and manner of recitation, the *ginān*s are reminiscent, on the one hand, of the *pada*s and *bhajan*s of the north Indian *bhakti* and *sant* traditions and, on the other, of Sufi poetry in the Indic vernaculars. On account of their distinctive linguistic and cultural background, the *ginān*s represent an important regional and ethnic element in a broader corpus of Ismaili devotional literature that includes works in Arabic, Persian and even Burushaski, a language of the northern areas of Pakistan.[4]

The Role of *Gināns* in Ismaili Religious Life

Before examining the historical background and principal features of the *ginān* literature, it will be useful to discuss briefly its role within the context of the Khoja Ismaili community's religious life and in individual piety, that is, the interaction between these texts and the people who memorize them, recite them and listen to them. The intention here, therefore, is to focus on the 'relational, contextual, or functional quality'[5] of the *ginān* literature.

Although initially associated with the preaching of Ismaili doctrines and ideas, today, several centuries later, the *ginān*s continue to exercise a significant influence in the religious life of the Nizari Ismailis, not only in the subcontinent but also in other parts of the world where they have immigrated. When Wladimir Ivanow, the Russian orientalist, was conducting his researches on the Ismailis of India in the early part of the 20th century, he noted 'the strange fascination, the majestic pathos and beauty' of the *ginān*s as they were being recited, and observed further that their 'mystical appeal equals, if not exceeds that exercised by the Coran on the Arabic-speaking peoples.'[6]

The reverence shown to the *ginān* as written word should not, however, mislead us. Though they have been embodied in a written textual form, the *ginān*s are primarily an oral tradition.[7] Their greatest impact is through the ear. They are intended to be chanted and recited aloud according to prescribed *rāga*s (melodies) and folk tunes. Singing *ginān*s, alongside the performance of ritual prayers, is one of the mainstays of the worship service in the mornings and evenings when the community congregates in the *jamāʿat-khāna* for prayers. Memorization of at least a few *ginān*s and their tunes constitutes an essential part of the religious education of Khoja Ismaili children. In fact, like much Indian devotional poetry, the *ginān*s, through much of their history, were transmitted orally and only committed to writing rather late. As I have shown elsewhere, even after being recorded in Khojkī, the community's special script, oral knowledge of *ginān* texts was still necessary to ensure correct reading of an ambiguous alphabet.[8] Nowadays, the oral and memorized text continues to be functionally more important than the written text, which appears to be more of an *aide-mémoire* for the man or woman who leads the congregation in recitation.

While the recitation of one or more *ginān*s constitutes an important ritual in itself, individual *ginān* verses or sometimes entire *ginān*s are also an integral part of other rituals of worship. Consequently, manuscripts, lithographs or books containing *ginān*s are frequently classified and arranged according to ritual usage. There are entire genres of *ginān*s intended for recitation with specific prayers and religious ceremonies held in the mornings or evenings. For instance, before the faithful begin their early sessions of morning meditation, a selection of verses on aspects of the mystical experience are recited in order to evoke the appropriate mental and spiritual disposition within the meditators. Some *ginān*s are heard only on certain religious festivals and holidays: the *ginān Sāt swargnā kāīṁ khuliyā che dwār* (*The Doors of the Seven Heavens have Swung Open*) on the birthday of Prophet Muḥammad; *Dhan dhan ājno dahaḍo* (*Happy and Blessed is this Day*) on the birthday of the Imam; and *Navaroznā din sohāmaṇā* (*On this Auspicious Day of Navrūz*) at the beginning of the Persian New Year. Finally, on a night of special spiritual significance such as *Laylat al-Qadr* on which the Qur'an was first revealed, appropriate *ginān* verses alternate with the names of God and other religious formulas in an entrancing meditative chant called the *zikr* (Arabic, *dhikr*).

Beyond their role in worship, the *ginān*s permeate in many ways communal and individual life. At a communal level, the commencement of any function or meeting, be it religious or secular, is marked by a short Qur'an recitation followed by one from the *ginān*s. The intent of such recitations is to bestow auspiciousness on the occasion. During sermons, religious discussions and in religious education materials, *ginān* verses are often cited as proof-texts. Occasionally, a special concert called *ginān meḥfil* or *mushā'iro* takes place, much like the *qawwālī* and other Sufi devotional recitations, during which professional and amateur singers sing *ginān*s with musical accompaniment. In deference to the reluctance among orthodox-minded Muslims to permit the use of musical instruments in explicitly religious contexts, such concerts are not usually held within the premises of *jamā'at-khāna*s. Again, outside the context of formal worship or liturgy, community institutions responsible for religious education may sponsor *ginān* competitions in which participants are judged on their ability to sing and properly enunciate *ginān* texts. Such competitions are a popular method among religious educators to encourage the learning of *ginān*s among young students and adults. At a personal and family level, too, *ginān*s are used in many different contexts: individual verses can be quoted as proverbs; verses can be recited in homes to bring *baraka*, spiritual and material blessing; housewives, in a usage that stresses the links between the *ginān*s and folk tradition, often recite them while working or as lullabies; audio cassettes with *ginān*s sung by 'star' singers or recordings of *ginān mehfil*s can be found in many an Ismaili home and even their cars!

That the *ginān*s, a literary corpus originating within a folk tradition, should have attained a devotional role is by no means unprecedented in the history of north Indian vernacular literatures. Poems and hymns attributed to prominent religious personalities associated with the *bhakti*, *sant*, Sufi as well as the Sikh traditions have come to play a pivotal role in the devotional life of religious communities all over north India. What is unusual in the case of the *ginān* literature are the questions raised, both within and outside the community, regarding the 'Islamic' character of this literary corpus and its relationship with the Qur'an, as the primary scripture of the Islamic tradition. The need to clarify these issues became urgent in the late 19th and 20th centuries.

From this time onwards, on account of a complex interaction of political and historical factors, questions of religious identity became crucial for Ismaili and other Muslim communities who practised forms of Islam which did not correspond with the assumed standards of Islamic orthodoxy and orthopraxy.[9] Furthermore, in this period, lines between Hindu and Muslim groups were gradually being firmly delineated, with different facets of South Asian culture increasingly coming to be viewed from the perspective of religious communalism. Language, literature, music, dance, architecture, etc., became variously politicized within the realms of colonial or nationalist discourse as elites tried to preserve their privilege in the colonial and post-colonial state through the manipulation of symbols which had mass appeal.[10] The twin processes of Islamization – defined as the adoption of Perso-Arabic cultural elements and mores – among Muslims and

Sanskritization among Hindus resulted in cultural distancing between Muslims and Hindus. Several regions of the subcontinent, including Bengal, home to the majority of the Muslim population, witnessed the emergence of grass-roots Muslim reformers, such as the Faraizis, who targeted a whole range of practices, customs and ideas prevalent among Muslims and recognized as local or indigenous and, therefore, decidedly 'un-Islamic' in their opinion.[11] In such an atmosphere, Muslim literatures in indigenous Indic languages, particularly those that displayed characteristics considered to be syncretistic, stood in danger of being regarded with suspicion and branded as 'Hindu' and 'non-Islamic.'[12]

The response of the Nizari Ismailis of the subcontinent to these developments has been a complex one. First, as noted, the *ginān* literature came to be perceived within the community as a kind of commentary on the Qur'an. This was the clarification given by Ṣulṭan Muḥammad Shāh Aga Khan III, the 48th Imam of the Ismailis, in his pronouncement giving guidance on this issue: 'In the *ginān*s which Pīr Sadardin has composed for you, he has explained the gist of the Qur'an in the language of Hindustan.'[13] According to this interpretation, the *ginān*s serve as secondary texts generated in the vernacular for transmission of the teachings of a primary scripture, the Qur'an, for non-Arabic speaking peoples. It is therefore commonly believed in the community, reflecting the traditional preoccupation of the Ismailis with the esoteric, that the *ginān*s serve to penetrate to the inner (*bātin*) signification of the Qur'an rather than the external (*zāhir*) aspects.

In this manner, while affirming the primacy of the Qur'an in its theology, the community has been able to preserve a significant role for the *ginān*s. Viewed within the context of Islamic religious literature, the community's perception of the *ginān*s as playing a mediating role between the faithful and the Qur'an is not without its parallels. In parts of the Islamic world influenced by Persian culture, Mawlānā Jalāl al-Dīn Rūmī's *Mathnawī*, popularly called the 'Qur'an in Persian,' is regarded as a vast esoteric commentary on the Qur'an, many of its verses being interpreted as translations of Qur'anic verses into Persian poetry. Similar interpretations exist about the poetic masterpiece so influential among Sindhi-speakers – Shāh ʿAbdu'l Laṭif's *Risālo*, the 'sacred book for Sindhis, admired and memorized by Muslims and Hindus equally.'[14]

In a second development, terms and idioms within the *ginān*s that could be perceived as 'Hinduistic', and hence likely to provoke questions regarding their identity as Islamic literature,[15] have been replaced by Perso-Arabic ones considered to be more in consonance with the greater Islamic tradition. In recent editions of *ginān* texts published by community institutions, for example, the word 'Harī' is replaced by 'ʿAlī', and so on. *Ginān*s in which the *pīr*s elucidate Ismaili concepts through reformulations of Hindu mythologies are recited less frequently, such as the *Dasa Avatāra* (*The Ten Avatāras*), a central, early text of the Satpanthi tradition.[16] Such changes, while generally accepted within the community, have also generated much debate on the appropriateness of interpolations of texts which presumably have been handed down intact through the centuries. They also raise the question of what constitutes a 'Hindu' element as opposed to an 'Islamic' one, especially when terms from Indic languages with no specific theological connection to the Hindu tradition have been replaced by Perso-Arabic ones. Such questioning and debate, symptomatic of tensions between localized, ethnic, or vernacular expressions of Islam and pan-Islamic forces, reveals the strength of the Nizari Ismaili community's attachment to the *ginān*s. While their functions may change and evolve over time, they will nevertheless remain a part of the communal religious life. They provide us with a particularly vivid and powerful reminder of the significant, and unfortunately underestimated, role played by Indic vernacular literatures in the development of Indo-Muslim civilization.

Origins of the *Ginān*s

The origins of these religious poems, as is the case with much *bhakti* and *sant* poetry, are so hopelessly entangled in historical obscurities that there are simply too many questions for which we cannot provide satisfactory answers. The community's legendary accounts and traditional histories assert that these *ginān*s were composed by a series of preacher-saints or *pīr*s sent to the subcontinent from Iran by the community's Imams for the express purpose of propagating the Ismaili form of Islam in Gujarat, Sind and Punjab. According to these traditions, the *pīr*s' mission began in the 5th/11th or 6th/12th century. This would mean that the *ginān*s were not associated with the earlier attempts, in the 4th/10th century, to establish Ismaili political dominion in the subcontinent, specifically in Sind and Multan.[17] We do, in fact, have archaeological and other evidence to support the existence of a long-standing relationship between the Ismaili Imams in Iran and their communities in India,[18] making it quite plausible that some of these *pīr*s did come from Iran or at least had some sort of a connection with that region. In any case, a critical aspect of the *pīr*s' activities was the creation of a new literature – the *ginān* literature – geared for those embarking on *satpanth* (the true path), the Indic vernacular term utilized by the *pīr*s to refer to Ismaili Islam.[19]

We possess remarkably little reliable information about these *pīr*s who are believed to be the authors of the *ginān*s. Since they very likely maintained a low profile in order to avoid undue attention and possible persecution, works by contemporary Muslim historians and travellers contain no direct references to them or their adherents. Ismaili accounts, some of them incorporated in the *ginān* literature, surround them with layers of myth, legend and hagiography that have been compounded by centuries of transmission.[20] Nevertheless, in these accounts, the *pīr*s stand out as figures of dominating importance who are accorded reverence not unlike that accorded to a Hindu *guru* or a Sufi *shaykh*. They are depicted as mystical teachers leading their followers to the truth. In an environment permeated by Sufi *tarīqa*s and *bhakti* groups revolving around religious personalities, the Ismaili *pīr*s must have been quite inconspicuous.[21]

For our purposes here, it suffices to be acquainted with some of the most important figures to whom the *ginān*s are attributed. Pīr Satgūr Nūr, regarded in the traditions as the earliest *pīr*, is believed to have worked mostly in Sind and Gujarat. The tombstone at the shrine dedicated to him at Navsari in Gujarat gives his death date as 487/1094. However, this information is not very useful for the shrine itself is a much later development. There are, in fact, many enigmatic and perplexing questions about this earliest of the *pīrs* who is supposed to have composed at least nine short *ginān*s as well as a *granth*, that is, a long *ginān* with a title. He was followed by Pīr Shams, a preacher associated with the Ismaili Imam Qāsim Shāh (c.710–772/c.1310–1370). Popular tradition has identified Pīr Shams, who possesses a shrine in Multan, with Shams-i Tabrīzī, the mysterious mentor of the great Muslim mystic, Maulānā Jalāl al-Dīn Rūmī (d. 672/1273).[22] To this *pīr* are attributed 108 short *ginān*s as well as ten *granth*s, many of which are in various Punjabi dialects. Pīrs Satgūr Nūr and Shams laid the foundation of the community, the consolidation of which is associated with a later figure, Pīr Ṣadr al-Dīn. His mausoleum is near Ucch in present-day Pakistan.

Placed by the Russian orientalist W. Ivanow between the second half of the 8th/14th century and the beginning of the 9th/15th century, Pīr Ṣadr al-Dīn is the most well-known among the *pīr*s. The number of works ascribed to him is linguistically diverse and extremely large (218 *ginān*s and 18 *granth*s),[23] leading Ivanow to comment that only God knows how far this attribution is correct.[24] He contributed in various ways to developing the community's organization: he is believed to have established the first *jamāʿat-khāna*s and given the title *khawāja* (lord, master) to his followers. The term *Khoja*, by which Nizari Ismailis are popularly known in the subcontinent, is a corruption of this title. Pīr Ṣadr al-Dīn was succeeded by his son, Ḥasan Kabīr al-Dīn (d. c. 875/1470?), renowned in the community for his emotional poems in which he passionately expresses his yearnings for beatific vision. To this religious figure are attributed at least 79 short *ginān*s and seven *granth*s. On the death of Pīr Ḥasan Kabīr al-Dīn there was considerable dissension within his family over the succession to the office of *pīr*. His brother, Pīr Tāj al-Dīn who was actually the nominated successor, was rejected by a section of the community in favour of Ḥasan Kabīr al-Dīn's son, Imām-Shāh. Tāj al-Dīn's mysterious death plunged the community into a crisis leading to the secession and declaration of autonomy by Nar Muḥammad Shāh (d.c. 941/1534), a son of Imam-Shāh (d. 919/1513), who organized the Imām-Shāhī sect. Both father and son composed *ginān*s: Imām-Shāh has fifteen *granth*s and 162 short *ginān*s while Nar Muḥammad Shāh has two important *granth*s to his name. On account of the schism, the Imam repudiated the Imām-Shāhīs and sent a Persian text, the *Pandiyāt-i jawānmardī* (*The Counsels of Chivalry*) in place of a *pīr* to guide those who remained loyal to him (see Plate v).[25] The mainstream Khoja faction, though continuing to recite the compositions of Imām-Shāh and his son, regard them as less authoritative works. With the resolution of the Imām-Shāhī crisis, the age of the great *pīr*s comes to an end. However, *ginān*s continued to be composed till the early 20th century by persons known as *sayyids*.[26] The most notable of these is a woman saint, Sayyida Imām-Begum (d. 1283/1866), whose ten *ginān*s are extremely popular today.[27] She is buried in the Mian Shah cemetery in Karachi, next to the grave of her suitor.

In the absence of concrete evidence, much of the attribution based on the community's traditions cannot be authenticated. The *ginān*s, like much medieval Indian devotional poetry, were initially transmitted largely through oral tradition. They appear to have been put into writing only much later in their history, giving rise to vexing questions concerning their authorship as well as their transmission. Indeed, for many *ginān*s, the traditional attribution of authorship can be challenged on linguistic and literary grounds. Ivanow feels that in some cases the attribution of a *ginān* to a certain *pīr* may, in fact, reflect that it is a work written by later devotees about the *pīr* rather than by him.[28] Azim Nanji, too, suggests that sometimes the actual composition of a *ginān* may have been the work of later disciples.[29] It is, therefore, quite possible that composers of some *ginān*s may have attributed them to their favourite *pīr* as a way of spiritually identifying themselves with their mentors. Whatever the case may be, clearly more research needs to be undertaken before we can clarify the origins of these religious poems and answer questions that seem at present to be unanswerable.[30]

However important questions of origins and authenticity of the *ginān* literature may be to the scholar, the community has never approached the issue with the same 'scientific' concerns. Naturally, for most adherents, authorship by a recognized *pīr* is crucial to the validity of a *ginān* as well as its teachings. However, for them, authorship is determined solely on the basis of community tradition. Ultimately, as is the case with medieval Indian *bhakti* and *sant* poetry, the communal attribution of a certain composition to a particular author depended upon the inherited consensus of the audience of this literature. Once a piece was in circulation and acknowledged as 'religious', it belonged to its audience which made of it what it willed.[31]

General Characteristics

Viewed within the context of Islamic civilization in the subcontinent, the *ginān*s clearly belong to a larger corpus of Indo-Muslim literatures, 'popular' or 'folk' in orientation and utilizing Indic vernacular languages. Studies of South Asian Islam clearly demonstrate that vernacular literatures in the folk idiom, rather than literature in classical Islamic languages, Arabic and Persian, were responsible for spreading Islamic precepts in the region.[32] Literatures in the vernaculars were instrumental in explaining fundamental Islamic concepts to the native populations in terms that were familiar and accessible to them.[33] The subcontinent's many languages, folk songs, metres, poetic idioms, symbols and traditional music were all harnessed for this task. In the process, the authors who formulated these literatures, indigenized the Islamic tradition to the local Indian cultural environment.

The Ismaili *pīr*s, too, seem to have adopted a similar approach in their interaction with native populations, presenting Islam, in its Nizari Ismaili form, in a manner that would be accessible to their predominantly Hindu audiences. They utilized myths and concepts prevalent in the Indian religious milieu in order to provide a locally intelligible expression to fundamental Ismaili principles.[34] For example, through a process of mythopoesis, they created an ostensible correspondence between the Vaishnava

Hindu concept of *avatāra* and the Ismaili concept of the Imam. Such mythopoesis is found in other local Indo-Muslim traditions as, for example, in Bengali *puthī* literature. The tenth *avatāra* of Vishnu, renamed in the tradition as Nakalankī, 'the stainless one,' was identified with 'Alī, the first Shi'i Imam. Other basic Hindu figures were redirected to Islamic personalities: Brahmā, for example, was identified with the Prophet Muḥammad, while the Prophet's daughter, Fāṭima, was identified with Shakti and Sarasvatī.[35] Typically, in *ginān*s, such as the 'classic' *Dasa Avatāra*, the *pīr*s, many of whom even took on local Indian names, represented themselves as guides who knew the whereabouts of the awaited tenth *avatāra* of Vishnu, meaning the Ismaili Imam.[36] Thus, their concern for facilitating a smooth transition and a continuum from one religion to another led the *pīr*s to portray Ismaili Islam as the completion or culmination of the Hindu tradition.[37] Strange as it may appear, this approach was not unparalleled in Islamic theology for, in another cultural environment, namely the Middle East, Islam had already been represented as the fulfilment of Judaism and Christianity.

In keeping with the emphasis on indigenization, the *ginān*s, the literary vehicles which the *pīr*s utilized for their preaching, exhibit many characteristics typical of medieval Indian devotional literatures. Indeed, the similarities are so strong that it is very likely that works could have been appropriated from one tradition to another, resulting in the phenomenon of 'portability' (discussed in the introductory chapter).[38] The structural features of the *ginān*s may be summarized as follows.

Language and Vocabulary

The *ginān*s favour the subcontinent's vernacular languages as appropriate expressions of faith. Although the composers of the *ginān*s were of Iranian origin, not a single *ginān* can be found in Persian. Although Ismaili tradition claims the use of 36 Indian languages in the *ginān*s, we can discern, in fact, only six major languages with several of their dialects: Punjabi, Multani (Saraiki), Sindhi, Kachchi, Hindustani/Hindi and Gujarati. Generally, these languages occur in their medieval form, making comprehension difficult for the contemporary audience. In fact, some *ginān*s in archaic Sindhi may represent the earliest surviving examples of the language that have come down to us.[39] On the other hand, many *ginān*s contain idioms and expressions that are clearly too 'modern' to have been used by the saint to whom they are attributed. Such anachronisms are the result of the vagaries of transmission during which works of folk literature are notoriously prone to distortion and interpolation.

In this regard, we should note that a substantial portion of the *ginān* literature, as we know it now, underwent 'editing' before being printed in the Gujarati script at the beginning of the 20th century. During this process, the vocabulary of many *ginān*s seems to have incorporated elements from Gujarati, the language spoken by a substantial segment of the community.[40] The use of two or more Indic languages in a single *ginān*, may also indicate that, as they spread, *ginān*s originating in a certain area were probably translated entirely or suitably adapted to the needs of a new linguistic region. Vocabulary from one North Indian language, it seems, was replaced by synonyms from another. For example, the *ginān* which begins *Amar te āyo more shāhjījo* (*The Command has come from my Master*) has, in one version, all its Sindhi elements changed to Punjabi equivalents so that it begins *Hukam āeā mede shāhadā.*[41] Consequently, in such cases, the original text or language of a *ginān* becomes difficult, if not impossible, to determine. The theological vocabulary, too, tends to be mostly Indic in origin. For example, indigenous Indian terms, such as *niranjan, hari, nirākār, rām,* occur frequently in reference to God instead of the Arabic 'Allah.' Arabic and Persian theological terms, though they occur, tend to be limited. Frequently, however, they appear in strangely distorted forms. As noted, in more recent times, certain expressions in the *ginān*s have also been altered so that they are more in consonance with changes in the community's religious identity. Thus, as the community identifies itself more closely with the larger Islamic world, vocabulary items of Indic or Sanskritic origin perceived to be of 'Hinduistic' origin have gradually been replaced by Perso-Arabic ones that are considered to be more compatible with an 'Islamic' character.

Prosody and Verse-forms

Alongside the use of Indic languages, the *ginān*s make use of traditional Indian prosody in which verse forms, metrics and musical beat (*tāl*) are closely allied. Like much North Indian verse, the poetry in the *ginān*s belongs to the class of *jāti chand* in which scanning is based on the number of long and short *mātrā*s (metrical instants) in a line.[42] However, as Azim Nanji correctly points out, ginanic prosody 'suffers from great inexactitude owing to negligence in transmission and linguistic acculturation.'[43] The most popular metres in the *ginān*s are the *dohā*, the *caupāī*, the *soraṭha*, all employed in verse-forms of the same name.[44] In lengthier *ginān*s, usually of a more didactic nature, the *dohā* and *caupāī* are frequently used together in the same work. This combination is entirely in keeping with Indian literary conventions – it is found in works attributed to luminaries such as Kabīr, Mūḥammad Jaisī, Tulsīdās and Sūrdās.[45] The *sloka*, the epic stanza with two verses of sixteen *mātrā*s, also occurs with great frequency.

In addition to the verse forms we have just described, others have been adopted from the realm of folk poetry: the *sī ḥarfī* or *chautisa* in which each verse begins with a letter of the alphabet; the *kāpāītī*, a type of folk song sung by women to accompany their work at the spinning wheel; the *kāfī*, a typically Sindhi form involving the repetition of the initial verse after each succeeding verse. From Gujarati folk culture was adopted the *garbī*, traditionally associated with the worship of the mother-goddess among Hindu Gujaratis. Combining both verse and dance,[46] the *garbī* was especially favoured by Pīr Shams, who is credited with at least 28 compositions in this genre.

Regardless of the verse-forms used, most *ginān*s also have a refrain, usually called a *tek* or *varaṇī*, the constant repetition of which is integral to holding together the different ideas expressed in the various verses of a *ginān*. If a *ginān* does not possess a formal refrain, then, as is the case with *bhakti* and *sant* poetry, the first verse is used for this purpose. The last verse of most *ginān*s usually contains a *bhanitā* (sometimes called *chāp*) or signature line, which identifies the composer of the work. Though reminiscent of the *takhalluṣ* of Persian poetry, the *bhanitā* is, in fact, a characteristic feature of medieval North Indian poetry.[47]

The number of verses in a *ginān* varies tremendously: the shorter compositions may contain four to ten stanzas while the longer ones may comprise of over five hundred. Usually the short *ginān*s do not possess a title; in such cases, the first verse or refrain often serves as a title equivalent for identification purposes. The longer *ginān*s, however, have individual titles that may reflect the central theme or subject of the work. For example, a long mystical poem on the spiritual quest of the soul is appropriately titled *Būjh Niranjan* (*Knowledge of the Attributeless Deity*) and a didactic piece giving instruction in moral and religious matters is called *Moman Chetāmaṇī* (*A Warning for the Believer*). These titled *ginān*s, popularly designated *granth*s to distinguish them from the short untitled compositions, may in some cases exist in minor (*nāno, ninḍo*) and major (*moṭo, vaḍho*) versions. However, in quite a few cases the minor version's relation to the major is simply in title.[48] Again, some *granth*s may possess a sort of an appendix or addendum, commonly called *vel* (lit. creeper).

Though they are poems, the *ginān*s exhibit a great variety in style. Many, like the *Būjh Niranjan*, are didactic in tone, imparting instruction on religious and other matters. Others are narratives, containing hagiographic and legendary accounts of the *pīr*s.[49] Several are in the form of parables or stories that are meant to be interpreted mystically: the *ginān* called *Kesrī sinh swarūp bhulāyo* (*The Lion Forgot his Lion-form*) for example, describes a lion who has forgotten its true identity on account of its upbringing among a flock of sheep, while the *granth* called *Hans Hanslī nī Vartā* (*The Parable of the Goose and the Gander*) is about the mystical encounter of a male and female goose. Some are dialogues: the *Bāī Budhāī* (*Lady Budhāī*) are a series of poems comprising the conversation of Pīr Imām-Shāh with his sister Budhāī on religious and theosophic subjects, and the *granth Hasan Kabīr-adīn ane Kānipā no Samvād* (*The Conversation between Hasan Kabīr al-Dīn and Kānipā*) records the discussion of the Ismaili *pīr* with Kānipā, a Hindu sage and ascetic, on various religious issues. Yet others are short ecstatic compositions describing the joys and agonies of mystical love.

Music and Recitation

Like most Indian devotional poetry, the *ginān*s are meant to be sung and recited with each *ginān* having its own *rāga* or musical modes. Music is, therefore, a distinctive and integral feature of each *ginān*. For example, the *ginān* called *Āe rahem rahemān* (*Come, O Merciful, Benevolent One*) is in *rāga kāfī* with its *tāl* (beat cycle) as *dīpchandī*, that is, fourteen beats; *Ab terī mahobat lāgī* (*Stricken by Love for You*) is in *rāga kālingrā, tāl kaherwā* (eight beats).[50] Given the state of our sources, we will perhaps be unable to determine whether *pīr*s who composed the *ginān*s were also responsible for setting them to music or whether this was the task of disciples. Tradition, however, informs us that at least one composer of *ginān*s – the woman saint Sayyida Imām-Begum – was familiar with Indian music as well as an accomplished player of the *sitar* and *sarangī*.[51]

The use of *rāga*s in the *ginān*s is essential for the evocation of moods appropriate to certain occasions, or to the theme of the work, or to the rituals of which it is part. Some *ginān*s, it seems, are associated with *rāga*s appropriate to the time of day they are meant to be sung. Thus, *ginān*s – such as the genre of the *prabhātīya* – intended for recitation early in the morning are likely to be sung in morning *rāga*s. Though some *ginān* texts, both manuscript and printed, indicate the particular *rāga* for a composition, for the most part the *rāga*s of the *ginān*s are transmitted orally. As a consequence, there may be several melodic variations for a particular *ginān*, often differing from one geographical region to another. In recent years, some of these traditional *rāga*s have even been affected by melodies from popular Indian film music. But, fortunately, for the preservation of the traditional music, this trend has faded. On account of a growing awareness of the importance of singing a *ginān* properly, several individuals have attempted to record the *rāga*s of popular *ginān*s for dissemination within the community.[52]

Usually in the *jamāʿat-khānas*, the recitation of a *ginān* is led by a man, woman or even a child, accompanied by the entire congregation. Those who are unfamiliar with the text of a particular composition can usually participate in the singing of the refrain, a common structural element in most *ginān*s. The recitation, especially if it is well delivered, can often be very powerful in its evocation of emotional and religious feelings. Illustrative of the significance and effect of the oral/aural dimension of *ginān* recitation are the following comments by the Pakistani writer and poet G. Allana, as he reminisces about a childhood experience:

> My mother Sharfibai start[s] singing a *ginān*. Her voice was unmatched. Everybody listened to her bewitching voice singing a *ginān*. No other person, as is normally customary, dare join his or her voice with hers to sing in chorus, whether she sang a stanza of a *ginān* or the refrain of the *ginān*. The fragrance of that spiritual atmosphere still lingers in my mind. One seemed to live and be so near to the presence of the Omnipotent and the Omniscient One. The weight of life's burdens dissolved.[53]

The singing in unison of the entire congregation, which on Fridays and special religious holidays may number, in some areas, up to one thousand or more, can also be very powerful in its emotional and sensual impact. Even those who may not fully understand the meanings and significance of the words they sing may experience an emotion difficult to describe but which sometimes physically manifests itself through moist eyes or tears.

An oft-repeated story within the community concerns the penitence and redemption of Ismail Gangji, a not exactly pious individual from Junagadh, induced one evening while he was sitting in the *jamāʿat-khāna* listening to the recitation of a *ginān* stanza.

> He heard the stanza very attentively and tears poured through his eyes. Immediately on conclusion of the ginan recitation, this faithful [one] got up, went to the honourable Mukhi [a religious official], Rai Rahmatullahbhai, and sought forgiveness of all his sins. This was the moment signifying the day he started his life anew.[54]

Subsequently, he became the chief minister to the *nawāb* of

Junagadh. According to one community publication, Ismail Gangji even had the unique honour, following his death in 1883, of receiving the title of *pīr* from the Imam on account of his high spiritual status.

As a rule, the recitation of *ginān*s in the *jamāʿat-khāna* is not accompanied by musical instruments. However, basing our assumptions on the performance of poetry from literary traditions parallel to the *ginān*s – the *bhakti*, *sant* and Sufi traditions – it is likely that in the past musical accompaniment may have featured in the recitation of *ginān*s. As noted earlier, outside the *jamāʿat-khānas*, that is, in more social gatherings called *ginān meḥfil* or *mushāʿiro*, the *ginān*s are often recited to the accompaniment of musical instruments, usually the Indian harmonium and the *tabla* (drum).

Manuscripts and Texts

The *ginān*s began as oral literature, being recorded in writing only much later in their history. Although there are many manuscripts, very few date earlier than the 12th/18th century: the earliest extant manuscript dates to 1736.[55] However, since this manuscript, like others, is mentioned as being copied from older ones, it is likely that the practice of writing *ginān*s began earlier. The absence of earlier manuscripts can be explained by various factors. The subcontinent's climatic conditions as well as its prolific insect life certainly do not assist the preservation of manuscripts. Again, it was probably customary to destroy old and deteriorating manuscripts once they had been re-copied by scribes. Finally, piety itself has been no less of a problem: Ivanow remarks that in the early 20th century, after the printing of certain *ginān*ic texts, 'the manuscripts from which the edition was prepared were buried in the ground!'[56]

Ginān manuscripts are written in Khojkī, a script peculiar to the subcontinent's Ismaili communities. A 'proto-Nagari' script dating back to the early 2nd/8th century, Khojkī belongs to the group of *Laṇḍā* or 'clipped' alphabets found in Sind, Punjab and north-western India. These scripts were mostly used by trading communities for keeping accounts and recording transactions.

On account of their mercantile functions, these scripts tend to be crude by literary standards, often being simply a type of shorthand. They lack complete vowelling systems as well as sufficient characters to represent unambiguously the full range of consonants. However, a small number of scripts – including Khojkī – actually evolved into vehicles of literary expression through refinement of their writing systems.

The use of Khojkī, a 'local' script, to record the *ginān*s, was an integral part of the *pīr*s' attempt to make religious literature more accessible by recording it in a script with which the local population had the greatest familiarity. That the adoption of a 'local' script for preserving religious literature may have been customary with various groups in medieval India is further evident from the Sikh adoption of Gurmukhī as an 'official' script for its religious literature. Significantly, Gurmukhī, like Khojkī, is a polished and refined version of a *Laṇḍā* alphabet whose adoption was of great significance for the Sikh community. Only by adopting a script of their own could the Sikhs develop a literary culture that was suited to their faith and language.[57]

Much more was involved in the use of the Khojkī script than access to religious literature. The script, by providing an exclusive means of written expression shared by Ismailis living in three regions (Sind, Punjab and Gujarat) was instrumental in developing cohesion and group identity within a widely-scattered and linguistically diverse community. This function of the script – that is, to strengthen ties within a group – is again paralleled not only by the role of Gurmukhī in developing Sikh identity but also that of Moḍī, another clipped alphabet, in fostering and strengthening ethnic identity among Mahrattas during the time of Shivājī.[58] No doubt Khojkī facilitated the flow and the transmission of religious literature from one area to another. Use of the script may have also served to confine religious literature within the community – this precaution being necessary to avoid persecution from outsiders not in agreement with the community's doctrines and practices.

Important as Khojkī was to the preservation and recording of *ginān*ic manuscripts, it was gradually abandoned in favour of the

Gujarati script. For all practical purposes, Khojkī is no longer a 'living script' and few of the community's younger members even know of its existence. There were several factors behind this move which we have discussed elsewhere.[59] In the first decades of the 20th century, as collections of the *ginān* literature began to be printed, Khojkī texts were switched to the Gujarati alphabet. At the same time, the *ginān*s themselves were edited. For this purpose, manuscripts were for the first time collected at community-wide level, and their texts collated.[60] However, the goals and the methods of this editing were very different from those of scholarly textual criticism, for very often the religious outlook of the editors would inspire changes in the texts. Finally, these edited texts were printed at the community's central press, the Ismaili Printing Press (also known then as the Khoja Sindhi Press) in Bombay.

Although the *ginān*s continue to be printed in the Gujarati script to this day, changes in the community's linguistic status in different areas of the world have made the use of other alphabets also necessary. Since many younger members of the diasporic community in East Africa and in the West cannot read Gujarati, *ginān* texts are often transliterated into the Latin alphabet. The transliteration systems are, however, quite chaotic and sometimes inaccurate. Again, with the growing stress on Urdu in Pakistan, young Pakistani Ismailis are now familiar only with the Urdu script, making it imperative for Pakistani *ginān* publications to use that script.

Themes and Motifs

Unlike Ismaili literature in Arabic and Persian, the *ginān* literature is not overly concerned with lengthy and learned expositions of theological and doctrinal issues. Nor is it concerned with philosophical and intellectual controversies and the systematic refutations of false doctrines. Its character tends to be 'popular' rather than pedantic or scholarly. Its themes are many and diverse, ranging from descriptions about the beginnings of creation and laments of the soul as it proceeds on a spiritual quest, to ethical precepts concerning proper business practice. These themes cannot be too rigorously separated from each other for, typically, in a single *ginān* they mingle and blend together. Nevertheless, in order to better understand the nature of the literature, it may be useful to isolate some major motifs.

The first category of motifs relates to the overall portrayal of Islam, specifically in its Nizari Ismaili form, as the culmination of the Vaishnava Hindu tradition. The 'classic' of the tradition, the *Dasa avatāra*, which represents the integration of Ismaili thought within a Vaishnava framework, is permeated with motifs from this category.[61] Within this category may also be included *ginān*s that deal with accounts of traditional figures of Hindu mythology. Figures such as Harishcandra, Draupadī and the Pāndava brothers have served Hindus as models of proper behaviour and conduct. In order that some of these figures might be of benefit to the new converts, they were assimilated into the Ismaili tradition by being re-interpreted with Ismaili perspectives. For example, the *ginān* called *Amar te āyo* (*The Command has Come*) Harishcandra is carried over from the Hindu tradition, where he is a model of righteousness and *dharma*, into the *ginān* tradition, where he becomes the paradigm of the true Muslim who is ready to sacrifice everything for his religion. Finally, we also include here *ginān*s that are hagiographic accounts of the great Ismaili *pīr*s and their activities. The *granth*s, *Satgūr nā Vivā* (*The Wedding of Satgūr*) and *Putlā* (*The Idols*) are accounts of the conversion activities of Pīr Satgūr Nūr, while some of the *garbī*s describe the travels and activities of Pīr Shams.

The second category of motifs addresses a variety of cosmological and eschatological themes. To mention a few, the *granth Bāvān Ghāṭī (Fifty-two Passes)* deals with the questioning of the soul as it passes through fifty-two stages in the afterlife; another granth *Brahmā Gāyantri* deals with the creative process from a pre-eternal divine light (an integration of Hindu creation myths into an Ismaili context);[62] the *Nakalank Gītā* (*The Hymn of Naklank*) is a mystical cosmogony; and *Ūnch thī āyo* (*Coming from an Exalted Place*) is a lament of the soul's fate in the material world and a plea for the intercession of Prophet Muḥammad.

The third category consists of motifs of an ethical or a moralistic nature, providing instruction for the proper conduct of worldly life. The most important *ginān*s exemplifying these motifs include *Soh Kiriya* (*One Hundred Obligatory Acts*); *Bāvan Boḍh* (*Fifty-two Advices*) and *Moman Chetāmaṇī* (*A Warning for the Believer*). The last of these also incorporates parables and stories of a number of Prophets from the Qur'an.

The fourth category relates to motifs concerning a wide variety of religious rituals and festivals. There are, for example, *ginān*s that are recited on specific occasions such as the birthdays of the Prophet and the Imam, the beginning of the New Year with the Iranian festival of *Navrūz*, or at certain religious ceremonies such as funerals, etc.

The fifth and perhaps the most important category include motifs related to mysticism and the spiritual life among the Ismailis. The Ismailis have been notable in Islamic thought for the emphasis they give to the *bāṭin*, the esoteric or spiritual aspects of the faith, to complement the *ẓāhir*, the exoteric or external. Ismaili literature has been concerned throughout its development with the spiritual life of the human soul, especially its search to transcend the shackles of material bondage. The ultimate destiny of the soul is to return to its origins in the transcendent and ineffable God. Such a journey becomes feasible by means of the spiritual relationship that exists between the individual believer and the Imam. As keeper of the mysteries of the *bāṭin* (the esoteric), the Imam becomes the supreme guide in the spiritual quest.[63]

Naturally, these mystical aspects of the faith made their appearance in the *ginān*s. There are, for example, compositions that are guides for an individual's spiritual progress being composed in the same vein as Sufi manuals. The most important examples are two *granth*s, the *Būjh Niranjan* (*Knowledge of the Attributeless Deity*)[64] and the *Brahmā Prakāsh* (*Divine Illumination*), both of which include descriptions of mystical stages and advice on how to attain them. Other *ginān*s are literary expressions of mystical experiences, comparable to poems written by Sufi mystics on spiritual stages and states. Such *ginān*s are very popular in the community on account of their appeal to the individual's spiritual development. And finally there are *ginān*s that are basically petitions or supplications (*ventīs*) for spiritual enlightenment and vision (*darshan, dīdār*). These *ventīs*, incidentally, are analogous to the petitionary genre called *vinaya* so popular among the *bhakti* and *sant* poets, as well as the long tradition of devotional prayer and poetry in Shiʿism.[65]

It is in those *ginān*s dealing with mystical themes where we encounter the greatest number of similarities to the poetry of the *bhakti, sant,* Indian Sufi and Shiʿi traditions. The similarities are most prominent in the common set of symbols and metaphors employed in these literatures. In mystical *ginān*s, for example, the soul is always represented in the feminine mode as a wife anxious for the return of her husband or a bride awaiting her bridegroom. The woman-soul symbol, as is well-known, is a conventional feature in most North Indian devotional poetry written in vernacular languages.[66] Again, like *sant* and Sufi poetry, the *ginān*s draw on a host of symbols taken from the world of nature, agriculture or folk culture to garb their message with a material form. Thus, for example, in the *ginān* called *Huṅ re pīasī tere darshan kī* (*I Thirst for a Vision of You*) the symbol of the fish writhing in agony outside its home in water, is used to underline the importance of love, symbolized by water, as the emotive principle of existence (see Appendix, v). On a thematic level, the concept of *viraha*, 'longing-in-separation,' that is so common in *bhakti* and *sant* poetry, also plays a prominent role in the *ginān*s where the Imam represents the longed-for beloved. The emphasis on interior religion, personal experience and the efficacy of an inner mode of worship against the mindless performance of rituals – themes characteristic of *sant*[67] and Sufi literature – are also conspicuous in the *ginān*s. In this regard, the *ginān*s stress the efficacy of love as a force on the mystical path as opposed to barren learning and intellectualism, ideas that are generally prevalent in medieval Indian devotional poetry. Their anti-intellectual bias often takes the form of attacks on *mullā*s and *paṇḍit*s who symbolize dry, fossilized learning. In contrast, the *ginān*s extol the virtues of the *pīr* as a spiritual guide or preceptor on the path to enlightenment, echoing yet again the importance of the *guru* or *shaykh* in Hindu and Islamic mystical thought.

Our survey of the *ginān* literature and its characteristics and themes is of considerable importance in placing this genre within the context of the Indo-Muslim literary tradition. The significant similarities and parallelisms to which we have alluded serve to reveal the intimate connection of the *ginān*s to the religious and literary milieu from which they emerged. They do not necessarily imply direct borrowing, but merely emphasize the interaction that was going on at the various levels of Indian society at the time. The assimilative character of the *ginān* literature is, in fact, illustrative of the nature of Nizari Ismailism as a whole: a religious tradition with a remarkable ability to integrate disparate elements from a variety of cultural contexts as a means of elaborating its own universal concepts.

Notes

* This chapter is a revised version of 'The Ginān Literature of the Ismailis of Indo-Pakistan,' first published in D. Eck and F. Mallison, ed., *Devotion Divine: Folk Sources of the Bhakti Tradition.* Gröningen and Paris, 1991, and incorporates some passages from 'The Ismaili *Ginān*s as Devotional Literature,' in R.S. McGregor, ed., *Devotional Literature in South Asia: Current Research, 1985–88.* Cambridge, 1992.

1. From *Mahān Ismāīlī sant pīr Sadaradīn racit gīnānono saṁgrah* (*Collection of Ginans Composed by the Great Ismaili Pir Sadruddin*), (Bombay, 1969), p. 61 (English translation mine).

2. An alternative, though highly unlikely, derivation from the Arabic *ghanna* (to sing) is mentioned by G. Khakee, 'The Dasa Avatāra of the Satpanthi Ismailis and the Imam Shahis of Indo-Pakistan' (Ph.D. thesis, Harvard University, 1972), p. 3.

3. For a summary of the main themes in the *ginān* literature, see my article 'Ginān' in Mircea Eliade, ed., *Encyclopedia of Religion* (New York, 1987).

4. The Nizari Ismaili community of Northern Pakistan, in particular Hunza, Gilgit and Chitral, possesses its own literary tradition of devotional poetry known generically as *manqabāt.* For a survey of Ismaili devotional literature in Arabic and Persian, see Faquir M. Hunzai, trans., and Kutub Kassam, ed., *Shimmering Light: An Anthology of Ismaili Poetry* (London, 1996).

5. I borrow this expression from William A. Graham's study of sacred

texts, *Beyond the Written Word: Oral Aspects of Scripture in the History of Religion* (New York, 1987).

6. W. Ivanow, 'The Sect of Imam Shah in Gujrat,' *JBBRAS*, New Series 12 (1936), p. 68.

7. The *ginā̄ns* provide a particularly strong case for religious texts functioning as oral phenomena. The significance of the oral-aural dimensions of the written word for the history of religions has been most ably explored by Graham in *Beyond the Written Word* and his article 'Scripture,' in Eliade, ed., *Encyclopedia of Religion.*

8. Ali S. Asani, 'The Khojki Script: A Legacy of Ismaili Islam in the Indo-Pakistan Subcontinent,' *JAOS*, 107 (1987), pp. 439–49. [Chapter 6 of this volume].

9. For a detailed discussion of this issue, see Ali S. Asani, 'The Khojahs of South Asia: Defining a Space of Their Own,' *Cultural Dynamics* 13, (2001), pp. 155–68.

10. See Paul Brass, 'Ethnic Groups, Symbol Manipulation and Ethnic Identity among Muslims of South Asia,' in D. Taylor and M. Yapp, ed., *Political Identity in South Asia* (London and Dublin, 1979), pp. 35–77.

11. For a discussion of the reformist Faraizi movement in Bengal, see Rafiuddin Ahmed, *The Bengal Muslims, 1871–1906: A Quest for Identity* (Delhi, 1981) pp. 39–105.

12. See Ali S. Asani, 'Muslims in South Asia: Defining Community and the "Other,"' *BRIIS*, 2(2001), pp. 108–10.

13. Quoted in *Ginā̄ne Sharīf: Ismāʿīlī pīroe āpel pāk dīnnī roshnī* (Karachi, 1966), p.[2], (original in Gujarati; my translation).

14. Annemarie Schimmel, 'Sindhi Literature' in J. Gonda, ed., *A History of Indian Literature*, vol. 8, pt. 2 (Wiesbaden, 1974), p. 14.

15. Aziz Ahmad, for example, judges the 'literary personality' of the *ginā̄ns* to be 'un-Islamic,' in his *An Intellectual History of Islam in India* (Edinburgh, 1969), p. 126.

16. Writing in the early years of this century, Menant observes: 'Le *Desavatar* est le livre le plus sacré de la littérature religieuse des Khodjas: on en récite des passages au lit de mort des fidèles; au *Jamat Khana* quand on commence la lecture du dixième chapitre la congrégation se lève et reste debout en s'inclinant chaque fois que le nom d'Ali est prononcé.' 'Les Khodjas du Guzarate,' *Revue du Monde Musulman*, 10 (1910), p. 224.

17. See S.M. Stern, 'Ismāʿīlī Propaganda and Fatimid Rule in Sind,' *Islamic Culture*, 23 (1949), pp. 298–307, and Abbas Hamadani, *The Beginnings of the Ismāʿīlī Daʿwa in Northern India* (Cairo, 1956).

18. The Iranian town of Kahak, which once served as a centre for the Ismaili Imams, contains in its cemetery the graves of several Indian Ismailis who died during their pilgrimage to see the Imam. See W. Ivanow, 'Tombs of some Persian Ismaili Imams,' *JBBRAS*, New Series 14 (1938), p. 57.

19. The term *panth*, an Indic term meaning path, doctrine or sect, is popularly used in the names of groups that crystallized around the different religious personalities of medieval India. For example, followers of the poet Dādū call their movement *Dādūpanth*, while those of Kabir use the term *Kabirpanth*. The term *satpanth* used by the Ismaili *pīrs* echoes the Qur'anic concept of *ṣirāt al-mustaqīm* (the right path).

20. For a discussion of the 'historicity' of these *pīrs* and the use of *ginān*s as sources of information concerning the arrival and establishment of Nizari Ismaili Islam in the subcontinent, see Azim Nanji, *The Nizārī Ismā'īlī Tradition in the Indo-Pakistan Subcontinent* (New York, 1978), pp. 33–96.

21. Some of the *pīrs* were so successful representing themselves as spiritual leaders that today the non-Ismailis of Punjab and Sind revere them as Sufi masters of Sunni persuasion. W. Ivanow, 'Satpanth (Indian Ismailism),' in *Collectanea*, vol. 1 (Leiden, 1948), p. 10.

22. See Nanji, *The Nizārī Ismā'īlī Tradition*, pp. 61–5; and W. Ivanow, 'Shams Tabriz of Multan,' in S.M. Abdallah, ed., *Professor Muhammad Shafi Presentation Volume* (Lahore, 1955), pp. 109–18. Annemarie Schimmel, *The Triumphal Sun: A Study of the Works of Jalāloddīn Rumi* (rev. ed., London, 1980), p. 22, cites information provided by Rūmī's biographer, Aflākī, as well as recent discoveries by Mehmet Onder, the former director of the Mevlana Muzesi in Konya, which indicate that the real Shams-i Tabrīz was murdered by some people, with the connivance of Rūmī's son 'Alā' al-Dīn, in a fit of jealousy and then hastily buried.

23. See Zawahir Noorally, *Ginans, Our Wonderful Tradition* (Canada, n.d.), [p. 7], and Ismail K. Poonawala, *Biobibliography of Ismā'īlī Literature* (Malibu, Calif., 1977), pp. 302–3.

24. W. Ivanow, *Ismaili Literature: A Bibliographical Survey* (Tehran, 1963), p. 177.

25. For a detailed discussion of this text, see W. Ivanow, ed. and trans., *Pandiyāt-i jawānmardī* or 'Advices of Manliness' (Leiden, 1953).

26. Particularly prominent among the *sayyid*s were the Kadiwālā Sayyids, so-called since they resided in the village of Kadi in Cutch. The Kadiwālā Sayyids are said to be descendants of Pīr Ḥasan Kabīr al-Dīn through his son Raḥmatullāh Shāh (d. 925/1519). Mumtaz Ali Tajddin

Sadik Ali, 'Sayyida Bibi Imam Begum,' *Hidayat* (July, 1989), p. 16.

27. Sadik Ali notes that he came across a manuscript with at least 32 compositions attributed to Sayyida Imām-Begum in Lassi, a neighbourhood of greater Karachi. Ibid., p. 17.

28. Ivanow, 'Satpanth,' p. 41.

29. Nanji, *The Nizārī Ismāʿīlī Tradition*, p. 62.

30. For detailed discussion concerning the authorship of the *ginān*s, see Ali S. Asani, 'The Ismaili *ginān*s: Reflections on Authority and Authorship,' in F. Daftary, ed., *Mediaeval Ismaʿili History and Thought* (Cambridge, 1996) pp. 265–80 [Chapter 5 of this volume].

31. Faisal F. Devji, 'Conversion to Islam: The Khojahs,' unpublished paper submitted to the University of Chicago, 1987, p. 9.

32. See Annemarie Schimmel, 'Reflections on Popular Muslim Poetry,' *Contributions to Asian Studies*, 17 (1982), pp. 17–26; Richard Eaton, 'Sufi Folk Literature and the Expansion of Islam,' *History of Religions*, 14, no. 2 (1974–75), pp. 115–27; and Ali S. Asani, 'Sufi Poetry in the Folk Tradition of Indo-Pakistan,' *Religion and Literature*, 20 (1988), pp. 81–94.

33. Annemarie Schimmel, *As Through a Veil: Mystical Poetry in Islam* (New York, 1982), p. 136. This role of vernacular literatures is evident in many regions of the subcontinent. For example, Richard Eaton in his *Sufis of Bijapur, 1300–1700* (Princeton, NJ, 1978, p. 174) points out that folk literature in Dakhini Urdu composed by Chishti Sufis played a profound role in the gradual acculturation of the region's lower classes to the Islamic tradition. Likewise, Asim Roy talks of the masses of Muslim believers in Bengal who would have been debarred from the Islamic tradition had it not been for the 'cultural mediators' of the 16th and 17th centuries who made available the religious tradition to Muslim folk in familiar and intelligible terms in the Bengali language. Asim Roy, *The Islamic Syncretistic Tradition in Bengal* (Princeton, 1983), p. 72.

34. Aziz Esmail and Azim Nanji, 'The Ismāʿīlīs in History,' in S.H. Nasr, ed., *Ismāʿīlī Contributions to Islamic Culture* (Tehran, 1977), p. 252.

35. For a discussion of the mythopoeic character of the *ginān* literature, see Nanji, *The Nizārī Ismāʿīlī Tradition*, pp. 110–20.

36. For a translation and transliteration of the *Dasa Avatāra*, see G. Khakee, 'The Dasa Avatāra of the Satpanthi Ismailis and Imam Shahis of Indo-Pakistan' (Ph.D. thesis, Harvard University, 1972).

37. The *pīr*s' manner of representing the relationship between Islam and the Hindu tradition echoes the traditional Muslim conception of Islam as the culmination of the Judaeo-Christian religion. The Ismaili *pīr*s were by no means unique in expressing such a formulation. For

parallel developments in Bengali Islam, see Roy, *The Islamic Syncretistic Tradition*, pp. 87–110.

38. We have some evidence that at least one *ginān*, the *Būjh Niranjan*, was originally a Sufi poem that was appropriated into the Ismaili tradition. See Ali S. Asani, *The Būjh Niranjan: An Ismaili Mystical Poem* (Cambridge, Mass., 1991), pp. 19–46.

39. Schimmel, *Sindhi Literature*, pp. 4–5.

40. See Asani, 'The Khojki Script,' for a discussion of the linguistic composition of the *ginān*s.

41. For the Punjabi version of this *ginān*, consult manuscript Ms Ism K 22, ff. 327r-327v, in the Harvard collection of Ismaili literature in Indic languages. See also Ivanow, 'Satpanth,' p. 40.

42. S.H. Kellogg, *A Grammar of the Hindi Language* (3rd ed., London, 1938).

43. Nanji, *The Nizārī Ismāʿīlī Tradition*, p. 20.

44. The *caupāī* metre consists of a quatrain each of whose four lines comprises 16 *mātrā*s. These 16 *mātrā*s are arranged into four 'feet' each containing a fixed number of *mātrā*s. The *caupāī*'s rhyme scheme follows the pattern A A A A or A A B B. The *dohā*, a much admired metre in North Indian poetry, consists of two lines, each containing 24 *mātrā*s. Each of the two lines is sub-divided into two *caran*s (divisions) of 13 and 11 *mātrā*s. An important feature of the *dohā* is the pause *viram* which may occur as a harmonic pause or caesura after *caran*s of 13 *mātrā*s or a sentential pause after the 11 *mātrā caran*s. The *soraṭha* is simply an inverted *dohā*, that is, the first *caran* consists of 11 *mātrā*s while the second possesses 13.

45. M.S. Mahesh, *The Historical Development of Medieval Hindi Prosody* (Bhagalpur, India, 1964).

46. According to Gujarati custom, participants in the *garbī* revolve in a circle, maintaining rhythm by clapping. If the *garbī* is being performed as part of a devotional practice, then a pot (*garbo*) containing offerings is usually placed in the centre.

47. Charlotte Vaudeville, *Kabir*, vol. 1 (Oxford, 1974).

48. Ivanow, *Ismaili Literature*, p. 174.

49. The *granth*s *Satgūr nā Vīvā* and *Putlā*, for example, describe the activities of Pīr Satgūr Nūr, one of the tradition's earliest *pīr*s.

50. See G. Hyder Alidina, *Standardized Ginans* (unpublished monograph, Karachi, 1985), pp. 2–5. To compensate for differences between the poetic and musical metre of a *ginān*, extra syllables such as '*re*' and '*ejī*' are often inserted during recitation.

51. Sadik Ali, 'Sayida Bibi Imam Begum,' p. 17.

52. Foremost in these attempts is Dr G. Hyder Alidina of Karachi who has almost single-handedly undertaken the monumental project of researching and recording *rāgas* of *gināns*. He has produced cassette recordings of these, under the title of 'Standardized Ginans.'

53. G. Allana, *Ginans of Ismaili Pirs* (Karachi, 1984), vol. 1, p. 2.

54. *The Great Ismaili Heroes* (Karachi, 1973), pp. 98–9. The verse that was effective in bringing about Ismail Gangji's 'conversion' is reputed to be one from the Gujarati *ginān*, attributed to Pīr Ṣadr al-Dīn: *Sheṭh kahe tame sāṁbhaḍo vāṇotar* (*The Chief Merchant Says to the Traders*).

55. Nanji, *The Nizārī Ismāʿīlī Tradition*, pp. 9–11, and Zawahir Noorally, *Catalogue of the Khojki Manuscripts in the Collection of the Ismailia Association for Pakistan.* Unpublished paper (Karachi, 1971), MS 25.

56. Ivanow, 'Satpanth,' p. 40.

57. S.S. Gandhi, *The Sikh Gurus* (New Delhi, 1978), pp. 174–5, quoting Gokal Chand Narang.

58. B.A. Gupte, 'The Modi Character,' in *Indian Antiquary*, 34 (1905), pp. 27–30.

59. Asani, 'The Khojkī Script.'

60. Azim Nanji mentions in *The Nizārī Ismāʿīlī Tradition*, p. 10, that he was given information to the effect that Aga Khan II (d.1885) had assigned the task of collecting manuscripts to some of his followers in order that the *gināns* be properly preserved.

61. For an analysis of this text, see Khakee, 'The Dasa Avatāra'.

62. Ivanow, *Ismaili Literature*, p. 179.

63. For an overview of spirituality among the Ismailis, see Henry Corbin, *Cyclical Time and Ismaili Gnosis*, trans. R. Mannheim and J.W. Morris, (London, 1983); also Azim Nanji, 'Ismāʿīlīsm,' in S.H. Nasr, ed., *Islamic Spirituality: Foundations* (New York, 1987), p. 185.

64. For critical edition and translation of this text, see Asani, *The Būjh Niranjan.*

65. J. Hawley and M. Jurgensmeyer, *Songs of the Saints of India* (Oxford, 1988), p. 6.

66. J. Hawley, 'Images of Gender in the Poetry of Krishna,' in Caroline Bynum et al., ed., *Gender and Religion: On the Complexity of Symbols* (Boston, 1986), pp. 231–56.

67. See, for example, Charlotte Vaudeville, 'Kabir and the Interior Religion,' *History of Religions*, 3, 2 (1964).

3

Bridal Symbolism in the *Ginān*s*

Evelyn Underhill, in her classic study of mysticism, while discussing the difficulties mystics encounter in communicating their spiritual experiences, writes:

> ... it is not strange that certain maps, artistic representations or symbolic representations should have come into being which describe or suggest the special experiences of the mystical consciousness and the doctrines to which these experiences have given birth. Many of these maps have an uncouth, even an impious appearance in the eyes of those unacquainted with the facts which they (the mystics) attempt to translate.[1]

These comments are particularly applicable to descriptions of the crowning point of the mystical experience – the union of the soul with the Absolute. Like most esoteric states, the unitive experience is essentially ineffable and beyond the realm of ordinary human language. Yet, when constrained to describe it, many mystics frequently resort to the metaphor of the spiritual marriage of the soul with God. This particular metaphor, a special favourite of those for whom mysticism is an intimate and personal mode of communion,[2] has been used, since the earliest periods of human religious history, to evoke the consummating event of the spiritual quest.[3] Admittedly, most mystics have been cognizant of the dangers of employing this particular symbolic expression: it is liable to be misunderstood or misinterpreted by the uninitiated and provides opportunity for harsh criticism from those who view the mystic path with disfavour.[4]

The popularity of spiritual marriage as a symbol among mystics of all periods and cultures is not difficult to explain. Mystics, though aware of the inadequacy of symbols and images as vehicles of expression, nevertheless employed them to provide material clothing for the spiritual. Only in this manner could they hint at or suggest to their fellows, albeit imperfectly, the nature of their experience. In their search for symbols best suited to represent the business of 'being in love with the Absolute,' it was but natural for them to turn to the sphere of human love and marriage. Both worldly experiences offer parallels to the mutual love and permanent bond that ties the soul to God. Moreover, the conception of marriage in many medieval (and some modern societies) with its aspects of duty, perpetuity, finality and loving obedience, 'make it an apt image of a spiritual state in which humility, intimacy and love were the dominant characteristics.'[5]

Our concern here is with the application of the spiritual marriage symbolism in a rather unusual Islamic context, specifically with the mystical literature of the Nizari Ismaili community of the Indian subcontinent. We do, however, have to point out two distinctive characteristics of Nizari Ismaili theology which are relevant to our discussion here. Firstly, the Nizari Ismailis believe, in common with other Shiʿis, that the message of Islam can be truly understood and implemented by the Muslim community only under the leadership of a divinely-guided Imam. This Imam, the Shiʿi Muslims declare, must be a specifically designated descendant of the Prophet Muḥammad through his daughter Fāṭima and his cousin and son-in-law ʿAlī. At present, the Nizari Ismailis remain the only Shiʿi group with a physically manifest Imam, namely Aga Khan IV, recognized as the 49th direct descendant of the Prophet Muḥammad. The contemporary community's conception of the Imam is a result of beliefs transmitted through the centuries, interpreted and adapted by each generation in diverse cultural milieus. However, through the flux of change and diversity, obedience and devotion to the Imam have remained the cardinal pillars of faith. For Nizari Ismailis, only the Imam's spiritual insight and knowledge can provide the faithful with the correct interpretation (*ta'wīl*) that penetrates beyond the formal and literal meaning of the divine word embodied in the Qur'an.[6] Secondly, the Nizari Ismailis are notable for the precedence they give the *bāṭin*, the esoteric or spiritual aspects of the faith over the *ẓāhir*, the exoteric or external. Their literature has been perenially preoccupied with the spiritual life of the human soul, especially its search to transcend the confines of physical existence and fulfil its ultimate destiny. This, according to the Qur'anic saying 'From God we are and to Him we return' (2: 156), is for the soul to return to its origin in God. Such a spiritual journey, according to Ismaili thought, is only feasible by means of the spiritual relationship that exists between the inner reality of the individual believer and the inner reality of the Imam as the locus of the divine light (*nūr*). As keeper of the mysteries of the *bāṭin*, the Imam becomes the supreme guide and facilitator of the individual's spiritual quest.[7]

Clearly, the Imam is the focus, and even the fountainhead of mystical life in the community. He is the sole connecting link with the 'other,' standing as he does on the threshold between the temporal world and the world of spiritual reality.[8] Each aspirant desiring to enter the spiritual path must necessarily concentrate on cultivating his or her own individual spiritual relationship with the Imam. It is a bond that is based on mutual love and devotion, its personal dimension being enhanced by the presence of a visible and living Imam. Love and devotion to the Imam are, in fact, among the Ismailis necessary conditions for the attainment of spiritual vision and mystical union for which the believer yearns.[9]

The relationship of the Imam to his disciple (*murīd*), as well as the quest for spiritual enlightenment in the context of this relationship, have been central themes in the community's literature. Ismaili literature is far from being a homogenous corpus. It is as linguistically diverse as the community itself, with each cultural region producing its own distinctive literary artifacts.[10] In the Indian subcontinent, the Nizari Ismailis tradition developed a unique literary genre consisting of approximately 1,000 hymn-like poems, called *gināns*. Composed in several Indic vernaculars, they are meant to be sung in various Indian *rāgas* (musical modes). The *gināns*, though probably dating back to medieval times, continue to function today as one of the mainstays of religious life of the Nizari Ismaili community of the Indian subcontinent; their poetic appeal forms the main content of religious experience within the community.

The Imam-*murīd* relationship, with its mystical and emotional elements, is the subject of many a *ginān*. The mystical experiences that the *pīrs*, the authors of these religious poems, underwent in the course of developing their own spiritual relationships with the Imam, were recorded in poetic form. Indeed, certain *gināns* can be considered to be literary expressions of mystical experiences. At the same time, these mystical *gināns* play an important role in nurturing an individual's understanding of the nature of his or her relationship with the Imam. The ultimate goal of this relationship, as portrayed in the *gināns*, is *dīdār* (vision of the Imam). The *dīdār* is not conceived of in anthropomorphic terms; rather it refers to the inner, mystical vision of the Imam's spiritual light (*nūr*).[11] It is this vision that re-unites the soul with the lofty and sublime origin from which it is separated. For the majority of Ismailis, life is painfully incomplete without the experience of the Imam's *dīdār*.

The most common symbolic expression used in the *ginān* literature for the Imam-*murīd* relationship is that of a woman separated from her beloved – the woman representing the pining human soul, while the beloved represents the Imam in his spiritual reality. Typical of this use of the woman-soul is the *ginān* *Tamakū sadhāre soh din* (*The Day that You Left*), attributed to the 8th/14th century Pīr Ṣadr al-Dīn (see Appendix, II). This poem in the form of a woman's lament at the departure of her beloved, highlights the agonies of separation in a language that is intended to inspire the novice on the spiritual journey.

> Beloved, it has been long since the day you left
> (and) anxiously I wait for you.
> My merciful lord and kindly master,
> O my beloved, how will I spend these days without you?[12]

The utter selflessness, humility and devotion that are necessary prerequisites for success on the spiritual path are also strikingly portrayed in the *gināns* by the symbol of the woman as a wife awaiting the return of her husband. It is not uncommon to find *gināns* using Indic terms for husband or lord (*nar, nāth, swāmī*) in reference to the Imam. This symbol of the wife is best exemplified in the *ginān* called *Swāmī rājo more man thī na viserejī* (*My Heart will Never Forget the Master, the King*) also attributed to Pīr Ṣadr al-Dīn, in which the woman-soul is portrayed as performing her 'wifely duties' towards her husband (see Appendix, III). The idea of servitude is also expressed by representing the soul as the servant or slave of the lord. A popular *ginān Darshan dīyo morā nāth* (*Grant me Your Vision, my Lord*), composed by the female saint Imām-Begum, is based entirely on this theme, with the supplicating servant craving for *dīdār/darshan* (vision) of the Lord.[13] In accord with the tendency to portray the human soul as female, the servant, too, is always a *dāsī*, a female slave, never a *dās* or male slave.

Yet the most dramatic symbol employed in the *gināns* recalls the image of the woman separated from her beloved. More precisely, the woman-soul is likened to a bride awaiting her marriage. A host of terms and rituals, normally associated with the marriage ceremony in Indian society, are used to garb the spiritual experience with a form that arouses immediate associations and is readily understood. The *ginān* that best reflects the use of the image of the bride and the spiritual marriage is in the form of a supplication (*ventī*). It is attributed to a male author of the 9th/15th century, Pīr Ḥasan Kabīr al-Dīn, who portrays himself as a bride longing for her divine bridegroom.[14] Comprising fifty verses in the Gujarati language, the *ginān* is often published under the evocative title of *Rūḥānī Visāl* (*Spiritual Union*), (see Appendix, I).[15] The emotions aroused by the exquisite use of symbols in this *ginān* as well as the wistful and plaintive *rāg* (melody) in which it is sung have undoubtedly contributed to its immense popularity within the community. In the subcontinent, it is sung particularly during occasions when the *jamāʿat* (congregation) decides to make a special effort, for a period of seven days and nights, of intense prayer and meditation for union with the Divine. These occasions, called *satāḍās* (literally 'heptads') are seen as periods of spiritual regeneration and renewed resolution to strive for spiritual progress. The *ginān* is sung, however, just before the meditation session to create an appropriate spiritual atmosphere and evoke a mood suitable to this significant occasion.

The central concept that underlies the *Rūḥānī Visāl*[16] is one of a primordial covenant between the yearning soul and the Divine Beloved. The *ginān* begins with an invocation to the absolute and indescribable Lord, the Origin of all beings who have been separated from Him through the process of creation and earthly manifestation. To this typically gnostic theme is added another element. The fifth verse alludes to a primordial gathering, obviously of great significance:

> Whoever in that gathering recognized You,
> Him You will make return.

The soul, longing to be united with her Lord, reminds Him of a promise that was made between them and urges Him to fulfil the promise, since she has been waiting too long:

> Lord, my attention is fixed upon You;
> It is You who occupy my thoughts.
> How can I capture another (like You)?
> Lord, return to fulfil Your promise to me;
> do not forsake me, even for a single moment.

The concepts of a primordial gathering and a promise in this *ginān* refer to a verse in the Qur'an (7:172), where God called the future humanity out of the loins of the yet uncreated Adam and addressed them with the words, 'Am I not your Lord (*alastu bi rabbikum*)?' and they answered, 'Yes, we witness it (*balā shahādnā*).' The idea of this primordial covenant between God and man is one that has made a deep impression on the spiritual outlook of Muslims.[17] In the words of Henry Corbin, 'The religious conscience of Islam is centred upon a fact of meta-history.'[18] This event in pre-eternity commemorates the establishment of a lasting bond or relationship between God and His creation. It is a relationship that the Muslim mystic conceives of being based on love and obedience.

> The goal of the mystic is to return to the experience of the 'Day of *Alastu*,' when only God existed, before he led future creatures out of the abyss of not-being and endowed them with life, love and understanding so that they might face Him again at the end of time.[19]

The motif of the primordial covenant, so characteristic of Islamic mysticism in general, is represented in our *ginān* by the use of symbols and imagery normally associated with betrothal and marriage. The most obvious of these symbols is the *nikāḥ*, the marriage rite among Muslims. The spiritual state of yearning and longing for divine union is compared to a woman's longing to get married.

> Age upon age I have been waiting anxiously,
> But yet the marriage (*nikāḥ*) has not taken place!

To add a dramatic note to the quality of longing, the woman is described as being in the bloom of youth (*bhar joban*) and unable to wait any longer for the wedding. In mystical terms, the bloom of youth refers to the state in which the soul feels it is mature for divine union. It is a state which is achieved through a long and painful process of spiritual evolution, during which the impure and wayward soul (in Sufi terminology, the *nafs al-ammāra*) is purified and tamed. It is only after the wayward soul is completely broken and transformed through the dynamic force of divine love that she is mature and 'ripe' enough to be accepted into the presence of the Husband. Thus, the term for bloom of youth (*bhar joban*) in this *ginān* refers to a state similar to the *nafs al-muṭmaʿinna*, 'the soul at peace.' It is in this state that the soul is ready to be 'called home to its Lord.'[20]

> Lord, sobbing and sighing, I plead with You.
> My heart pines in longing.
> O Lord, come soon,
> Lest (it is too late and) the bloom (of my youth) fades away.

In keeping with the overall theme of the covenant, the marriage is portrayed as one that has been promised to the woman by her Beloved. The use of the terms *dūhāg* and *sūhāg* in this connection are particularly significant. *Dūhāg*, depicting the state of waiting that elapses between the time the bride-to-be receives news of her approaching (traditionally arranged) marriage and the performance of the marriage ceremony, corresponds to a period of formal engagement. *Sūhāg*, on the other hand, corresponds to a state of married bliss. In the *ginān*, the soul complains about the unusually lengthy period of time that she has passed in the unfulfilled state of *dūhāg* and urges the Beloved to remedy the situation:

> O Lord, how long must I remain alone?
> The days pass in separation (*dūhāg*) from You.
> Change my state of separation to married bliss (*sūhāg*).
> Lord of the fourteen heavens, preserve my honour.

Again, the woman-soul reminds her Beloved that she has been entrusted to Him by her parents, and she exhorts Him to fulfil this trust by marrying her. Having been committed to marriage with the Beloved, the woman reminds Him that preservation of her honour (*lāj*), a goal so important in Indian society, depends on the fulfilment of the promise. Here the relationship with the Lord is not seen as one that is hindered by other competing relationships. It is a unique association that goes back to pre-eternity, innate and natural to the soul. The marriage or union marking the culmination of this relationship has been promised, even guaranteed; it is inevitable that the Beloved fulfil the promise. His only freedom is in determining the time for the inevitable marriage. The relationship, as a binding contract between two parties, thus downplays the importance of the free gift of divine grace without rejecting it completely.

In another verse, the bride-soul observes in desperation that she cannot marry anyone else, for the coconut, which is a public declaration of the bridegroom's honourable intentions and commitment of marriage, has already been sent to her. Having willingly accepted the Beloved's proposal, now it would be disgraceful for her to look at another. It is only the Beloved who can soothe the agonies of the soul. The soul, in its search for divine union, must be willing to sacrifice and risk everything for the sake of the Beloved. Hence, in a very bold move, the bride-soul in our *ginān* leaves her parental home and comes to the Beloved's residence with a water pot (*hail*) on her head. Through this Gujarati custom which permits young women to choose their own spouses, the bride offers herself of her own accord to her Beloved. If rejected, she runs the risk of losing all honour and standing in society and perhaps ruining her chances of ever receiving a marriage offer. She pleads with the Beloved to accept her offering, and hence herself, by taking down the water pot from on top of her head. This offer of love also indicates that the marriage is important not just for the sake of preserving the woman's honour and the mere fulfilment of a contract, but it is fervently desired by the soul as an end in itself.

An important facet of the pleas for marriage is the constant use of terms associated with the rites and rituals of the marriage ceremony. The bridegroom is urged to come and collect the bride from her parental home with the traditional marriage procession while she, in anticipation, beautifies herself with *aṁbar* (clothes) and *ābhūshan* (ornaments). The theme of the bride preparing herself for the Beloved is a significant allusion to an important facet of the mystical path – the preparation the soul has to undertake before it is ready to experience the unitive experience.[21] The Beloved is also urged to set up a *chorī* or boundary of sacredness, within which the marriage is to take place. Significantly, in this *ginān*, the *chorī* is to be set up in the midst of the universe, giving the marriage a cosmological tone. Another verse refers to the *chauk* (*chok*) *bāzār*, an ornamental square of coloured flour in which the bride and bridegroom sit for a short while for a certain number of days before the wedding. The soul ascends to the *chauk* remembering the name of the Lord – the image of the bride constantly thinking about her Beloved correlates with the practice of meditation – 'breath upon breath, I contemplate.' Through the power of the divine name, all obstacles on the spiritual path are removed and salvation (union with the Divine) is attained.

The role played by the parents represents symbolically the role of the physical world in the spiritual quest. The parents and relatives, rather than being obstacles on the path to spiritual fulfilment, seem to play a supportive role in the bride's pleas for marriage. For the sake of the family honour, they urge their daughter to get married, and do not want to keep her any longer than is necessary in the family home. It is the parents who entrusted their daughter to her husband-to-be, arranged the marriage, and they are perfectly happy to see it actualized. While this may be in stark contrast to the views of the 'ascetic' forms of mysticism which regard the world and family as obstacles to the spiritual path, it alludes to a fundamental propensity in Ismaili thought to regard the physical world to exist in a state of complementarity with the spiritual. The world of matter is the arena in which the context for a spiritual life is shaped; without acting in it, the spiritual quest is regarded as unworthy.[22]

The synthesis between the spiritual and the material in a mystical symbol has often led to the conclusion that mystical love poetry refers to earthly love. Poetry composed by Persian mystics has sometimes been interpreted in this manner. In the *Rūḥānī Visāl*, despite the use of imagery of human love and marriage, there can be no doubt of its religious and spiritual character. This lack of ambiguity is partly achieved by the absence of any erotic images and symbols. It is also the result of the overall cosmological tone of the *ginān* and the inclusion of clear spiritual advice, especially in the last verses. Denouncing ignorance, the bride-soul pleads with the believers (Gujarati *rikhīsaro*, Arabic *mu'mins*) to acquire virtue, meditate regularly and love the Lord, so that divine union may be achieved. True knowledge is taken to mean that which enables the soul to keep its attention on the Lord. The lack of knowledge and indulgence in activities such as backbiting remove the fixation of the mind on the Lord and hence are hazardous to the attainment of bliss. The soul is dear to the Lord when He knows not only that she thinks of Him constantly but also that she is aware of Him in every one of her actions. Hence the traditional Indian image of the loving, devoted wife, constantly thinking about her beloved, is an excellent means of portraying the psychological orientation necessary in the spiritual quest.

The symbols of the bride and marriage are by no means the only symbols used in the *ginān*s in connection with the mystical experience. A host of other symbols from the world of nature that depict states of dependence, selflessness and devotion are also employed quite effectively. An especially popular one among the *pīrs* was the symbol of the fish writhing in agony when it is out of the water. Love, as symbolized by water, is portrayed through this symbol as the emotive principle of life.[23] Symbols exalting in the efficacy of an inner mode of worship and interiorized religion are also emphasized in consonance with the traditional Ismaili pre-occupation with correlating the interior with the exterior, the spiritual with the material, the *ẓāhir* with the *bāṭin*.[24] Within this rich treasure of symbols and images, however, the symbol of the woman separated from her lover or the bride longing for her groom is pre-eminent in its importance. So strongly has the human soul of the *ginān*s been glued to this symbol, that the *pīrs*, the mostly male composers, often reversed gender when they spoke for the soul and its experiences. Typically, the composer of the *Rūḥānī Visāl*, says in its final stanza:

> Pīr Ḥasan Kabīrdīn, becoming a woman, supplicates
> And holds the hand of her husband ʿAlī.

The *pīr* specifically states that he has taken on a feminine role to petition ʿAlī, the first Shiʿi Imam, who here symbolically and spiritually represents all the Ismaili Imams. This gender reversal is noteworthy, for, it implies that gender itself is endowed with religious significance. Adopting a feminine consciousness seems to lead to a fuller spiritual experience; selfless devotion and love are conceived as more innate to the feminine mode. This is, of course, of considerable importance in our understanding of the psychology of religious experience. It raises the question of finding out in what way the feminization of the male believer and the use of the marriage symbol is institutionalized through devotional worship. These are issues certainly worthy of analysis but beyond the scope of our discussion here.[25]

The *ginān* literature of the Nizari Ismailis of the subcontinent has its own place within a cultural and religious context beyond the specific confines of the community. Its cultural context was that of pre-modern north India, specifically the regional cultures of Sind, Gujarat and Punjab. In its religious context, it belongs to the vast corpus of Islamic mystical literatures produced in the subcontinent by a large number of mystically-inclined Muslim groups. The literature's partiality to, and preference for, the use of bridal symbolism can best be appreciated by considering it within both these contexts.

By casting the soul in the feminine mode, the *pīrs*, though representatives of an Islamic community with strong historical and political links to the Perso-Arabic world, demonstrated an awareness and sensitivity to cultural and literary conventions of their Indian audience. While the woman-soul or bride symbolism of the *ginān*s seems unique in the broader corpus of Ismaili literature, it is extremely common and popular in Indian literature. Medieval Indian poets of the Hindu *bhakti* tradition, under the influence of the Krishna devotional movement of north India, almost always wrote their poems from the point of view of the *gopīs*, the young women who herded cows and were madly in love with Krishna.[26] Being male in traditional north Indian society meant superior social standing – a standing that in devotional poetry could only be a prerogative associated with the Divine. Indeed, according to Hindu ideals of marriage, the husband was representative of divine power. Moreover, the Hindu tradition perceived women as innately closer to the intimacy and naturalness of spirit that it is the purpose of *bhakti* to cultivate.[27] Thus it was only logical for Mīrābāī, medieval India's foremost female poet-saint, to declare that in the presence of the Lord Krishna all of humanity is reduced to womanhood.[28] To become a woman before Krishna was, indeed, the goal of spiritual life among some Vaishnavite devotional cults.[29]

To what extent do the woman-soul and the bride-soul symbols found in the Ismaili *ginān* literature fit into the topography of other Islamic mystical literatures? Annemarie Schimmel has remarked that in classical Sufi poetry from the Arab and Iranian world, the woman is, with a few exceptions, almost always a negative symbol, representing something that is dangerous to the spiritual health of the soul.[30] Many a Sufi would agree with the statement of the great Persian mystic, Mawlānā Jalāl al-Dīn Rūmī, 'first and last my fall is through woman.'[31] And yet, on the other hand, several Sufis, including Rūmī himself, while depicting the union of the soul with God, resort to the imagery of marriage of the bride-soul with the Divine, designating physical death as a spiritual wedding 'in which the soul is finally reunited with her primordial Beloved.'[32] Other mystics, notably Ibn 'Arabī, reinterpreted the significance of the feminine element by suggesting that God's essence is best recognized through the feminine aspect.[33] In the Indian subcontinent, Sufi poetry written in the indigenous languages such as Hindi, Sindhi, Punjabi, etc., however, it is conventional to represent the soul as a woman, either as a *virahinī* (a woman yearning to be reunited with her lover), a faithful wife or a loving bride.[34] In some regions such as Punjab and Sind, Sufi poets identified themselves with the heroines from the many folk romances which they endowed with mystical interpretation. They depicted these heroines in the long and painful search for the union with the Beloved.[35] The soul explicitly portrayed as a bride also makes her appearance as a symbol in many *qawwālīs*, the popular songs recited at the shrines of Muslim saints in the subcontinent. Thus, in a *qawwālī* attributed to Amir Khusrau (d. 726/1325), the renowned poet of the Chishti order expresses his mystical love through a young bride longing to offer herself up in utter devotion to her groom.[36] Bridal symbolism also occurs in the poetry of some of the earliest Sufi poets writing in Urdu. Again, in the provinces of Sind and Punjab, one frequently finds in poems of the *bārahmāsa* genre that the poet identifies himself as a bride waiting to be reunited with God or with the bridegroom of Medina, that is, the Prophet Muḥammad.[37]

Seen within this larger context, the highly-developed use of bridal-soul symbolism in the *ginān*s falls into perspective. Clearly, like the Ismaili *pīr*s, other Muslim authors also felt the need to indigenize their symbolism to the literary tastes of their local Indian audiences. The symbol of the longing woman or the bride, taken over from Hindu devotional poetry, is a powerful one in which many of the emotions experienced by the soul in its quest for union can be intensely compressed and tenderly expressed. It was, on the whole, a perfect 'Indian' vehicle in which Indo-Muslim mystics, Shiʿi and Sunni alike, could convey their message most effectively and with maximum impact on their audiences.

Notes

* This chapter was originally published as 'Bridal Symbolism in Ismaili Mystical Literature of Indo-Pakistan,' in Robert Herrera, ed., *Mystics of the Book: Themes, Topics and Typologies.* New York, 1993, pp. 389–404.

1. Evelyn Underhill, *Mysticism: A Study in the Nature and Development of Man's Spiritual Consciousness* (12th ed., New York, 1930; repr., 1961), p. 125.

2. Ibid., p. 138.

3. Ileana Marcoulesco, 'Mystical Union,' in Mircea Eliade, ed., *Encyclopedia of Religion* (New York, 1987).

4. Evelyn Underhill points out that the other common form of expressing mystical union, favoured by mystics she calls the 'transcendent-metaphysical' types, is deification, a form of expression she considers at least as dangerous as that of the spiritual marriage. Ibid., p. 415.

5. Ibid., p. 163. Underhill also notes the interesting case of the mystic Richard St. Victor who found the symbolism of marriage so appropriate to spiritual life that he devised a daring and detailed application of it by identifying the soul's mystical development to four stages of betrothal, marriage, union or wedlock, and fruitfulness, pp. 139–40.

6. Azim Nanji, 'Ismāʿīlism,' in S.H. Nasr, ed., *Islamic Spirituality: Foundations* (New York, 1987), p. 185.

7. For an overview of spirituality among the Ismailis, see Henry Corbin, *Cyclical Time and Ismaili Gnosis,* trans. R. Mannheim and J.W. Morris (London, 1983); also Nanji, 'Ismāʿīlism.'

8. Aziz Esmail, 'Satpanthi Ismailism and Modern Changes Within it With Special Reference to East Africa' (Ph.D. thesis, University of Edinburgh, 1971), pp. 459–60.

9. The bond of love between the Imam and his followers is readily apparent to anyone who is acquainted with modern Nizari Ismaili communities. The Nizari Ismailis consider their Imam to be their 'spiritual father and mother,' while the Imam in turn refers to his followers as 'my beloved spiritual children.' It is crucial to bear in mind this spiritual basis for the love and devotion shown to the Imam for it goes a long way in explaining the centrality of the Imamate for Ismailis, and why they have upheld their faith in the Imam despite severe persecution over the centuries.

10. Some of the languages in which Ismaili literature is recorded include Arabic, Persian, Urdu, Hindustani, Sindhi, Gujarati, Punjabi, Burushaski, Shina and Khowar.

11. Esmail, 'Satpanth Ismailism,' pp. 459–60.

12. Translated from the text in D. Velji, 72 *Ginans. Part I: Transliteration of Holy Ginans* (Nairobi, 1972), pp. 3–5.

13. Text in Roman transliteration from *Wonderful Tradition* (Kampala, 1968), pp. 40–1.

14. According to Aziz Esmail, *ginān*s attributed to Pīr Ḥasan Kabīr al-Dīn are marked by an acute sense of contriteness and dereliction, which finds expression in numerous and intense prayers and outbursts of passionate longing for beatific vision. 'Satpanth Ismailism,' p. 33.

15. *Rūḥānī Visāl. Ventī Pīr Ḥasan Kabīrdīn* (Karachi, 1976).

16. The text of the *ginān* used in this analysis is contained in the edition referred to above. As is the case with most printed *ginān* texts, it has not been critically edited and hence may vary in minor details from versions found in original manuscripts. This does not, however, affect its use in this study for the text is faithful in its representation of the symbolism associated with the Imam-*murīd* relationship.

17. Annemarie Schimmel, *Mystical Dimensions of Islam* (Chapel Hill, 1975), p. 24.

18. Henry Corbin, *Histoire de la philosophie Islamique* (Paris, 1964), p. 16.

19. Schimmel, *Mystical Dimensions*, pp. 24, 184. Love-intoxicated Sufis such as Ibn al-Fārid and Gisūdarāz refer to true lovers drinking the wine of love at the day of the covenant, while Maulānā Rūmī represents the pre-eternal covenant by the image of the *samā*ʿ or mystic dance:

> A call reached Not-Being; Not-Being said:
> 'Yes, yes.
> I shall put my foot on that side, fresh and green and joyful.'
> It heard the *alast*; it came forth running and intoxicated,
> It was Not-Being and became Being (manifested in) tulips and
> willows and sweet basil.

20. Ibid., p. 112.

21. Cf. Verse 51 from the *ginān Sloko nāno* (*The Shorter Collection of Couplets*) where the *pīr* addresses the woman-soul embarking on the mystic-journey:

> Strive for the Truth
> And decorate yourself with the Truth;
> Take love as the *kohl* (make-up) for the eye
> And place the Beloved as a garland round the neck.

Text from *Shrī Nakalank Shāstra. Pīr Sadardīnno saloko nāno.* 1st ed. (Bombay, 1923), p. 10.

22. Nanji, 'Ismāʿīlīsm,' p. 197.

23. A typical example of the use of the fish symbol occurs in the *gināns* *Huṅ re pīasī tere darshan kī* (*I Thirst for a Vision of You*) and *Ūncā re koṭ bahu vecana* (*A High and Lofty Fortress*). See Appendix, V and VII, for translations of these *gināns*.

24. Azim Nanji, *The Nizārī Ismāʿīlī Tradition in the Indo-Pakistan Subcontinent* (Delmar, NY, 1978), p. 178.

25. It would be interesting to look into the implications of the woman symbol from the viewpoint of Jungian psychology. For a discussion of this symbol in Gnostic thought, see Wayne A. Meeks, 'The Image of the Androgyne: Some Uses of a Symbol in Earliest Christianity,' *History of Religions*, 13, no. 3. See also M. Eliade, *The Two and the One* (New York, 1965), pp. 78–122.

26. For a discussion of gender reversal in this tradition, see John Hawley, 'Images of Gender in the Poetry of Krishna,' in Caroline Bynum et al., ed., *Gender and Religion: On the Complexity of Symbols* (Boston, 1986), pp. 231–56.

27. Ibid., p. 238.

28. Ibid., p. 235.

29. Ibid., p. 236.

30. *Mystical Dimensions of Islam*, p. 428. In the Arabic and Persian mystical literature, the representation of the longing soul in the image of a woman occurs in the rare cases of Mary, the mother of Jesus, and Zulaykha, the wife of Potiphar.

31. Ibid., p. 429.

32. Annemarie Schimmel, *My Soul is a Woman: The Feminine in Islam* (New York, 1997), p. 110.

33. Ibid., p. 102. See also R.J.W. Austin, 'The Sophianic Feminine Tradition in the Works of Ibn ʿArabi and Rumi,' in Leonard Lewisohn, ed., *The Heritage of Sufism* (Oxford, 1999), vol. 2, pp. 233–45.

34. Ibid., p. 434; Lajwanti Rama Krishna, *Panjabi Sufi Poets, A.D. 1460–1900* (Karachi, repr. 1977), p. xxi; and Ali S. Asani, 'Sufi Poetry in the Folk Tradition of Indo-Pakistan,' *Religion and Literature*, 20, no. 1 (1988), pp. 85–6.

35. Ali S. Asani, 'Folk Romance in Sufi Poetry from Sind,' in A. Dallapiccola and S. Lallemant, ed., *Islam and the Indian Regions* (Stuttgart, 1993), vol. 1, pp. 229–37; Annemarie Schimmel, *Pain and Grace: A Study of Two Mystical Writers of Eighteenth Century Muslim India* (Leiden,

1976) and Lajwanti Ram Krishna, *Panjabi Sufi Poets.*

36. Regula Qureshi, *Sufi Music of India and Pakistan: Sound, Context and Meaning in Qawwali* (Cambridge, 1986), p. 26.

37. See Ali S. Asani and Kamal Abdel-Malik, *Celebrating Muhammad: Images of the Prophet in Popular Muslim Poetry* (Columbia, S.C., 1995), pp. 19–36.

4

The *Gīt* Tradition: A Testimony of Love*

The Nizari Ismailis are distinctive among contemporary Muslim communities for the veneration which they accord their leaders, the Imams, known as the Aga Khans.[1] The Imams' claim to spiritual and temporal leadership of the community is based on their descent from the Prophet Muḥammad through his daughter Fāṭima and son-in-law, ʿAlī. It is this fact of their physical descent from the Prophet and the first Shiʿi Imam ʿAlī that is the most important factor contributing to the veneration that the Ismaili Imams receive from their followers. This essay explores the symbols and images that contemporary Nizari Ismailis employ in their folk songs or *gīts* to express their veneration for the Imams. Though a popular medium of devotional expression, these songs have hithertofore never been studied as a genre of religious literature.

The tradition of composing *gīts*, as we know in its present form, has been associated particularly with Nizari Ismaili communities of South Asian origin, whether residing in the subcontinent itself or in diaspora in East Africa, Europe and North America. Unfortunately, we know precious little about its development. As is the case with many folk traditions that have been orally transmitted, its historical origins are quite obscure. Moreover, the *gīts* themselves have never been systematically collected and documented. In the community's perception, the *gīts* are quite distinct in nature and function from the *gināns*, the hymn-like poems and songs, which have been examined in the previous chapters.[2] Over the course of time, this corpus came to be gradually 'frozen,'[3] the last *gināns* probably having been composed at the turn of this century. *Gīts*, on the other hand, are perceived to represent a 'living' tradition of piety in the community. They provide an outlet for individuals to express their religious devotion by utilizing their own poetic idiom and musical creativity. The popularity of these *gīts* is so widespread that today *gīt* cassettes and records can be found whenever Nizari Ismailis of South Asian origin reside. Sold through the religious book depots associated with every major community centre, these recordings have become ubiquitous in many an Ismaili home.

Both women and men have been actively engaged in the development of the *gīt* tradition. Significantly, hardly any of them are musicians or song-writers by profession, although quite a few have received some kind of formal training. Depending on their personal background and inclination, most tend to focus on the creation of either lyrics or melodies; a few, however, are talented enough to be involved in both aspects. Others may 'specialize' in *gīt* performance, singing compositions created by others. In several cases, involvement with the *gīt* tradition is a family affair transmitted from one generation to the next. Thus Anaar Kanji, a leading *gīt* singer in the Canadian Ismaili community, traces her musical talents back to her great-grandparents, especially her great-grandfather who used to sing songs for silent Indian movies in Zanzibar. Another singer, Kamal Taj, a Pakistani immigrant to the USA and by profession an engineer, is a protégé of his father Taj Kavi who played a leading role in the *gīt* tradition in Pakistan. Although for the most part, the evolution of the tradition has been on an individual or personal basis, in recent years, community institutions, such as the Ismaili Tariqa and Religious Education Boards, have also become involved in sponsoring *gīt* recordings by community-based groups, orchestras and bands.

Usually *gīts* are composed and sung to commemorate festive events such as Imamat Day (the anniversary of the Imam's accession),[4] the birthday of the Imam,[5] or to express joy during his

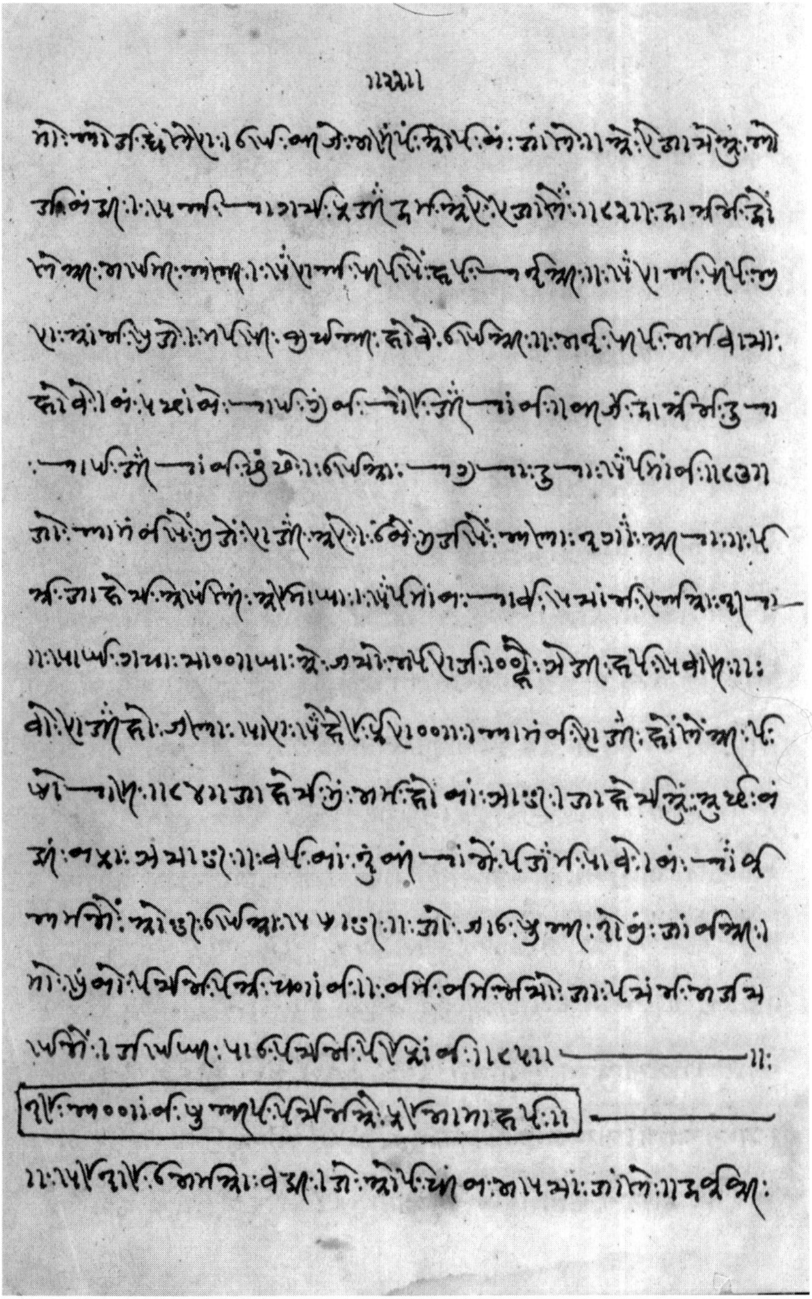

I. From *Kalām-i Mawlā*, a Hindustani translation written in Khojkī script of an Arabic-Persian poem attributed to Imam 'Alī (KH42, p.22, dated 1851, copied by Khoja Alarākhiā Kurjī of Bombay).

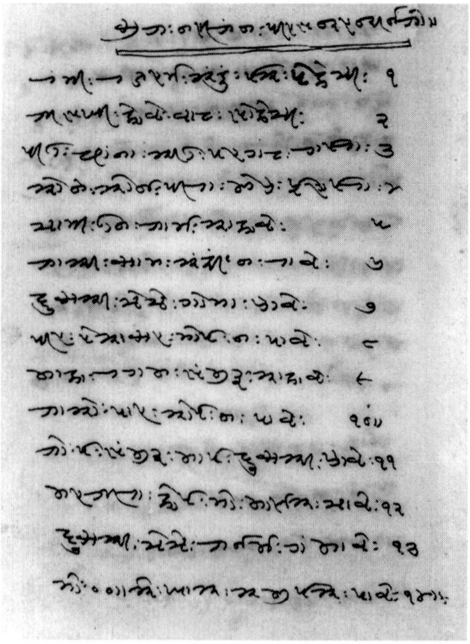

II. From *Būjh Niranjan*, a *ginān* attributed to Pīr Ṣadr al-Din, from a Khojkī manuscript (KM117, folio 173a, copied in late 19th/early 20th century).

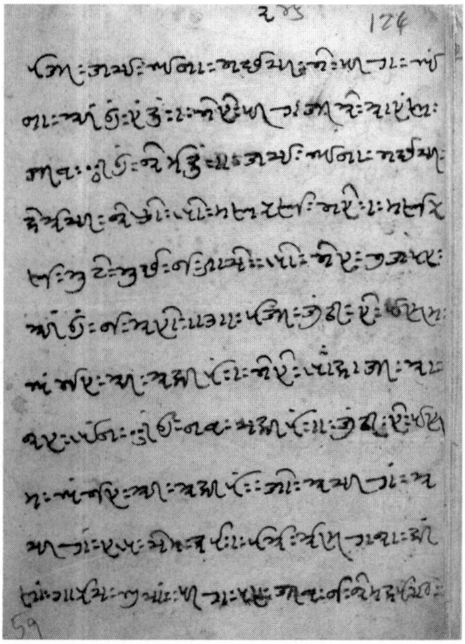

III. From *Hun re pīasī tere darshan kī*, a *ginān* attributed to Sayyid Khān, from a Khojkī manuscript (KH84, p.259, dated 1867, copied by Khoja Jāfar Dhālānī).

IV. Arabic text written in Khojkī script of the 'Throne-verse' *(ayāt al-kursī)* from the Qur'an (2:255), followed by invocatory prayers (KH101, pp.90-91, copied in late 19th century).

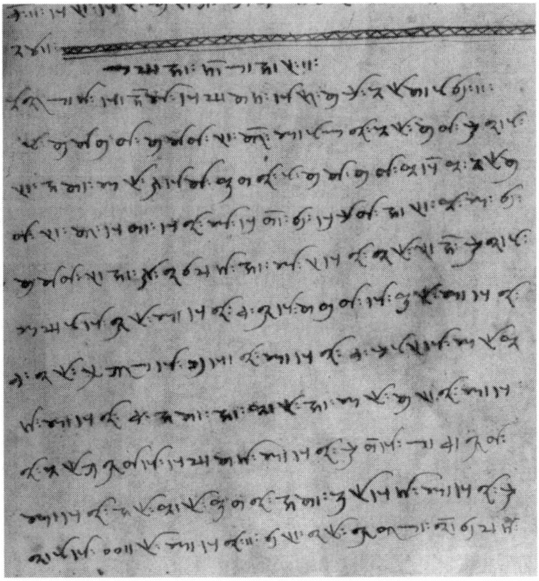

V. From the Persian text written in Khojkī script of the *Pandiyāt-i jawānmardī* attributed to the Imam Mustanṣir-bi'llāh II (d. 885/1480), (KH48, vol.3, dated 1802-1830 in Shah Bandar, Sindh).

VI. On the left: the *Shahāda* inscribed in Arabic within a circle, surrounded by invocations to Allāh, Muḥammad, 'Alī, Fāṭima, Ḥasan and Ḥusayn.
On the right: text of *Nāde 'Alī,* an invocatory prayer addressed to Imam 'Alī, with the representation of his sword *dhu'l-fiqār* (from a Khojkī manuscript, KH21, pp 308-309, dated 1817-1823, copied in Surat, Gujarat, by multiple scribes including the daughter of Pīr Ghulām 'Alī Shāh).

formal visits to a particular congregation or country. In 1982–3, dozens of *gīts* were composed during the Silver Jubilee honouring the Imam's 25th anniversary. *Gīts* have also been composed in conjunction with Muslim festivals such as the *ʿīd al-adhā* and *ʿīd al-fiṭr*. For example, as part of *ʿīd* celebrations in Zanzibar, a major centre of Ismaili settlement in East Africa in the late 19th and early 20th centuries, the Ismailis organized grand parades, complete with floats, through city streets and alleyways. Seated on the float at the head of the parade would be groups of singers, usually young ladies, singing *gīts*.[6] In addition to such celebrations, *gīts* are also sung in special musical assemblies called *gīt meḥfils* or *mushāʿiras*, often featuring specially-invited singers of international repute in the Ismaili world. Frequently *gīts* are specifically composed or their rhythm adapted to accompany the performance of dances popular in the community such as the Gujarati *ḍānḍiyā*, *garba* and *rās*.

In terms of their formal or structural characteristics, *gīts* draw heavily from popular culture, especially the folk song traditions of India and Pakistan. Consequently a diversity of forms, metres, rhymes and melodies prevail. Common forms include the Gujarati *garbo*, the Urdu *ghazal* and *qawwālī*, as well as the Sindhi *kāfī*. In addition, devotional songs attributed to poets from the North Indian *bhakti* and *sant* traditions have provided inspiration for some compositions, as have popular songs from Hindi movies. A few *gīts* from the Ismaili immigrant communities of East Africa, especially in Zanzibar, have also been affected by the *tārāb* musical tradition of the Swahili. Not surprisingly, in recent years, even Western 'popular' discotheque music has become a growing influence. The *gīts* are equally versatile, linguistically. Naturally, South Asian languages such as Gujarati, Hindi, Sindhi and Urdu predominate, but a few are also in Swahili. Among the Ismailis of the United States, attempts have been made to create *gīts* in the English language. Finally, we must also note occasional instances of the incorporation of entire Arabic phrases, usually from the Qur'an or of some theological import, into some poetic compositions.

As already intimated above, *gīts* function primarily as a means for composers and singers to express their feelings of devotion to the Imam. At the same time, they permit those who listen to them to participate in this devotion which is so central in the Nizari Ismaili path of Islam. According to this, the Imam is a representative of a divinely-ordained institution, the Imamate, whose function is to provide the faithful with the correct interpretation of the divine word embodied in the Qur'an beyond its formal or literal sense.[7] Believed to be an intermediary between the temporal world and the world of spiritual reality, the Imam holds an immense actual and symbolic significance.[8] An individual's spiritual development is considered feasible only by means of the relationship that exists between the inner reality of the individual believer and the spiritual reality of the Imam as the locus of divine light (*nūr*). As keeper of the mysteries of the *bāṭin* (the esoteric), the Imam became not only the guide but also the object of the spiritual quest.[9] It is as a result of his supreme spiritual status that the Imam has become the focus of love and devotion in the community. Indeed for many of his followers, love and devotion to the Imam are absolutely necessary for the attainment of the spiritual vision (*dīdār*) and union for which the believer yearns.

How is the special relationship between the Imam and his disciples expressed in the *gīts*? Given the rudimentary state of research on the *gīts* and the constraints of space, we can only provide a brief survey of the more important themes and symbols based on a sample of 80 *gīts* from various parts of the Ismaili world.[10]

As is the case with most types of devotional poetry where the object of devotion becomes the focus of praise, and also in common with the tradition of Shiʿi poetry in general, the *gīts* extol and glorify the virtues of the Imam.[11] As *Imām-i zamān* (the Imam of the time), he is the beloved of God (*maḥbūb allāh kā*),[12] the king of the two worlds, (*shāh-i do ʿālam*),[13] and a symbol of divine dignity (*shān-i khudā*).[14] A recent English *gīt* describes the Imam as the *nūr* of *Al-Raḥmān*, 'the light of the Merciful.'[15] The Imam is the prince of the believers (*amīr al-muʾminīn*) and their lord (*ākā*).[16] According to one Sindhi composition, he is the protector and keeper of the community; his blessings and prayers are truly extraordinary.[17] In short, his spiritual status is considered unique (*nirālo*) in the entire world.[18]

As one would expect, the Imam's role as a guide for the faithful in this world and the next constitutes an important theme in the *gīts*. It is expressed in many different ways. On account of his spiritual knowledge, he is praised as the only true interpreter of God's word, the Qur'an, and hence the holder of its secrets (*rāz*). A few *gīts* emphasize the historical legitimacy of this role by alluding to the events of the Ghadīr Khumm incident when, according to Shiʿi history, the Prophet Muḥammad declared ʿAlī to be the first Imam by taking his hand and saying, 'He whose master I am, ʿAlī is also his master.' The Arabic for this theologically significant phrase – '*Man kuntu mawlāhu fa ʿAliyyun mawlāhu*' – is often incorporated into several lyrics, including a *qawwālī* recited by the famous Sabri brothers for a record to commemorate the Silver Jubilee of the present Imam.[19] With this declaration, says one Urdu *gīt*, the religion [of Islam] was completed (*kāmil mazhab ho gayā*).[20] Along similar lines, other *gīts* highlight the Imam's physical and spiritual ancestry from the Prophet through his daughter Fāṭima and son-in-law, ʿAlī, by employing epithets such as *nūr-i nabī* (light of the Prophet) or *nūr-i ʿAlī* (light of ʿAlī) for it is this illustrious and luminous ancestry that legitimizes the Imam's spiritual role.[21] Sometimes, as in one Gujarati composition, this light imagery is extended further so that the Imam is described as *panj tan no e prakāsh*, 'the light of the five holy persons' of Shiʿi Islam, that is Muḥammad, ʿAlī, Fāṭima, Ḥusayn and Ḥasan.[22] Another piece in Urdu, entitled *Tārīkh-i Imāmat* (*The History of the Imamate*) treats the ancestry theme by tracing, in a musical form, the genealogy of all the Nizari Ismaili Imams together with a historical synopsis of their reigns, beginning with ʿAlī and ending with the present Imam, Karīm al-Ḥusaynī.[23]

Far more commonly associated with the Imam's role as a guide are appeals to his intercessory or intermediary powers. Anyone who appeals to God in the Imam's name will surely, on account of God's love for the Imam, get his or her prayers answered and transgressions forgiven. As one Urdu poet puts it, 'Whoever has grasped his skirt (i.e., gained his protection) is forgiven on the day of resurrection.'[24] He is, in the words of a Sindhi poet, the prince of mercy (*raḥmat jo rāṇo*).[25] The Imam is also *mushkil gushā*, 'the solver of difficulties,' for he helps his faithful devotees withstand all hardships.[26] A very common image in this connection is the Imam as the pilot or captain who navigates the ship of his disciples across the whirlpools of turmoils in the ocean of worldly existence until it safely reaches the shore of salvation in the other world.[27]

Yet the most interesting and intriguing depictions of the Imam's relationship to his disciples takes place within the context of images associated with the *virahinī* or a loving and yearning woman, usually symbolized as a young bride or bride-to-be, who is tormented by the absence of her husband or lord. The *virahinī* has enjoyed great popularity in a wide variety of religious contexts, including the Hindu, Sikh and Islamic traditions, where she was often identified as a symbol for the human soul.[28] As I have discussed elsewhere (in Chapter 3), she is also conspicuous in the *ginān*s where she yearns for the Imam. That she should appear in the *gīt*s devoted to the Imam, the longed-for beloved, is hardly a surprising development. Such usage is entirely in keeping with Indian literary conventions according to which the human soul is always represented in the feminine mode before the divine beloved who is male.[29]

The *virahinī* of the *gīt*s is typically a poignant woman who is afflicted by the fiery pangs of yearning for her beloved Imam. In a Gujarati *gīt* she laments:

> What yearning afflicts me,
> From which there is no escape.
> Come quickly, my sweet beloved,
> Come and quench the fires in my soul.
> How can I bear this separation (*viraha*)?
> What yearnings have afflicted me today?[30]

This love for the Imam has driven her to the point of distraction, for she knows that she can no longer survive without him; he is her life-breath and life-support, just as a fish or a lily flower cannot survive outside water.[31] She neglects her daily chores and at night she is restless without sleep. She complains: 'Love for my lord consumes me body and soul!'[32] In this state, worldly existence has become a cage or prison from which the Imam is her refuge and comfort. Hence she hopes fervently for a glimpse (*darshan* or *dīdār*) of his resplendent face. Addressing the Imam as 'Alī, she implores him:

> Please listen to me, O 'Alī,
> Just cast a glance towards me, O 'Alī.
> No longer can I tolerate this cage,
> No more strength do I have for the deceits of the world.
> I come seeking refuge in you, O 'Alī.[33]

To stress the humility of the disciple before the spiritual guide, the *virahinī* is often represented as a humble peasant woman living in a small hut or cultivating a small field. But she is convinced that out of love (*prīt*) her beloved, overlooking her low status as well as her numerous sins and faults, will visit her home or village.[34] An Urdu *gīt*, based on this image, is appropriately titled *Maulā mere ghar ānā, āke kabhī jānā nā* (*Come to my house, Lord, and then never leave!*)[35] So ardent is the *virahinī*'s hope for a visit that the *papīhā* bird flies far and wide, singing *Maulā ghar āye* (*Lord, come home!*).[36] In an amusing reminder of our modern times, a Gujarati *virahinī* even resorts to urging the beloved Imam to catch the earliest possible airplane back to her![37]

Naturally the visit of the Imam represents for the *virahinī*, and indeed the community of the faithful, an occasion of much celebration and festivity. As the long-awaited meeting (*mulaqāt*) approaches, the Imam's lovers gather and everywhere there is rejoicing: *gīt*s are being sung to welcome him and *ḍānḍiyā* (Gujarati stick dances) are being played;[38] a hundred thousand flowers are gathered to make fragrant garlands for him;[39] the path along which he will walk is decorated with lamps and scattered with pearls;[40] even the birds are chirping away songs of happiness.[41] The *virahinī* sings to her female companions (*sakhīāṅ*) to apply henna to their hands and feet. Some of the henna, she reminds them, is to be saved so that she can apply it symbolically on the Imam's hands.[42]

Lurking behind every happy meeting are the sorrowful thoughts of departure and further separation. This is an event that causes great sadness among the Imam's devotees. The *virahinī* constantly pleads with her beloved not to leave and stay with her eternally or to take her along with him wherever he goes.[43] In a Gujarati song, she lovingly forbids him to leave because it will surely break her heart.[44] And once the Imam has departed, she can no longer bear the pain of separation:

> Every second I recall the times we met,
> The feelings of separation (*biraha*) cannot be expressed.[45]

The composers of *gīts*, notwithstanding the imagery they borrow from the realms of human love, realize that their relationship with the Imam is a spiritual one, between their souls and the spiritual reality of the Imam. They, therefore, avoid erotic or sensual imagery involving descriptions of physical love or beauty. They thus attempt to portray the *virahinī*'s love in an interiorized or spiritualized manner. She knows that even though her beloved may be in a worldly manner far from her, he is spiritually ever-present in her heart which contains his portrait:[46]

> You may be physically distant from my eyes,
> But within my heart and soul there is only you.[47]

> Lord, I see you on the throne in my heart;
> Dear girlfriends, that's how I conceal my soul's thirst.[48]

Indeed the Imam's spirit pervades the *virahinī*'s entire being and she declares:

> Your fragrance permeates every pore of my body,
> In my every breath I take your name.[49]

References to breath and the name frequently occur in the *gīts* and allude to the well-known meditational practice of *dhikr* in which the disciple repeats one of the names of God. It is within the heart that the Imam's lovers attain the goal of their quest, the *nūrānī dīdār*, the vision of his spiritual light. This much-longed for experience forms the most significant leitmotif in Ismaili literature as it is the real goal of the Imam's disciples. As one poet expresses it:

Lord, today, I plead with you and ask only that you grant me *nūrānī dīdār*.[50]

Not surprisingly, some poets have employed the image of eyes and vision to allude to spiritual enlightenment and mystical union. In a rather striking line that appropriately sums up the intensely devotional nature of the *gīts*, the *virahinī* sings:

O crow! Eat up my entire body,
Peck up my flesh into little shreds,
But please don't eat my eyes,
For I still hope to meet my beloved [Imam].[51]

Notes

* This chapter was originally published as 'A Testimony of Love: The *Gīt* Tradition of the Nizari Ismailis,' in A. Giese and J.C. Burgel, ed., *God is Beautiful and He Loves Beauty (Festschrift in Honour of Annemarie Schimmel)*, Bern, 1994, pp. 39–51.

1. The hereditary title 'Āghā Khān' was first bestowed by the Qājār Shah of Iran shortly after 1817 on the 46th Ismaili Imam, Ḥasan 'Alī Shāh (d. 1881).

2. In addition to the articles collected in this volume, see Ali S. Asani, 'The Ismā'īlī *Ginān* Literature: Its Structure and Love Symbolism' (B.A. thesis, Harvard College, 1977); V.N. Hooda, 'Some Specimens of Satpanth Literature', in *Collectanea*, vol. 1 (Leiden, 1948), pp. 55–137; Wladimir Ivanow, 'Satpanth', in *Collectanea*, vol. 1, pp. 1–54; and *Ismaili Literature: A Bibliographic Survey* (Tehran, 1963), pp. 174–81; Azim Nanji, *The Nizārī Ismā'īlī Tradition in the Indo-Pakistan Subcontinent* (Delmar, NY, 1978), pp. 7–24, 120–30; Ismail K. Poonawala, *Biobibliography of Ismā'īlī Literature* (Malibu, Calif., 1977), pp. 298–311.

3. Nanji, *The Nizārī Ismā'īlī Tradition*, p. 17.

4. The present Imam assumed office on July 11, 1957.

5. This festival, commonly called *sālgirah khushiālī*, is at present celebrated on 13th December, the birthday of the present Imam.

6. Anaar and Shiraz Kanji, personal communication.

7. Azim Nanji, 'Ismā'īlīsm,' in S.H. Nasr ed., *Islamic Spirituality: Foundations* (New York, 1987), p. 185.

8. Aziz Esmail, 'Satpanthi Ismailism and Modern Changes Within it

With Special Reference to East Africa,' (Ph.D. thesis, University of Edinburgh, 1971), pp. 459–60.

9. For an overview of spirituality among the Ismailis, see the three essays by Henry Corbin in *Cyclical Time and Ismaili Gnosis*, trans. R. Mannheim and J.W. Morris (London, 1983). See also Nanji, 'Ismāʿīlism.'

10. The *gīts* I have used for this study derive from two major sources: (1) A photocopy of a handwritten notebook containing *gīts*, kindly provided to me by Anaar Kanji of Vancouver, which was presumably compiled for the private use of a singer; the *gīt* lyrics are written in the Gujarati script. It is subsequently referred to in this essay as '*gīt* notebook,' with the first line of the cited *gīt* serving as a title equivalent. (2) Transcriptions from the following commonly available *gīt* cassettes: *Ur na Umango, Ecstasy of the Heart*, vols. 1 & 2 (India); *Yaadon ka Nazrana*; *Surobitan*; *Nazr-e Shah Karim* by Sabri Brothers (sponsored by Tajico group); *Prem Sandesh* (Pakistan); *Rangeet* (Pakistan); *Preetam Pyare Geets* (UK); *Silver Melodies*, vol. 1 (Jubilee Arts); *Geeto'n ki Shaam* (Anaar Kanji); *Shan-e-Karim Geets*, nos. 1–8 (Canada), *Shahadat-e-Ishq* (USA); *Antargeet* (Chicago); and *Nooran Ala Noor*, *Tarikh-e-Imamat* by Kamal Taj and Group (USA); *Padhramni Mubarak 1991*, *Selected Silver Songs in Jhankar* (Pakistan).

11. The strong emphasis on love and devotion in the *gīts* is reflected in the titles of many *gīt* cassettes, for example, *Prem Sandesh* (*The Message of Love*); *Preetam Pyare Geets* (*Gīts for the Dear Beloved*); *Shahadat-e-ishq* (*Testimony of Love*), and so on.

12. *Ur na Umango*, vol. 1, '*Ham par karam kijiye.*'

13. *Gīt* notebook, '*Ay shāhe zamān karīm.*'

14. Ibid., '*Tashrīf lāe darshan diā.*'

15. This *gīt* occurs in a cassette most likely recorded in the United States; unfortunately the copy in my possession does not have a title.

16. *Silver melodies*, '*Maulā jaldī jaldī āvo.*'

17. *Padhramni Mubarak 1991*, '*Aj to ace sāīn sajan pāk waṭan merī.*'

18. *Yaadon ka Nazrana (Gift of Remembrance)*, '*Sārī ʿālam men munjo maulā nirālo.*'

19. Nazr-e Shah Karim, '*Qaul tarānā.*'

20. *Ur na Umango*, vol. 1, '*Ham par karam kijiye.*'

21. *Padhramni Mubarak 1991*, '*Aj to ace sāīn sajaṅ pāl waṭan merī.*'

22. *Gīt* notebook, '*Dejo vadhāmanā.*'

23. *Nooran ala noor. Tarikh-e-Imamat.* Kamal Taj and Group.

24. *Ur na Umango*, '*Ham par karam kijiye.*'

25. *Padhramni Mubarak 1991*, '*Aj to ace sāīn sajan pāk waṭan meṅ.*'

26. *Silver melodies*, '*Hameṅ ghurūr hai allāh nūr hai.*'

27. *Gīt* notebook, '*Pār karo morī nayā*' and '*tashrīf lāe.*'

28. The most renowned use of the *virahinī* in Indian literature occurs, of course, in poetry dedicated to Krishna. In this poetry, the *gopīs* (cowmaids) and in particular Rādhā, express their longings for union with their elusive beloved. The *virahinī* appears in many genres of vernacular Sufi poetry ranging from the romantic epics of Awadh to the folk songs of Punjab and Bengal. In the poetry of the Muslims of Sind, she appears as the bride longing for her beloved Prophet Muḥammad.

29. See John Hawley, 'Images of Gender in the Poetry of Krishna,' in Caroline Bynum et al., ed., *Gender and Religion: On the Complexity of Symbols* (Boston, 1986), pp. 231–56.

30. *Ur na Umango*, vol. 1, '*Viraha tāro kem sahevāy.*'

31. *Gīt* notebook, '*Karīm Shāh huṅ ghelī banī.*'

32. Ibid., '*Nūrānī jalvā mujhko Karīm Shāh dīkhā.*'

33. *Geeto'n ki Shaam*, '*Zarā sāṁbhar mārī 'alī.*'

34. *Gīt* notebook, '*Karīm Shāh ās purone amārī.*'

35. *Surobitan.*

36. *Surobitan, 'Dūr dūr papīhā bole.'*

37. *Gīt* notebook, '*Nahīre āvo to maulā.*'

38. Ibid., '*Bhale āvyā īmāme zamān.*'

39. Ibid.

40. *Ur na Umango*, vol. 1, '*Viraha tāro kem sahevāy.*'

41. *Silver melodies*, '*Āvī āvī jubīlī shāndār.*'

42. *Gīt* notebook, '*Meheṅdī te vāvī antarmāṅ.*'

43. Ibid., '*Laī jā tūṅ mane tārī sāthe.*'

44. Ibid., '*Hāṅre nathī jāvuṅ vilāyat.*'

45. *Silver melodies*, '*Zarā sun le tūṅ dil kī pukār.*'

46. Ibid., '*Mane vahālo vahālo āgā karīm dhaṇī.*'

47. Ibid., '*Laī jā tūṅ mane tārī sāth.*'

48. *Ur na Umango*, vol. 1, '*Viraha tāro kem sahevāy.*'

49. *Ur na Umango*, vol. 2, '*Mane choḍī na jājo mārā prān.*'

50. *Gīt* notebook, '*Maulā āj hāth joḍīne.*'

51. *Ur na Umango*, vol. 2, '*Kāgā sab tan khāyo.*'

5

Reflections on Authority and Authorship of the *Gināns**

Among the literary genres associated with the Ismaili tradition, the *gināns* of the Khoja communities of South Asia are unique.[1] Composed in several Indic languages and dialects, these hymn-like poems have been strongly influenced by North Indian traditions of folk poetry and piety. They thus represent a distinctive regional strand within a larger corpus of Ismaili literature that is mostly in Arabic and Persian. Not surprisingly, the *gināns* are markedly different in their style and ethos from the more scholarly Arabic and Persian Ismaili treatises that have usually attracted the attention of researchers.

The apparently 'syncretistic' manner in which the *gināns* employ Indian or Hindu mythological and theological concepts to present religious ideas has raised questions about their 'Islamic' character. For example, a prominent scholar of South Asian Islam felt that the *gināns* possessed a 'literary personality' regarded as 'un-Islamic,' presumably on account of their vernacular and 'syncretistic' characteristics.[2] Such judgements have, in turn, provoked debate within the community concerning the validity of using externals of culture such as language and idiom as yardsticks for measuring Islamic identity. Ironically, in earlier times, when the religious identity of the Khoja community was the subject of intense dispute, the courts of colonial British India drew on evidence from these very hymns to determine that the Khojas were indeed Muslims of the Nizari Ismaili persuasion.[3]

For historians of religion, the *ginān*s are of particular interest for the prominent role they play in the religious life of Ismaili Khoja communities in the Indian subcontinent and elsewhere.[4] Like many genres of Indian devotional poetry, they are intended to be sung in designated *rāga*s or melodies. The singing of *ginān*s constitutes a prominent item during prayer meetings held every morning and evening in the *jamāʿat-khāna*s (halls of congregation). As Tazim Kassam points out, the singing of *ginān*s in the context of Khoja religious practice is a phenomenon generally characteristic of the Indian religious landscape.[5] Participation in *ginān* singing, especially in a large congregation, can have a powerful emotional and sensual impact on individuals, even those who may not fully understand the meanings and significance of the words they sing.

Beyond their supportive role in worship, the *ginān*s permeate communal and individual life in many ways. At a communal level, functions or meetings, be they religious or secular, frequently begin with a short Qurʾan recitation followed by one from the *ginān*s. Verses from the *ginān*s are often cited as proof-texts during sermons, religious discussions and in religious education materials. Occasionally, for both entertainment and religious edification, special concerts are organized, during which professional and amateur singers recite *ginān*s to musical accompaniment.[6] Again, outside the context of formal worship, community institutions responsible for religious education may sponsor *ginān* competitions in which participants are judged on their ability to sing and properly enunciate *ginān* texts. At a personal and family level, too, *ginān*s are used in many different contexts: individual verses can be quoted as proverbs; verses can be recited in homes to bring *baraka*, a spiritual and material blessing; housewives, in a usage that stresses the links between the *ginān*s and folk tradition, often recite them while working or as lullabies.

As I have discussed elsewhere,[7] the *ginān*s enjoy a significant status in the Khoja Ismaili community, for they are commonly perceived as a source of mystical knowledge. The *ginān*s have been described as 'an unbounded and immeasurable sea of knowledge, a unique storehouse of wisdom and guidelines for everyday life.'[8] They contain instruction on a broad range of themes, including the religious obligations of the believer, ethics and morals, eschatology, the mystical life and the spiritual quest of the soul. Indeed, their function as vehicles for imparting religious teachings and precepts is reflected in their very name which is derived from the Sanskrit word *jnāna*, meaning 'knowledge' or 'sacred wisdom.'

In the community's traditional self-image, the *ginān*s originated in mediaeval times, approximately around the 5th/11th or 6th/12th centuries, when they were first composed by Iranian preacher-saints, called *pīr*s. The *pīr*s were sent to North India by Ismaili Imams from Iran on missions to convert local people to Ismaili Islam and to provide spiritual guidance for the newly-created convert communities. These preacher-saints, tradition asserts, in order to overcome cultural and linguistic barriers facing potential converts, composed *ginān*s to explain the gist of the Qur'an and the Ismaili faith to Indian populations in their native languages and idioms. These poetic compositions provided the faithful with an understanding of the 'true meaning' of the Qur'an, serving to penetrate its 'inner (*bāṭin*) signification.' The *ginān*s were, in effect, 'secondary' texts generated in the vernacular to transmit the teachings of a 'primary' scripture – the Qur'an – to non-Arabic speaking peoples.[9]

The authority of the *ginān*s and the veneration accorded to them is entirely due to their being perceived as substantiations of the truth of the faith as taught by the *pīr*s. These preachers were no ordinary missionaries and evangelists; in the community's understanding, they were spiritually enlightened individuals whose religious and spiritual authority the Ismaili Imams had formally endorsed by bestowing on them the title of *pīr*.[10] The *ginān*s extol the virtues of love for, and unquestioning obedience to, the *pīr* and his teachings, for he is the true guide (*sat guru*) who can guide the faithful on the path to salvation.[11] Since the Imams resided in Iran, the *pīr*s became tangible symbols of the Imams' authority in South Asia with total control over the community and its members.

W. Ivanow describes their theological position as being the 'link between God and man, really the "door", *bāb,* of the Imam, without whose guidance and instruction all efforts of the individual may remain futile and useless.'[12] Not surprisingly, the *pīrs* stand out in the tradition's history as figures of dominating importance, next only to the Imam.[13] In fact, in many contexts the *ginān*s do not always distinguish between the *pīr* and the Imam, both being merged in doublets such as *gur-nar* and *pīr-shāh,* meaning 'guide' and 'lord.'[14]

The most vexing question confronting scholars of the *ginān*s concerns their provenance and authorship. As is the case with many of the poet-saints of mediaeval India, we possess remarkably little accurate historical information about the reputed authors of the *ginān*s and their activities. What we do have, however, are hagiographic and legendary accounts, some of which are incorporated in the *ginān*s themselves. Notwithstanding the admirable attempts made by Azim Nanji to analyse this 'mythic' material, the historical personalities of the *pīrs* remain 'dim and obscure.'[15] In the case of many *pīrs*, we do not possess even basic biographic information such as birth and death dates. In fact, there are doubts concerning the historical existence of Pīr Satgūr Nūr, claimed in traditional accounts to have been the first to be sent to India as early as the 4th/10th or 5th/11th century.[16] According to Azim Nanji, this *pīr* remains at best a symbolic and archetypal figure.[17] We are on slightly firmer ground with his successors, Pīrs Shams, Ṣadr al-Dīn and Ḥasan Kabīr al-Dīn, but only just. In addition to a host of problems associated with their biographies, there is much confusion about the exact identities of the first two.[18] A fourth figure, Imām-Shāh (d. 919/1513), about whom we possess somewhat more reliable information, was allegedly the founder of a 'schismatic' movement that resulted in the formation of the Imām-Shāhī subsect.[19] Consequently, the Ismaili Khoja tradition only accords him the status of *sayyid,* a rank inferior to that of *pīr.* To these four personalities, who reportedly lived between the 6th/12th and 9th/15th centuries, are attributed the vast majority of *ginān*s.

The *ginān*s contain very little evidence to corroborate religious claims that they were composed during the historical period traditionally associated with these early *pīrs*. On the contrary, the linguistic and grammatical features of the *ginān*s, as well as their idioms and style, point to later origins. W. Ivanow, though averse to offending the sentiments of his Ismaili friends, declared that in his opinion *ginān*s attributed to a certain *pīr* seem to be more *about* him than *by* him, and that there was no doubt about their being composed much later.[20] Christopher Shackle and Zawahir Moir, in their recent study, remark:

> No realistic discussion of the ginans is possible without first facing the realization that they are, at least in their present form, of quite recent origin. The linguistic evidence, which reveals a notable lack of discernibly archaic features, is itself a quite sufficient demonstration of the truth of this assertion.[21]

They go on to state quite confidently that many, perhaps most, of those *ginān*s which are attributed to the early *pīr*s are in fact compositions from a later period in the community's history, the so-called 'age of the *sayyids*,' which extended from 1500 to 1850 CE.[22] A growing number of studies on works ascribed to individual *pīr*s arrive at similar conclusions concerning authorship. Tazim Kassam's analysis of the *Brahmā Prakāsh* (*Divine Illumination*), a work attributed to Pīr Shams, points to a much later date of composition than that of the period identified with the *pīr*.[23] My own study of the *Būjh Niranjan* (*Knowledge of the Attributeless One*) attributed to Pīr Ṣadr al-Dīn, demonstrates with an array of evidence that this *ginān* was not composed by him but rather by an anonymous individual affiliated with the Qādirī Sufi order.[24] Similarly, evidence from Pyarali Keshwani's study of the *ginān*, *Sī Ḥarfī* suggests a possible Sufi origin for that work as well.[25] Clearly, we are treading here on delicate ground where the results of scholarly research are in open conflict with the truth claims of religious tradition.

The situation becomes even more complex when one discovers in manuscripts and printed texts that the same *ginān*s are attributed to two or more authors. The *Sī Ḥarfī* (*Thirty Letters*) for example, has been variously attributed to Aḥmad Shāh, Nar Muḥammad Shāh and Imām-Shāh.[26] Then again the *ginān* called

Allāh ek khasam subuka (*God is One, That is Everyone's Testimony*) has two authors, Pīr Ṣadr al-Dīn and Pīr Ḥasan Kabīr al-Dīn, raising the possibility of either a combined authorship or perhaps the latter transmitting the work of his predecessor.[27] A few *ginān*s have as their authors individuals whose names are associated with Hindu mythological figures such as Sahadeva, the youngest of the five Pandava brothers, and Harishcandra, a king known for his legendary generosity.[28] In several compositions the author's name simply consists of an honorific title, such as *sat gur brahmā* (the divine guide), *bār gur* (the guide of the twelve), or a compound of terms like Pīr Satgūr Nūr, 'the true guide of the light.' The identity of authors also becomes obscure on account of similar sounding names such as Pīr Indra Imāmdīn, Imām-Dīn and Sayyid Imām-Shāh. Tradition believes these names to refer to the same individual, but on the basis of poetic style we may in fact be dealing with three different persons. Finally, there are a few anonymous *ginān*s, not attributed to any particular *pīr*. The obvious example in this category is the ever popular *Kalām-i Mawlā* (*The Discourse of Mawla ʿAlī*) claimed to be an anonymous translation into Hindustani of an Arabic or Persian work allegedly transmitted from the first Shiʿi Imam, ʿAlī b. Abī Ṭālib (d. 40/661).[29]

What are we to make of this confused state of affairs? The tradition's claims of authorship of *ginān*s by *pīr*s rest on the fact that in almost every composition there occurs a *bhanitā* or 'signature verse.' This verse, which normally occurs towards the end of the *ginān*, customarily contains the name of a *pīr*. When the *pīr*'s name is mentioned during recitation, it is customary for members of the congregation to demonstrate their respect and devotion by bowing their heads slightly and silently invoking blessings on him. The *bhanitā* is not a poetic feature unique to the *ginān*s. It is in fact an essential element of many genres of South Asian religious poetry including the *pada*, the most popular form of devotional verse in north India. As in the *ginān*s, the *bhanitā* containing the name of the poet occurs in the last one or two verses of mediaeval devotional poems as an oral signature. And as is also the case with the *ginān*s, these signatures have been generally interpreted as indications of authorship.

In a ground-breaking study on the role of the *bhanitā* in North Indian devotional poetry, John Hawley convincingly demonstrates that this verse signifies authorship in other ways than simply 'writer,' as we commonly use the term in English.[30] Citing definitions of the word 'author' from the Oxford English Dictionary ('a person on whose authority a statement is made ...,' and 'a person who has authority over others ...') he argues that the occurrence of a poet's name in a poem points in the direction of authority rather than strictly authorship.[31] For example, in the hymns of the *Guru Granth Ṣāḥib*, the sacred scripture of the Sikhs, one hears only the name of Guru Nānak, the first *guru* of the community, even in verses known to have been composed by other *gurus*. Guru Nānak's name clearly serves as a symbol of authority rather than personal identity. When the *gurus* after him composed poetry, they did so in his name, invoking his authority.[32]

In support of his contention, Hawley analyses the *bhanitā* in the poetry attributed to prominent poet-saints of the North Indian *bhakti* tradition such as Ravidās, Sūrdās and Mīrābāī. In every case, he shows the many ways in which the authority of the poet in the signature-verse is more significant than the actual fact of composition:

> In devotional Hindi poetry, to give an author's name is not so much to denote who said what as to indicate the proper force of an utterance and the context in which it is to be appreciated. The author's name is no mere footnote. It anchors a poem to life, a personality, even a divinity that gives the poem its proper weight and tone; and it connects it to a network of associations that makes the poem not just a fleeting flash of truth – not just new and lovely – but something that has been heard before and respected, something familiar and beloved.[33]

The *bhanitā* serves as a means of 'anchoring' the poem by invoking a poet-saint's authority. In this connection, Hawley also points out that the *bhanitā* may also be called *chāp*, 'stamp or seal,' a term that indicates its function authoritatively, that what has been said is true and bears listening to.[34] It functions, in a way, as an authoritative seal of approval for the poem.

Several of Hawley's other observations on the *bhanitā* are

relevant to our discussion on authorship of the *ginān*s. A cursory examination of signature-verses in the *ginān*s shows that the name of the relevant *pīr* is invariably associated with verbs which mean to speak, to say, to utter, to instruct or to teach. It is on account of phrases such as '*pīr* so-and-so says' that those who revere these hymns, as well as those who study them, have assumed that these signatures signify the simple fact of a *ginān*'s authorship. Significantly, a substantial proportion of *bhanitā*s in Hindi devotional poetry, too, either explicitly contain the verb 'to say,' or some variant of it, or imply it in context. But this should not mislead us. In order to better understand this apparently confusing situation, we need to first examine the relationship of the poetic signature to the rest of the verse and, second, the relationship of the *bhanitā* itself to the rest of the poem.

We observe in the diction surrounding the *bhanitā*s of the *ginān*s that there is frequently a break in syntax between the name mentioned in the signature and the remainder of the verse. A similar situation exists in Hindi devotional poetry, where this 'grammatical hiatus' in the *bhanitā* transfers the responsibility for forming the grammatical connection between the signature and the verse to the listener.[35] Since verbs of actual 'authoring' rarely occur in the *bhanitā*s of the *ginān*s or any other mediaeval Indian devotional verse, the interpretation of these verses is fraught with ambiguity. This ambiguity is further compounded by the telegraphic style of poetry so greatly favoured by poets in the tradition. In this regard, Hawley remarks that the 'relation between the signature and the line of which it is a part can be an intricate matter indeed – not at all so simple as the linear "Sūrdās says" or "Ravidās says" would suggest.'[36]

As regards the relationship of the *bhanitā* to the entire poem, we can usually notice a subtle change in the direction of the poem when the poet's signature is revealed. The purpose of this shift, Hawley suggests in the examples of poetry he examines, is to convey not only 'authorship' but also to highlight authority.[37] Such a reorientation is characteristic of many *ginān*s where it is marked by dramatic changes in the narrative perspective of the *bhanitā*, frequently from the first or third person.[38] Sometimes there will be a prayer or petition:

> Pīr Sadruddin says: 'O master, it is to you that we owe all that we have eaten. If you are merciful, the soul will be delivered.'[39]

> Pīr Indr Imamuddin, with hope on his lips, has entreatingly said: 'Master, forgive the sins of your community!'[40]

But often the verse will consist of a command, an injunction, or a proverbial religious truth directly addressed to the listener:

> Pīr Tajuddin says: 'Magnify the Lord! Only true believers will be rewarded, O brother.'[41]

> 'O brother,' Pīr Imām-Shāh has said, 'Listen, O brother believers! Let those who would wake remain awake, for the Light has been revealed.'[42]

> Assemble, O congregations, and perform your devotions,' says Pīr Sadruddin.[43]

> Pīr Sadruddin has said: 'If anyone would make his mind understand, then what comes of washing clothes? Discovery comes through cleaning the heart.'[44]

The point to note here is that the *bhanitā*, whether it contains an intercessory petition, a command or a statement of religious truth, invokes in some manner the authority of the *pīr*.

If we now re-evaluate and re-examine the signature-verses of the *ginān*s as being invocations of authority, then some of the confusion on the 'authorship' issue begins to dissipate: the disproportionately large number of compositions attributed to the three or four *pīr*s who, in the community's self image, played a central or seminal role in the development of the tradition; the inconsistencies of style in works supposedly written by the same author; and the anachronisms of content. All of these points can now be better comprehended. Considering the *bhanitā* from this perspective makes it possible to understand that disciples of individual *pīr*s, like those of the *bhakti* poet-saints, could compose poems in the names of their spiritual guides as a way of expressing their spiritual affiliation, as well as their devotion and veneration to their mentors.[45] Furthermore, the *pīrs*' names served to 'anchor' the poems giving them validity and weight, confirming that the teachings contained within them were in conformity with those preached by the great masters. Significantly, the *ginān*s themselves contain some supporting evidence. An obvious example occurs in a popular *ginān, Āe Raḥem Raḥemān* (*Come, O Merciful, Benevolent One*), by the only known female composer Sayyida Imām-Begum (d. 1283/1866?). In the *bhanitā* of this composition, Imām Begum invokes the name of her *pīr*, Ḥasan Shāh, to validate her teachings, since she herself was not regarded as a *pīr*.[46] Similarly, the *ginān* called *Hans hansli ni vartan* (*The Parable of the Goose and the Gander*) contains a reference to the effect that it is being recorded by Vimras, a disciple of Pīr Shams. Elsewhere, the *pīr* asks the same disciple to recite *ginān*s to new converts, presumably in his name.[47] In several other cases, some verses specifically indicate that *ginān*s, attributed to Pīr Shams, were uttered by his devotees.[48]

That the name of the *pīr* in the *bhanitā* was conceived as a way of 'anchoring' a composition to the Ismaili *pīr* tradition is also illustrated by the case of the *Būjh Niranjan*. In my study of this text, I have shown that textual and linguistic evidence overwhelmingly indicates that this *ginān* was composed outside the Ismaili Khoja tradition, specifically in the Qādirī Sufi order.[49] As a mystical poem, outlining the various stages and experiences on the spiritual path, its general tenor has strong affinity to Ismaili mystical ideas. Historically, Ismaili and Sufi relationships, in the Iranian and Indian contexts, have been so intimate that there even developed a style of discourse in Persian that Ivanow has appropriately termed 'Sufico-Ismaili,' since works composed in it could be interpreted within both the Sufi and Ismaili perspectives.[50] Keeping in mind both the close Sufi-Ismaili links and the 'authorizing' role of the *bhanitā*, we may suggest that the name of Pīr Ṣadr al-Dīn, perhaps the most important personality in the Ismaili Khoja *pīr* tradition, was added to the *Būjh Niranjan* not as a way of establishing 'authorship' but as a way of validating its teachings and stating that they were in consonance with the *pīr*'s precepts. It is significant that the signature-verse, which is rather unusual in its phraseology, says: 'Know the path of Pīr Ṣadr al-Dīn which is eternally accepted.' The verse makes no claim of the *pīr* writing the poem; it simply endorses his path and thus his authority.[51] His name serves as a 'stamp of approval,' making the work legitimate for his disciples. With it, the *pīr*'s audiences could interpret the mysticism and esotericism of the *Būjh Niranjan* within a meaningful Ismaili context. To view the insertion of the *pīr*'s name as an act of plagiarism or forgery is to miss the point. As Hawley points out, 'the meaning of authorship in devotional India is not what we have come to expect in Europe and America since the Renaissance.'[52]

One more issue pertains to the subject of the origins and authorship of the *ginān*s. Ismaili tradition itself, as well as scholars who have studied the *ginān*s, concur that these religious poems began as oral literature and for a considerable period in their history were transmitted orally before being recorded in writing in Khojkī, a script peculiar to the community. Though at present very few *ginān* manuscripts date earlier than the 12th/18th century (the earliest recorded manuscript dates to 1149/1736[53]), Azim Nanji postulates that the tradition of written transcription may have begun around the 10th/16th century.[54] While no scholar to date has examined the corpus of *ginān*s from the perspective of its oral origins, we have little reason to doubt this theory, especially when we bear in mind parallel traditions of religious literatures in South Asia, such as the *sant*, *bhakti* and Sufi ones. Shackle and Moir consider a long period of oral transmission very plausible in light of the fact that some older members of the community today can still recite a repertoire of 200 or more *ginān*s by heart.[55] Nanji, citing evidence concerning the bardic role of the Bhatias of Sind, a caste from which many Khojas seem to have originated, speculates that the teachings of the *pīr*s may have been put to music and sung for adherents by professional bards.[56] My own examination of the role of the *ginān*s in the community's religious life indicates that even today, notwithstanding the existence of printed texts, the *ginān*s function primarily in their oral/aural dimension.[57]

If the *ginān*s did indeed originate as oral literature and were orally transmitted in their early history, then, from this perspective too, we need to re-evaluate the way in which we have been approaching the issue of their authorship. My late colleague Albert Lord argued that it is a myth to assume that in the oral tradition there are fixed texts which are transmitted unchanged from one generation to another, through an analysis of which one can trace 'original authors'.[58] Songs that are transmitted orally are both synchronically and historically 'fluid' in the sense that performers may change outward forms such as wording, which they consider 'inessential.' Only the basic idea or combination of ideas forming the core of the song remains fairly stable. In other words, Lord observes that:

> His [the singer's] idea of stability, to which he is deeply devoted, does not include wording, which to him has never been fixed, nor the inessential parts of the story. He builds his performance ... on the stable skeleton of narrative.[59]

Consequently, in the oral tradition, concepts such as 'author' and 'original' have no meaning at all, or they may have a meaning quite different from the one usually assigned to them.[60] The fluidity of the song makes it virtually impossible to retrace the song through the generations of singers to the moment when the first singer performed it; each performance is in a sense original.[61] It is only with the onset of the written tradition that the 'correct' text is fixed, sounding the death knell for the oral traditional process; singers become reproducers rather than recreators.[62]

Albert Lord's remarks may explain the tremendous variations in *ginān* texts as they are recorded in manuscripts and the 'great latitude' that seems to have existed in the rendering of the originals.[63] But more importantly, they serve as words of caution for societies permeated by the written tradition, who feel that for every text there must be an 'original' which can be demonstrably attributed to a certain author. If, during part of their history, the *ginān*s did indeed exist as an oral tradition, before they were reduced to writing, then by searching for evidence of 'original authors' in them, we may be asking questions that are illogical and inappropriate. 'Once we know the facts of oral composition,' Albert Lord writes, 'we must cease trying to find an original of any traditional song.'[64]

This essay suggests the need for new approaches to the issue of the authorship of the *ginān*s. It argues on several grounds for the need to redefine the manner in which 'authorship' as it applies to these religious poems has been usually viewed. Although the implications of its arguments may seem to challenge what tradition claims, the essay does *not* deny that the central core of the *ginān* literary tradition may have, in fact, been originally initiated by the *pīr*s and their disciples. Its intent is only to point out that, on account of factors intrinsic to the nature of their transmission over the centuries, the search for evidence within the *ginān*s themselves (as we have received them) to resolve questions of their 'authorship' will be a frustrating exercise that will only leave us dissatisfied. The application of conventional canons of textual criticism involving the tracing of transmission lines to an ideal archetype or autograph is futile and inappropriate. Between the actual composition of the *ginān*s and their first reduction to a written form lie several generations of singers, reciters and devoted redactors who have left their impress on most of these poems.[65] The more interesting and fruitful questions we need to ask about the *ginān*s concern their 'relational, contextual or functional' qualities.[66] By this we mean the interaction of these religious poems with the people who memorize, recite and listen to them. In the final analysis, the ability of the Nizari Ismaili Khojas to draw inspiration from the *ginān*s is based largely on the validation of these poems by communal consensus and usage. As is the case with medieval *bhakti* and *sant* traditions, the attribution of a certain composition to a particular person and the invocation of his or her authority, depends entirely on the consensus of the community within which the composition circulated. Ultimately, it is the community of believers which has the power to invest a text with religious meaning and determine the religious or theological framework within which it will be interpreted and understood. Texts become 'sanctified' only when a community can discover religious meaning and truth within them.[67]

Notes

* This chapter was originally published as 'The Ismaili *Ginān*s: Reflections on Authority and Authorship,' in Farhad Daftary, ed., *Mediaeval Ismaʿili History and Thought.* Cambridge, 1996, pp. 265–80.

1. The term 'Khoja' is used in this essay to refer to Nizari Ismailis originating in Sind, Punjab or Gujarat who hold Aga Khan IV to be their Imam. Believed to be a popularization of the Persian word *khwājā*, meaning lord or master, this term was bestowed on Hindu converts to Ismaili Islam in medieval times, apparently to replace the original expression *ṭhākur* or *ṭhākkar* (also meaning lord, master) used by the Hindu Lohāṇās. Between the mid-19th and early 20th centuries, various secessionist movements within the larger community resulted in the formation of small Sunni and Ithnāʿasharī (Twelver) Shiʿi Khoja groups as well. See Wladimir Ivanow, 'Khodja,' *SEI*, pp. 256–7, and Wilferd Madelung, 'Khodja,' *EI2*, vol. 5, pp. 25–7.

2. Aziz Ahmad, *An Intellectual History of Islam in India* (Edinburgh, 1969), p. 126. As a reaction to such perceptions, recent editions of *ginān*s published by the Ismaili community have purged terms that could be perceived as 'non-Islamic' or 'Hinduistic,' replacing them with those considered more in consonance with the Islamic tradition.

3. See, for example, the famous Khoja Case of 1866, presided over by the Bombay High Court Judge Sir Joseph Arnould, described in Asaf A.A. Fyzee, *Cases in the Muhammadan Law of India and Pakistan* (London, 1965), pp. 504–49. Evidence from the *ginān*s was also presented before Justice Russell of the Bombay High Court in the Ḥājjī Bībī Case of 1908.

4. Due to a combination of social, economic and political factors, the Ismaili Khoja community has, since the early 20th century, established itself in East Africa, Southeast Asia, Western Europe and North America.

5. Tazim R. Kassam, *Songs of Wisdom and Circles of Dance: Hymns of the Satpanth Ismāʿīlī Muslim Saint, Pīr Shams* (Albany, NY, 1995), p. 3.

6. In keeping with the reluctance among many Muslims to permit the use of musical instruments in explicitly religious contexts, such concerts are not usually held within the premises of *jamāʿat- khāna*s.

7. Ali S. Asani, 'The Ismaili *Ginān*s as Devotional Literature,' in R.S. McGregor, ed., *Devotional Literature in South Asia: Current Research 1985–88*, (Cambridge, 1992), pp. 101–12. (See also Chapter 2 of this volume).

8. See 'The Ismaili Tariqa Board: Two Special Evenings,' *Ismaili Mirror* (August, 1987), p. 33.

9. Viewed from this perspective, the 'mediating' role of the *ginān*s

has its parallels with other works of Islamic literature in the vernacular, such as Mawlānā Jalāl al-Dīn Rūmī's *Mathnawī* (popularly called 'the Qur'an in Persian') or the Sindhi poet Shāh 'Abd al-Laṭīf's *Risālo*, the collection of mystical poetry so sacred to Sindhi-speaking Muslims.

10. '*Pīrs* are appointed by the Imam of the Time, and only such persons can claim to call themselves *Pīrs*. The son, brother or a relative of a *Pīr* cannot on his own accord become a *Pīr* [through inheritance], unless he has been so designated by the Imam of the Time.' See *Collection of Gināns Composed by the Great Ismaili Saint Pīr Ṣadruddīn* (Bombay, 1952), foreword, p. 3.

11. Christopher Shackle and Zawahir Moir, *Ismaili Hymns from South Asia: An Introduction to the Ginans* (London, 1992), p. 21.

12. Wladimir Ivanow, 'Satpanth,' in W. Ivanow, ed., *Collectanea*, vol. 1 (Leiden, 1948), p. 31.

13. Aziz Esmail, 'Satpanth Ismailism and Modern Changes Within it With Special Reference to East Africa.' (Ph.D. thesis, University of Edinburgh, 1971), p. 14.

14. Shackle and Moir, *Ismaili Hymns*, p. 22.

15. Nanji, *The Nizārī Ismā'īlī Tradition*, p. 69.

16. Shackle and Moir, *Ismaili Hymns*, p. 7.

17. Nanji, *The Nizārī Ismā'īlī Tradition*, p. 61.

18. Ibid., pp. 50–83, and Kassam, *Songs of Wisdom*, pp. 143–205.

19. W. Ivanow, 'The Sect of Imam Shah in Gujrat,' *JBBRAS*, New Series, 12 (1936), pp. 19–70.

20. Ivanow, 'Satpanth,' p. 41.

21. Shackle and Moir, *Ismaili Hymns*, p. 15.

22. Ibid., p. 8.

23. T.R. Kassam, 'Syncretism on the Model of Figure-Ground: A Study of Pir Shams' Brahmā Prakāsa,' in Katherine K. Young, ed., *Hermeneutical Paths to the Sacred Worlds of India* (Atlanta, 1994), pp. 231–41, as quoted in her *Songs of Wisdom*, p. 9.

24. Ali S. Asani, *The Būjh Niranjan: An Ismaili Mystical Poem* (Cambridge, Mass., 1991).

25. P. Keshwani, '*Sī Ḥarfī:* A Ginanic Treatise: Text and Context,' (unpublished ms.); see especially Part II, Chapter 2: 'The Authorship of *Sī Ḥarfī*.'

26. Ibid., pp. 105–6.

27. See the text in Laljibhai Devraj, ed., *Sau ginānjī copaḍī cogaḍīevārī* (Bombay, 1903), pp. 48–50.

28. Tradition claims these Hindu mythological names are epithets of

the great Pīr Ṣadr al-Dīn. See Shackle and Moir, *Ismaili Hymns*, pp. 154, 191.

29. The Ismailia Association for India, *Kalāme Maulā* (8th ed., Bombay, 1963).

30. John S. Hawley, 'Author and Authority in the *Bhakti* Poetry of North India,' *JAS*, 47 (1988), pp. 269–90.

31. Ibid., p. 270

32. Ibid., p. 273.

33. Ibid., p. 287.

34. Ibid., pp. 285–6.

35. Ibid., p. 278.

36. Ibid., p. 278.

37. Ibid., pp. 282–5.

38. Shackle and Moir, too, remark on the directness of speech that characterizes the signature-verses of *gināns*, where it is a regular commonplace; see their *Ismaili Hymns*, p. 27.

39. Shackle and Moir, *Ismaili Hymns*, *ginān* no. 32.

40. Ibid., *ginān* no. 11.

41. Ibid., *ginān* no. 8.

42. Ibid., *ginān* no. 16.

43. Ibid., *ginān* no. 30.

44. Ibid., *ginān* no. 12.

45. A similar situation is found in the poetry of Mawlānā Jalāl al-Dīn Rūmī (d. 672/1273), the greatest mystical poet of the Persian language, who uses the name of his mentor Shams-i Tabrīz as his own poetic name or *nom de plume*.

46. *Sau ginānji copaḍi cālu ginān āgal na chapāelā bhāg trījo* (1st ed., Bombay, 1903), p. 108.

47. Nanji, *The Nizārī Ismāʿīlī Tradition*, p. 13.

48. See *gināns* no. 13, verse 8, and no. 37, verse 12, in Shackle and Moir, *Ismaili Hymns*, pp. 86, 132; and *ginān* 68, verses 11–12, in Kassam, *Songs of Wisdom*, p. 319. Kassam translates the word *ginān* here as 'wisdom.'

49. Asani, *Būjh Niranjan*, pp. 19–46.

50. W. Ivanow, *Ismaili Literature: A Bibliographical Survey* (Tehran, 1963), pp. 10 ff., 130–131, and 'Sufism and Ismailism: The Chirāgh-Nāma,' *Revue Iranienne d'Anthropologie*, 3 (1959), pp. 13–17. See also Azim Nanji's comments: 'The Nizārī *daʿwa*, when it entered the Subcontinent, already carried within its repertoire a strain of mysticism rooted in Ismāʿīlism

but tinged with the Ṣūfic terminology of the time,' in his *The Nizārī Ismā'īlī Tradition*, p. 126.

51. For a detailed contextual analysis of this *bhanitā*, see Asani, *Būjh Niranjan*, pp. 24–25.

52. Hawley, 'Author and Authority,' p. 287.

53. See Zawahir Noorally [Moir], *Catalogue of Khojkī Manuscripts in the Collection of the Ismailia Association for Pakistan* (unpublished, Karachi, 1971), Ms. 25; and Ali S. Asani, *The Harvard Collection of Ismaili Literature in Indic Languages: A Descriptive Catalog and Finding Aid* (Boston, Mass., 1992).

54. Nanji, *The Nizārī Ismā'īlī Tradition*, p. 12. A Gujarātī history of the community, *Khojā Vrttānt*, by S. Nanjiani (Ahmadabad, 1892), pp. 240–50, also notes that Pīr Dādū (d. 1593) was supposedly instructed by the Imam to collect the teachings of the earlier *pīrs* and produce a written record.

55. Shackle and Moir, *Ismaili Hymns*, p. 15.

56. Nanji, *The Nizārī Ismā'īlī Tradition*, p. 13.

57. Asani, 'The Iṣmaili *Gināns* as Devotional Literature,' pp. 104–6.

58. Albert Lord, *Singer of Tales* (Cambridge, Mass., 1968), p. 9.

59. Ibid., p. 99.

60. Ibid., p. 101.

61. Ibid., p. 100.

62. Ibid., p. 137.

63. Ivanow, 'Satpanth', p. 41.

64. Lord, *Singer of Tales*, p. 100.

65. I am aware that this statement may appear puzzling to some readers in light of my previous work on the *Būjh Niranjan*, in which I do consider questions of its provenance. That *ginān*, however, represents a rather unusual case for which there exists a written attestation from independent sources. The presence of a reasonably developed manuscript tradition justifies my approach in this particular case. At present, the only other work in the *ginān* tradition for which we have a manuscript existing outside the community is the *Sī Ḥarfī*. See Keshwani, '*Sī Ḥarfī*,' ch. 2.

66. This term comes from William A. Graham's study of sacred texts, *Beyond the Written Word: Oral Aspects of Scripture in the History of Religion* (Cambridge, 1987).

67. As testimony to the strength of communal authority, we note here that popular compositions attributed to individuals who technically did not have the 'official' status of *pīr*, namely the so-called 'unauthorized

pīrs' who are nevertheless accepted as part of the *ginān* literature. Examples of 'unauthorized' *pīrs* include Imām-Shāh (d. 919/1513) and his son Nar Muḥammad Shāh (d. ca. 940/1534), the pivotal figures of a 10th/16th century schismatic group, the Imām-Shāhīs, and the so-called Sayyids who disseminated religious teaching within the Ismaili communities in the 12th/18th and 13th/19th centuries. For all intents and purposes, most members of the community do not differentiate in status between these 'unofficial' *ginān*s and those by 'authorized' *pīrs*. Audience appeal is clearly more important in this case than considerations of religious history.

6

The Khojkī Script: A Legacy of Ismaili Islam in the Subcontinent*

The adoption of a communal script was one of the methods employed by several of the subcontinent's ethnic and religious groups to enhance communal solidarity. This chapter introduces a script heretofore little studied by scholars – the Khojkī script of the Nizari Ismaili Muslim community of Sind, Gujarat and Punjab. It outlines the salient features of the script's origins, development and significance, both historical and religious. Utilizing evidence culled from selected Khojkī texts, the article also examines ways in which Khojkī, originally a mercantile script, failed to develop into a precise system for literary expression.

Origin and Background

Khojkī (or Khojakī) is the name of the script that was used by the Nizari Ismailis of the Indian subcontinent to record their religious literature. Originating in Sind, the southern province of modern Pakistan and commonly used to transcribe several languages including Sindhi, Gujarati, Hindustani and Persian, the script was in active use within this particular Ismaili community from at least the 10th/16th century, if not earlier, until about the 1960s.[1] The name Khojkī is most likely derived from the word *Khoja*, a popularization of the Persian word *Khwāja*, meaning lord or master.[2] According to Ismaili tradition, the 9th/15th-century *dāʿī* (preacher, missionary) Pīr Ṣadr al-Dīn who bestowed this title on new Indian converts to Ismaili Islam, was also responsible for inventing the Khojkī script.[3]

Archaeological excavations at Bhambhore, the 2nd/8th-century Muslim settlement in lower Sind, however, have uncovered a 'proto-Nagari' script with characters remarkably similar to those found in modern Khojkī.[4] This script, clearly the prototype of Khojkī, has been identified as Lohāṇākī or Lārī, the script of the Hindu Lohāṇā community.[5] As it happens, the Lohāṇā community was one of the communities among whom the Ismaili missionary, Pīr Ṣadr al-Dīn (*circa* 751–803/1350–1400), was most active. Thus, while the Ismaili tradition that he invented Khojkī is clearly inaccurate – in any case, scripts evolve slowly because they are necessarily cultural and not individual products – the *pīr* may indeed have played a role in its elaboration, as we shall see below. That is speculative however. What is not speculative is that Khojkī is a refined and polished form of Lohāṇākī.[6]

Khojkī was one of the many scripts prevalent in Sind over a period of several centuries.[7] As early as the 3rd/9th and 4th/10th centuries, various Arab geographers and travellers referred to the fact that the inhabitants of Sind had many different scripts for writing their language.[8] Ibn al-Nadīm (d. 385/995) reports that approximately 200 scripts were employed in the region.[9] Al-Bīrūnī (d. 440/1048) provides more specific information about three of these scripts: a script called 'Malwārī' predominated in southern Sind, the 'Ardhā-Nāgārī' in some other parts and the 'Saindhava' in the ancient city of Bahmanwā or al-Manṣūra.[10] We can also be reasonably certain that after the Arab conquests of the 2nd/8th century, among this multitude of scripts, one or more forms of the Arabic script were also current.

Through a substantial portion of its history, there had been little incentive for the development of a single uniform script for the Sindhi language, principally because it was used only as a spoken language or for popular folk literature that was oral in character. Thus, during the long period of Muslim rule, Persian and not Sindhi was the favoured language in official, administrative and literary circles. As a consequence, the use of multiple scripts for Sindhi prevailed well into the 19th century CE. In a paper on Sindhi alphabets presented at the July 1857 meeting of the Royal Asiatic Society (Bombay branch), E. Trumpp, the German orientalist and author of a distinguished Sindhi grammar, noted the use of various alphabets, Muslims preferring Arabic characters loaded 'with a confusing heap of dots,' while Hindus employed a medley of alphabets known by the name of Banyāṅ.[11] The English adventurer, Richard Burton, also remarks that the 'characters in which the Sindhi tongue is written are very numerous,' and among the various alphabets in use he mentions 'that used by the Khwajah tribe,' presumably referring to Khojkī.[12] George Stack, in his *Grammar of the Sindhi Language*, published in 1849, tabulates thirteen script systems, including Khojkī, which were in use for transcribing Sindhi. His table reveals that the scripts used in Sind varied from one geographical region to another, and that different religious and caste groups favoured distinctive script styles.[13]

Khojkī and most of the scripts used for writing Sindhi belong to the group of Indian scripts which have been classified by Grierson under the heading 'Laṇḍā' or 'clipped' alphabets.[14] They were employed especially by the Hindus of Sind and Punjab for the purposes of commerce. In fact, in Sind, Laṇḍā was called Banyāṅ or Wāṇiko, indicating its use primarily as a mercantile and commercial script.[15] The Laṇḍā group, in turn, is related to the larger family of alphabets commonly employed by the subcontinent's mercantile classes, showing particularly close affinity to two members of this family: Ṭaṅkrī (Tākarī), a crude script system used in its many varieties by uneducated shopkeepers and the like in the lower ranges of the Himalayas and the Punjab hills; and Mahājanī (Mārwārī), the character originating in Mārwār and popularized among trading classes all over North India by the Mārwārī traders.[16] Another noteworthy parallel to the Laṇḍā group of Punjab and Sind exists in Gujarat where a variety of Gujarati character, known as Vāṇiāī (from *vāṇīo*, 'shopkeeper'),

Ṣarrāfī (from *ṣarrāf*, 'banker'), Bodīā (from *bodī*, 'clipped' or 'shorn'), is used exclusively by merchants and bankers.[17]

The mercantile origin of this extensive family of alphabets, to which Khojkī and its Laṇḍā analogues belong, may explain why the entire family was not well suited for literary purposes. Mercantile scripts have limited, specialized purposes; consequently they tend to be crude by literary standards. Often being a kind of shorthand, these scripts are not only imperfectly supplied with vowel signs but frequently omit the few vowels that they do possess, making them quite illegible or, even worse, liable to being misread.[18] Indeed, the omission of all vowels, except when initial, was the norm in ordinary mercantile correspondence.[19] Not surprisingly, there are numerous stories about the misreading of these mercantile scripts, the most popular being one of a Mārwārī merchant who went to Delhi; his agent wrote home: '*Bābū Ajmer gayo baṛī bahī bhej dīje* (The Babu has gone to Ajmer, send the big ledger)' but the letter was read as '*Bābū aj margayo, baṛī bahū bhej dīje*' (The Babu died today, send the chief wife [to perform his obsequies])'![20] Evidently, the inconvenience of the omission of vowel marks or *mātrā*s is not much felt in the limited scope of mercantile written communications such as *hunḍī*s (bills of exchange) in which almost identical sentences or phrases are constantly repeated.

A poorly developed vowel system, the chief characteristic of Indian mercantile alphabets, constitutes the major deficiency of the Laṇḍā scripts, many of which have no signs for internal vowels and have only two or three signs for initial vowels.[21] The Laṇḍā scripts are further handicapped by consonants that are far from being clear and that vary greatly from place to place. In most of them a single letter could often represent a number of different sounds. Indeed in a few cases some consonants seem to have been represented merely by ciphers, combinations of numbers and fractional parts; e.g. \\\ (3/4) for *n* and ४ (4) for *ch*.[22] Remarking on the capriciousness of Laṇḍā, Grierson observes that 'it is seldom legible to anyone except the original writer and not always to him.'[23] In this regard he also quotes a Sindhi proverb: '*Wāṇikā akhar ḅuṭā, sukā paṛhana-khān chuṭā,*' which means that the Wāṇiko [i.e., Laṇḍā] letters are vowelless; [as soon as the ink is] dry, they are released from reading [i.e., are illegible].[24] Burton comments that these alphabets are so useless that 'a trader is scarcely able to read his own accounts, unless assisted by a tenacious memory.'[25] Even Trumpp, who fiercely opposed the universal adoption of the Perso-Arabic writing system for transcribing Sindhi on the grounds that the alphabet was 'foreign,' confessed that an emendation of the native Laṇḍā system would be more useless by far than that of the Perso-Arabic character.[26]

Among this hodge-podge of commercial scripts – scribblings, we could truly say in many cases – a small number, including Khojkī, actually developed into vehicles of literary expression. Although for some scripts such as Khudawadī in Sind, Ḍogrī in Jammu and Chamīalī in Chamba, this evolution took place as a result of official government initiative and encouragement in the late 18th and early 19th centuries, for Khojkī the advance came about much earlier owing to (as we shall presently see) the script's affiliation with a minority religious community.

Expression in written literature, as in music, requires an instrument, and instruments require technical development. In Khojkī, two technical developments made a new range of expression possible. First was a system of medial vowel marks called *lākanā.* In the region of Sind, Khojkī was the only Laṇḍā script to have sustained and perhaps even developed the use of this medial vowel system.[27] It was this distinguishing characteristic of Khojkī that made the script suitable for its extensive use in recording a considerable corpus of Ismaili religious literature, in particular the genre known as *ginān.*[28] Incidentally, it is possible that the *dāʿī* Pīr Ṣadr al-Dīn, whom the tradition credits with the invention of the script, may have been responsible rather for introducing the *lākanā* and possibly other refinements to Khojkī.[29]

The second improvement in the Khojkī script concerns its capacity to retain the individuality of contiguous words written on the same line. In mercantile scripts, it is not only the omission of vowels which is responsible for the propensity to misread and misinterpret but it is also the non-separation of words from each other.[30] Because writing in mercantile scripts is, as a rule, continuous, adjacent words are often joined erroneously leading to alterations in the meaning of sentences. The 'mess' as Bendrey has termed it, is thus due to the arbitrary reconstruction of a group of letters by the readers.[31] This peculiarity, when combined with the absence of medial vowels, can be particularly fatal. As we have seen above, a phrase such as '*Bābū Ajmer gayo*' (The Babu has gone to Ajmer) could quite innocently be read as '*Bābū aj margayo*' (The Babu has died today). To prevent such misrenderings, Khojkī adopted a surprisingly simple solution: the use of colon-like punctuations to demarcate the ends of individual words.

Nonetheless, as will be seen below, the Khojkī script never evolved into an entirely satisfactory script system in spite of these refinements. The question therefore immediately arises: Why was it adopted for recording religious literature when more sophisticated and developed scripts such as Devanāgarī or the Perso-Arabic were available? The answer lies perhaps in the strong desire among religious groups in medieval India, both Hindu and Muslim, to make religious literature more accessible to the masses. The move away from the use of classical languages such as Sanskrit, Arabic and Persian; the corresponding blooming of the regional languages as vehicles of religious literature; the use of symbols and imagery taken from daily village life – all these are only a few examples of this trend. Certainly in its form, style and imagery, the Ismaili religious literature of the subcontinent (the *ginān*s) exhibits the same concern.[32] Consequently, in the Ismaili case the adoption of the Khojkī script, a 'local' script, was probably part of the attempt to make religious literature more accessible by recording it in a script with which the local population had the greatest familiarity. That the adoption of a 'local' script for preserving religious literature may have been customary with various groups in medieval India is further evident from the Sikh adoption of Gurmukhī as an 'official' script for its religious literature. Like Khojkī, Gurmukhī is a Laṇḍā script of Punjab which was improved and polished by the borrowing of vowel signs and refining of existing Laṇḍā characters.[33]

As a vehicle of Sikh religious literature, Gurmukhī contributed to the consolidation of the Sikh religion, becoming particularly important in the 18th and 19th centuries when the Sikhs exercised political hegemony over Punjab and Kashmir. S.S. Gandhi points out that the adoption of the Gurmukhī script was of great significance, for the Sikhs could develop their culture only by adopting a script which was their own and which was suited to their language. Furthermore, he observes, that the popularization of Gurmukhī was a 'well-calculated' move designed to make its readers, that is, converts to the Sikh religion, part with 'Hindu compositions written in [Devanāgarī] Sanskrit.'[34] The adoption of a common script to strengthen ethnic and linguistic ties was by no means confined to primarily religious groups. The political and cultural ascendancy of the Mahrattas, the major rivals to Sikh power in late Mughal India, was also marked by the selection of a single, uniform script for the Marathi language. This script, the Moḍī, was purportedly invented by the secretary to the great Maharashtrian hero, Shivājī.[35]

We may therefore surmise that much more was involved in the selection of the Khojkī script than access to religious literature. The script, by providing an exclusive means of written expression commonly shared by Ismailis living in three regions (Sind, Punjab and Gujarat), was influential in the development of cohesion and self-identity within a widely scattered and linguistically diverse religious community. No doubt the script facilitated the flow and the transmission of religious literature from one area to another.[36] Use of the script may have also served to confine religious literature within the community – this precaution being necessary to avoid persecution from outsiders not in agreement with the community's doctrines and practices.[37] In this respect, Khojkī may have served the same purpose as the secret languages, such as the so-called *Balabailān* language, utilized by Muslim mystics to hide their more esoteric thoughts from the common people.[38]

One final parallel between Khojkī and Gurmukhī deserves notice. Just as the Ismaili tradition associates its script with Pīr Ṣadr al-Dīn, a charismatic religious personality who is believed to have played a significant role in consolidating the young community,[39] so also the Sikh tradition associates Gurmukhī with the second Gurū, Aṅgad (1538–1552CE). According to Sikh tradition, Gurū

Aṅgad was responsible for improving the Gurmukhī script when he found that the Sikh hymns written in the original Laṇḍā form were liable to be misread. This is why the alphabet is called Gurmukhī, for it came forth from 'the mouth of the Gurū.'[40]

Khojkī in Modern Times: Uniformity and Demise

We possess remarkably little textual and historical evidence regarding the process by which the Khojkī script developed and evolved from a rudimentary commercial script of the 2nd/8th century to a more complex and plastic medium of expression. Not only is the study of the script still in its infancy, but many Khojkī manuscripts, our most important source of information about the script, have yet to be collected. Although at present there are three institutional collections of the manuscripts – two major ones, in Karachi at the Ismaili Tariqa and Religious Education Board for Pakistan and in London at The Institute of Ismaili Studies – these two collections remain largely inaccessible for research purposes. A third, much smaller collection in the Harvard University Library has been catalogued but is far from comprehensive in its scope.[41] Additionally, in spite of community-sponsored collection campaigns, mainly in Pakistan, there are many unexamined manuscripts, very likely in poor physical condition, in the possession of individual Ismaili families in various parts of the world. The absence of a comprehensive, centralized collection of Khojkī manuscripts thus becomes a formidable hurdle for any attempt to trace the evolution of the script. An equally serious obstacle is presented by the apparent absence of any pre-18th century manuscripts in the existing collections, for it was probably customary to destroy old and deteriorating manuscripts once they had been re-copied by scribes.[42] Finally, piety itself has been no less of a problem: Ivanow remarks that in the early 20th century, after the printing of certain *ginān*ic texts, 'the manuscripts from which the edition was prepared were buried in the ground!'[43]

Nevertheless, a cursory examination of existing Khojkī manuscripts reveals that even as late as the 19th century, the script was still undergoing refinement. Given the embryonic state of research on the script, it is not yet feasible to identify precisely the stages of evolution and refinement. The evidence does suggest, however, that the major improvements involved were mainly the development and the use of characters for sounds which were not satisfactorily represented. These sounds included the diphthongs, signs for which were added at a rather late stage to the original eight vowel graphemes after the pattern of the Devanāgarī alphabet, as well as the Arabic sounds which appear to have been incorporated only in the early 20th century.

The late 19th and early 20th centuries were of special importance in the history of Khojkī, for the advent of the printing press in the subcontinent during this period had a major impact. Already by the end of the 19th century, various lithographs were published in the Khojkī script under the auspices of individual members of the Ismaili community.[44] With the development of the printing press, the lithographs were gradually replaced by the printed form. Initially Khojkī material was printed by private printing presses such as the Ghulām-i Ḥusain Chāpākhānu in Bombay.[45] At this early stage, the printed material appears to have consisted of almost *verbatim* copies of the contents of the Khojkī manuscripts, particularly works belonging to the *ginān* genre, with very little editing.[46] In the first decade of the 20th century, however, most likely as a result of schisms within the Ismaili community,[47] the publication of religious literature was centralized and brought under the direct control of community institutions. Private attempts at publishing religious literature intended for general community use were discouraged and became less common. Under the auspices of the official community press, the Khoja Sindhi Printing Press in Bombay, Lāljī Devrāj began producing a large number of books, mostly *ginān* texts, in the Khojkī script. Devrāj was responsible for editing Khojkī manuscript material before it was put into print, and editions published by him have come to be regarded in certain Ismaili circles as an authoritative and bonafide source of *ginānic* literature. Notwithstanding his crucial role in the development of printed Khojkī literature, there are disconcerting aspects and questions regarding the methodology employed by Devrāj to edit Khojkī manuscripts. These have been discussed in detail elsewhere.[48]

The establishment of the Khoja Sindhi Printing Press, by making religious literature in Khojkī available in greater quantities, was an important impetus in promoting the use of the script. Books in the Khojkī script made their way to Burma and even to East and South Africa where substantial numbers of the Ismaili community had migrated for economic reasons. In the 1920s and 1930s, although the printing was still done by the Khoja Sindhi Printing Press (later known as the Ismaili Printing Press), the publication of Khojkī material was taken over by the Recreation Club Institute, which became the community institution responsible for the research and publication of religious material.[49]

Ironically, the introduction of printing may have also sounded the deathknell for the script. It soon became apparent that there were considerable expenses involved in manufacturing printing types specially for Khojkī. Moreover, the script itself, as will be seen below, still had some fundamental imperfections. A more significant factor leading to the script's demise was the lack of uniformity in the script in different geographical areas. For example, the character  represented the letter *dy* in Sind but *z* or *j* in Gujarat; or in one region the vowel *o* would be represented by the character , while in another area the character  served the same purpose. In short, regional variations were a serious problem in an era when literature was widely disseminated and printing was becoming standardized. Hence as early as 1910–11, the Gujarati script began to appear as an alternative, and by the 1930s it was quite commonly used in printing Ismaili religious texts. In fact it appears that most of the material until then available only in the Khojkī script was transcribed and printed in Gujarati characters.[50] In the following decades, the printing of books in Khojkī and instruction in the Khojkī script gradually ceased in all areas of the subcontinent where the Ismaili community lived except in the region of Sind, the home of the script.[51] There the script probably survived longer for two reasons. First, the partition of India in 1947 and later events increased the Gujarati and Urdu-speaking population of Ismailis in this region. Since these languages do not share a common script, there was still a need to have a single script in which different languages could be written. Second, the Sindhi Ismailis may have been reluctant to abandon a script so closely associated with their language, for Khojkī still represents one of the oldest forms of written Sindhi that has come down to us. Even in Sind, however, the Khojkī script did not survive beyond the early years of the 1970s when it gave way to the Perso-Arabic writing system in which both Sindhi and Urdu are now written. For all practical purposes, Khojkī no longer survives today as a 'living' script among the Ismailis of the subcontinent.

Even though it was adopted and used by Ismailis outside the region of Sind, Khojkī never lost its early association with Sind and its language. It remains customary for Ismailis from areas outside Sind to call the script 'Sindhī,' confusing it with that language.[52] This confusion is prevalent even in the area of religious education; to this day, in regions of Gujarat and Kāṭhiāwāḍ, classes providing instruction to children are called 'Sindhī', presumably a reminder of the time when a child attending religious classes learned the Khojkī script. However, to most young Ismailis today, the Khojkī script, if they are even aware of its existence, remains an obsolete legacy from the past. Since most important religious texts are available in Gujarati or Roman transcription, these Ismailis will rarely encounter a Khojkī text. Yet for the scholar, the script and the material it records is of considerable importance.

Literature in Khojkī throws light, for example, on the various aspects of the process of acculturation for it provides us with information concerning the ways in which the Ismaili movement adapted itself to the Indian cultural environment. In this respect Khojkī manuscript material is comparable to the Bengali and Dakhani Urdu material used by Asim Roy and Richard Eaton in their studies of the Islamization of Bengal and the Deccan, respectively.[53] It is also analogous to the Gurmukhī texts used by scholars of Sikhism to illumine the genesis of that tradition. For the scholar of post-classical Ismaili literature, recourse to Khojkī material has become especially critical with the growing awareness that there exists significant discrepancies between the modern printed version of the literature and its original manuscript form.

Again, because Khojkī records medieval literature composed in several Indic languages, Khojkī manuscripts form a valuable source of evidence for studying the development of literature in these languages. It is well known, for example, that several *ginān*s represent some of the earliest surviving specimens of literary compositions in Sindhī and Gujarati.[54] Finally, Khojkī manuscripts can be studied purely as specimens of special manuscript style developed in Sind, Gujarat and Punjab, principally to record literature to be recited during Ismaili religious ceremonies.

Inadequacies of the Khojkī Script

As a system of literary expression, the Khojkī script had serious limitations in three different areas. First, its vowel system, in spite of a slight refinement, was crude. Second, as to consonants, there were certain sounds, mostly of Arabic origin, for which the script had no characters at all (deficiency); the same sound could be represented by different characters (redundancy); and several sounds could be represented by the same character (ambiguity). And third, there was inconsistency in orthography and the use of orthographic signs. For the most part, these inadequacies can be explained by the script's mercantile origin and regional usage. Merchants originally developed the script for a narrow range of precise but technical purposes, and when the script was co-opted for recording Ismaili religious literature, its limitations created difficulties of expression and comprehension, only some of which were gradually remedied in subsequent centuries.

What follows is an investigation of these limited but serious difficulties as presented in the study of Khojkī texts of two important works from the Ismaili *ginān* literature, the *Dasa Avatāra* (The Ten *Avatāra*s) and the *Būjh Niranjan* (Knowledge of the Attributeless Deity).[55] The former, which has been described as the 'classic' of the Ismaili tradition in Indo-Pakistan,[56] is an example of the type of reformulation of Ismaili doctrine within a Vaishnavite framework that facilitated conversion, while the latter represents a theoretical and didactic exposition, in verse, of the various stages and states that the novice must experience in the course of his spiritual development.

1. The Vowel System

(a) The ū vowel

The Khojkī script does not distinguish between a long *ū* vowel and a short *u* vowel, whether these occur independently or with a consonant.[57]  the character for an independent *u* vowel could read either as long or short. Thus a word written as  can be transcribed either as *ūs* or *us*. The letter  used in Allana's table of the Khojkī script for an independent long *ū* vowel appears to be a theoretical form as it was not encountered in Khojkī texts of the *Das Avatār* and the *Būjh Niranjan*.[58] Furthermore, it does not occur in the 'official' Khojkī primers of 1932 and 1947. Similarly, the subscript sign which is combined with a consonant to indicate that the consonant is to be read with a *u* vowel, does not specify vowel-length. Thus  could be read as *kū* or *ku*. Consequently, the script relies on the reader's familiarity with a word in order to ensure that the vowel is read according to its correct length. Correct vowel length is, of course, crucial in poetry texts since it determines the length of syllable and affects metre. Given the ambiguity surrounding the length of the *u* vowel in Khojkī, the vowel should perhaps be represented as *ū̆* during the transcription and/or transliteration of Khojkī texts.

(b) The o vowel

The script also exhibits a confusion about the character used to depict an independent *o* vowel which is normally represented in modern Khojkī by the character . In the manuscript Kx, of the *Das Avatār*, the character  represents both the *o* and the *u* vowels, leading the editor to comment that only a knowledge of the language helps to determine appropriate reading.[59] The same confusion is apparent in manuscript K-4 of the *Būjh Niranjan*. Manuscripts K-3 and K-5 of the same work prefer to employ another method to represent the *o* vowel by using  or . This is obviously an adaptation from the Devanāgarī alphabet system.

Occasionally, K-5 even uses 𑈃, the letter for the independent *u* vowel in words where one would expect an *o* vowel. George Stack uses yet another character – 𑈆 – for the independent *o* vowel, but this character does not appear in actual Khojkī texts.[60] In view of this confusion, it is safe to conjecture that at an earlier stage in its history, Khojkī may have lacked a distinctive sign for the independent *o* vowel.

(c) The i vowel

The script has a single character 𑈂 to indicate both the independent short *i* and long *ī* vowels (as in *islām, lāiye, koī*).[61] Hence the need to use the transcription *ĭ* for any independent *i* vowel in a Khojkī text. Allana designates the character 𑈄 for an independent short *i* vowel, but that character is again not to be found in the Khojkī texts consulted.[62] Similarly, Stack uses the character 𑈄 for an independent short *i* vowel.[63] Though this character does indeed occur occasionally where one would expect a short *i* vowel, it is more commonly used to represent the independent *e* vowel. Again, as the section on orthography below will reveal, there is an ambiguity in the value of the symbol 𑈭 which is so often used to indicate a consonant followed by a short *i* vowel.

(d) The diphthongs

The script does not have any special symbols to represent the diphthongs.[64] The diphthong *ai* is usually changed to the vowel *e* while the diphthong *au* is changed to *o*. Stack uses the letters 𑈅 and 𑈇 for the diphthongs.[65] Allana remarks that the letters 𑈅 and 𑈇 were introduced later for the diphthongs *ai* and *au* respectively.[66] All of the characters mentioned by Allana and Stack are not employed consistently to represent the diphthongs, however. For example, the letter 𑈇 used by Stack to indicate *au* is absent from actual Khojkī texts or even primers. Among the texts of the *Būjh Niranjan*, only K-4 (c.1901) uses the letters 𑈅 and 𑈇. The rest of the texts, including the relatively later manuscript K-2 (1914), usually change the diphthongs to the *e* or *o* vowels. Manuscript K-3 of the same work uses yet another device for representing the *au* diphthong – the character , but this use is obviously borrowed from the Devanāgarī script system.

2. *The Consonant System*

(a) Deficiency

In an attempt to represent the sounds of the different languages and dialects for which it came to be employed, the Khojkī script eventually developed over 40 letters.[67] Some of these letters were especially incorporated into the script to represent sounds not native to Indian languages and which were peculiar to Arabic, the language from which most Islamic religious terminology is derived.[68] To this end, a Khojkī letter representing the sound closest to the Arabic sound in question was appropriately modified. Thus, to indicate the Arabic *shīn* (*sh*) which in the Arabic script is represented by three dots over the letter for *sīn* (*s*), three dots were placed over the Khojkī letter for *s*, to give the letter for the sound *sh*.[69] Similarly, to represent the Arabic *ʿain* in the Khojkī script, three dots were placed over the Khojkī letter *a* () or over the letter for the vowel *e* (), giving the script two letters for this sound, and .[70] The Arabic *ghain* was formed by placing three dots over the Khojkī letter for the *g* sound, . The four Arabic letters *dhāl*, *ze*, *ẓā* and *ḍād*, as happens in Urdu and Sindhī, were all pronounced as *z* and represented by the letter . This letter was formed by the familiar pattern of placing three dots over another consonant, in this case the letter for *j*. Indeed, as in many Indian languages it is very common to pronounce *j* or *jh* as *z* and vice versa.[71] Occasionally the letter was employed to represent the Arabic *qāf*, but this letter appears to have been a fairly recent addition to the script.[72]

A study of the Khojkī manuscripts reveals another kind of deficiency in the script's consonant system. In its early unpolished form, the script probably did not have a separate character for the consonant *y*. Manuscript Kx, of the *Dasa Avatāra*, dating from 1737, does not have a special letter for this sound.[73] In many Khojkī texts, the consonant *y* is quite consistently dropped or replaced by the vowels *a* or *e* or both.[74] A word such as *bhayā* would be written as *bhaeā*; *mayā* as *maeā*; and *piya* as *pīā*. Later Khojkī texts use the letter 𑈧 for the *y* consonant, a letter clearly adapted from the letter 𑈂 for the *i* vowel.

(b) Redundancy

While Khojkī originally did not have letters for certain Arabic sounds, it had developed special letters for the implosive sounds which are found only in the Sindhī language. This development was not unusual since Sindhī was the language for which Khojkī was originally used. But with the spread of the script to non-Sindhī speaking areas, the letters for these implosive sounds were given alternate sound values. The peculiar result was that a few sounds were represented by two letters. Thus 𑈤, the Khojkī letter for the Sindhī implosive *ḇ* (ٻ), became commonly used in Gujarat to represent the sound *b* (ب). Consequently, the Khojkī letter 𑈣 which originally represented the *b* sound was then used along with 𑈥 to represent the sound *bh* (ڀ). Likewise, 𑈜 the letter for the Sindhī implosive *d̤* (ڏ) is used for the sound *d* so that the aspirated *dh* is represented by two Khojkī letters – 𑈛 (used earlier to represent *d*) and 𑈝. Again 𑈑 the Khojkī character for the implosive *dy* (ڄ), was sometimes used in Gujarati-speaking areas for the sound *z* or *j*.[75] 𑈋 the Khojkī equivalent for the Sindhī *nġ* (ڳ) was used to represent *g* or even the conjunct *gr*.[76] The factors influencing the direction of this particular shift in the value of Khojkī characters in non-Sindhī areas certainly warrant further research. In light of the dual sound values (Sindhī and non-Sindhī) for the above letters, it is clear that the area of origin of a Khojkī text may be of considerable significance in determining its correct reading and transcription.

(c) Ambiguity

There is some confusion in the script about the character used to represent the sounds *ḍ*, *ṛ*, and *ṇ*. Compounding this confusion is the proclivity in Gujarati and Sindhī colloquial dialects to change the cerebral *ḍ* to the retroflexive *ṛ* when it comes between vowels. Indeed in the case of Musulmanī Gujarati, the regular *r* sound is liable to be changed to *ḍ* or *ṇ*.[77] Khakee notes that in manuscript K of the *Das Avatār*, the same letter, 𑈛, is used for all three sounds.[78] Manuscript K-3 of the *Būjh Niranjan* also uses 𑈛 for all three sounds.[79] Stack remarks that while most Indian languages have the same letter to represent *ḍ* and *ṛ*, Sindhī has a different one for each.[80] However, although his table does show a separate character for *ḍ* and *ṛ*, the character for *ṛ* and *ṇ* is the same.[81] Allana uses the letter 𑈙 to indicate the sound *ṛ*, but in modern Khojkī this character is almost exclusively used for the sound *ḍ*. Attempts seem to have been made at a much later stage in the script's development to clear the confusion by having separate and distinctive letters for these sounds. The Khojkī primers of 1932 and 1947 use 𑈙 for *ḍ*, 𑈚 to represent *ṛ* and 𑈛 to represent *ṇ*. Nonetheless, in most Khojkī texts the value of the character 𑈛 still remains uncertain.

3. Orthography

Since Khojkī script is chiefly phonetic and it was used over a wide area of diverse dialectical pronunciation without being standardized, it is common to find in Khojkī texts inconsistencies in the orthography of many words. One example of such an inconsistency is found in words in which the sounds *b* and *d* occur. In the spoken language, these two sounds are often aspirated and pronounced as *bh* and *dh*. It was, then, the aspirated sound which was often represented when the word was committed to writing. Thus, the Arabic word *dǖʿā* (prayer) was sometimes written as *dǖā* and sometimes as *dhǖā*, the latter spelling corresponding to the colloquial pronunciation of the word. Similarly *bāt* was sometimes written correctly and sometimes as *bhāt*.[82]

Another inconsistency in the orthography lies in the length of the vowels. It is true that in the case of a few vowels, Khojkī simply did not have the capacity to distinguish between short and long vowels. But there were vowels for which this distinction was possible, and yet the corpus of Khojkī literature pays very little attention to ensuring correct vowel-length. At one point in a text a word would be spelled with a long vowel, while at another the vowel of the same word would be reduced to a short one. The word *milanā*, for example, would be written as *mīlanā* or *milinā*.[83]

One final problem in the use of orthographic symbols is ambiguity. The script uses the superscript symbol / in conjunction with a consonant that is to be read with a short *i* vowel. The same symbol could also designate a vowel-less consonant, apparently serving the same function as the *halaṅt* in the Devanāgarī alphabet. Thus [Khojki] could be transcribed either as *pirem* or *prem*. The ambiguity surrounding the symbol / is more complex than this, however: Khakee in her study of manuscript Kx, of the *Das Avatār* remarks that in the manuscript this symbol is used to give a short *a* or a short *e* sound![84]

Another orthographic sign whose value, especially in handwritten texts, is uncertain is the superscript dot. In most Khojkī texts, it is usually placed above a long vowel to indicate nasalization. In this respect it is identical to the Devanāgarī *anunāsik*. In some manuscripts, however, the same mark is sometimes placed above a consonant, apparently to indicate that it is vowel-less. As one would expect of the Khojkī script, this practice is not consistently followed.

Notwithstanding the several flaws that have seriously limited its ability to function as a full-fledged literary alphabet, Khojkī performed the valuable service of recording and preserving the rich corpus of the subcontinent's Ismaili literature for a period extending over 300 years. Were it not for Khojkī, a substantial portion of this literature, particularly the unique genre of the *ginān*s, would have been possibly lost forever. Admittedly, the script's capriciousness contributed partially to the distortions and corruptions present in this literature. Although the script still poses difficult problems for scholars, these problems are surmountable through a systematic elaboration of the script's idiosyncrasies. Khojkī must certainly represent one of the more unusual items in the annals of Indo-Muslim civilization.

Notes

* This chapter was originally published as 'The Khojkī Script: A Legacy of Ismaili Islam in the Indo-Pakistan Subcontinent,' in *Journal of the American Oriental Society*, 107(1987), pp. 439–49.

1. G. Allana states in his *Sindhī Ṣuratkhatī* (Hyderabad, 1964), p. 4, that the Ismailis in Sind and Cutch began using the Khojkī script in the later half of the reign of the Sumra dynasty (1051–1351).

2. Although the term *Khoja* now most commonly refers to the Nizārī Ismaili followers of the Aga Khan, there are also Sunni and Ithnāʿasharī (Twelver) Khojas who, for various reasons, have seceded from the larger group and no longer follow Ismaili doctrine. The title *khwāja* appears to have been introduced to replace the original term *ṭhākur* or *ṭhākkar* (also meaning lord, master) used by the Lohāṇā Hindu caste, some members of which were converted to Ismaili Islam. *The Gazetteer of the Bombay Presidency* (vol. 9, part 2, p. 39) remarks that in north-east Kaṭhiāwāḍ, Khojas were still addressed by the Lohāṇā title *ṭhākkar* and wore their waistcoats in the Lohāṇā fashion. It must also be noted that among the Ismailis of the subcontinent, there are those who do not differ from the Ismaili Khojas either culturally or in terms of religious doctrines, but nonetheless are not Khojas, i.e. Momnās, Kunbīs or Shamsīs. These subgroups are converts from non-Lohāṇā castes. Cf. 'Khodjā,' *SEI*, p. 256.

3. Azim Nanji, *The Nizārī Ismāʿīlī Tradition in the Indo-Pakistan Subcontinent* (Delmar, NY, 1978), pp. 9, 74.

4. F.A. Khan, *Banbhore* (Karachi, 1976), p. 16; see especially figures 2 and 3.

5. G. Allana, *Sindhī Ṣuratkhatī* (rev. ed., Hyderabad, 1969), p. 20.

6. Ibid., p. 24.

7. Although the earliest extant Khojkī manuscript dates to 1736, there is considerable evidence that the tradition of writing in the script goes back much earlier. See Nanji, *The Nizārī Ismāʿīlī Tradition*, pp. 9–11, and Zawahir Noorally, *Catalogue of Khojkī Manuscripts in the Collection of the Ismailia Association for Pakistan* (unpublished, Karachi, 1971).

8. Allana, *Sindhī Ṣuratkhatī*, pp. 16–19.

9. Ibn al-Nadīm, *al-Fihrist* (Cairo, 1348/1929), pp. 27–8.

10. Abū Rayḥān al-Bīrūnī, *Kitāb al-Hind*, Eng. trans. E.C. Sachau, *Alberuni's India*, ed. A.T. Embree (New York, 1971), p. 173.

11. E. Trumpp, 'Abstract of the Society's Proceedings,' *JBBRAS*, 5 (1857), p. 685.

12. R. Burton, *Sindh and the Races that Inhabit the Valley of the Indus* (repr., Karachi, 1973), pp. 152–3.

13. George Stack, *A Grammar of the Sindhi Language* (Bombay, 1849), pp. 3–8.

14. G. Grierson, *Linguistic Survey of India* (Calcutta, 1903–28), vol. 8, pt. 1, p. 247.

15. Ibid., p. 14.

16. Grierson suggests that Laṇḍā, Ṭāṅkrī and Mahājanī are in fact descendants of one original alphabet that was current over the whole of north-western India. 'On the Modern Indo-Aryan Alphabets of North-Western India,' *JRAS* (1904), p. 67.

17. D. Diringer, *The Alphabet: A Key to the History of Mankind* (3rd ed., New York, 1968), vol. 1, p. 290.

18. J. Prinsep, 'Note on *A Grammar of the Sindhi language dedicated to the Rt. Honourable Sir Robert Grant, Governor of Bombay, by W.H. Whalen Esq.*,' *JASB*, 6 (1837), p. 352.

19. Grierson, *Linguistic Survey*, vol. 9, part 2, p. 338.

20. Ibid., p. 19, n. 1.

21. Diringer, *The Alphabet*, p. 295.

22. Prinsep, 'Notes,' p. 352.

23. Grierson, *Linguistic Survey*, vol. 8, part 1, p. 247.

24. Ibid., p. 14. In the same note he relates a story according to which a merchant wrote to his son to send 'the small account book with the cover' (*nanḍhī wahī puṭhe sūdhī*). The son read this as *nanḍhī wahū puṭa sūdhī* (Send the youngest daughter-in-law with [her] son)!

25. Burton, *Sindh and the Races*, p. 153.

26. E. Trumpp, *Grammar of the Sindhi Language* (Leipzig, 1872), p. 6.

27. G. Stack, *A Grammar of the Sindhi Language*, p. 2, note. Stack remarks that while he had been informed that the medial vowel marks were also used with other Sindhī scripts, he had not been able to locate any corroborative examples.

28. In addition to the *ginān*s, Khojkī manuscripts record *farmān*s (commands, guidances, given by the Imams of the Nizārī Ismailis), religious stories, popular Hindu *bhajan*s (devotional songs), as well as an assortment of *ghazal*s and *kāfī*s. For a detailed description of the contents of Khojkī manuscripts, see Ali S. Asani, *The Harvard Collection of Ismaili Literature in Indic Languages: A Finding Aid and Descriptive Catalog* (Boston, Mass., 1992), pp. 4–22. (See also chapter 7 of this volume)

29. Allana, *Sindhī Ṣuratkhatī*, p. 24. See also Nabi Bakhsh Khan Baloch. *Sindhī Bolī jī mukhtaṣar tārīkh* (Hyderabad, 1962), pp. 114–15.

30. Diringer, *The Alphabet*, p. 291.

31. Ibid.

32. See Ali S. Asani, 'The Nizārī Ismāʿīlī *Ginān* Literature: Its Structure and Love Symbolism' (B.A. thesis, Harvard, 1977).

33. Grierson, *Linguistic Survey*, vol. 8, part 1, p. 247.

34. S.S. Gandhi, *History of the Sikh Gurus* (New Delhi, 1978), pp. 174–5, quoting Gokal Chand Narang.

35. B.A. Gupte, 'The Modi Character,' *Indian Antiquary*, 34 (1905), p. 28.

36. A recent research trip to the subcontinent revealed a tradition among the Nizārī Ismailis which holds that there used to be a group of professional scribes, *Akhunds*, who would travel from one village to another for the purpose of transcribing 'fresh' copies of deteriorating manuscripts (*copḍās*) or supplying texts not available previously in the area. Some tenuous evidence of this practice is provided by manuscripts in the same hand and found in diverse places, but further research needs to be carried out to determine the authenticity of this tradition. Interview with Abdul Hussain Alibhai Nanji, Hyderabad, Pakistan, January 1982.

37. Nanji, *The Nizārī Ismāʿīlī Tradition*, p. 9.

38. See Ignaz Goldziher, 'Linguistisches aus der Literatur der muhammadanischen Mystik', *Zeitschrift der Deutschen Morgenländischen Gesellschaft*, 26 (1872), p. 765, and Alessandro Bausani, 'About a Curious Mystical Language,' *East and West* 4, no. 4 (1954).

39. Nanji, *The Nizārī Ismāʿīlī Tradition*, p. 72.

40. Grierson, *Linguistic Survey*, vol. 9, Part 1, p. 624. Cf. W. Owen Cole and P.S. Sambhi, *The Sikhs: Their Religious Beliefs and Practices* (London, 1978), p. 19.

41. See Asani, *The Harvard Collection of Ismaili Literature in Indic Languages*.

42. Personal communication from Zawahir Moir, London. The earliest extant manuscript in the Khojkī script dates to 1736. See Z. Noorally, *Catalogue of Khojkī Manuscripts*, MS 25, and Nanji, *The Nizārī Ismāʿīlī Tradition*, p. 10.

43. Wladimir Ivanow, 'Satpanth,' in *Collectanea* vol. 1 (Leiden, 1948), p. 40.

44. Two examples of Khojkī lithographs from this period are: (1) *Vasīle molājo sāṇ rasālo emām Jāafar Sādhik ane satī māheje rozeje dīān paḍaṇjo molājo moejejo*, published in 1895 by Kāsam bhāī Karīm Bhagat through the Datt Prasādh Press, Bombay; (2) *Sindh Hedhrābād tathā Jāmnagar jā faramān*, published in 1900 by M. (Muhammad?) Sāle Kāsam through the J.D. Press, Bombay.

45. The Ghulām-i Ḥusain Press was operated by Alādīn Ghulāmḥusain and his son, Ḥusain. Some of the Khojkī publications of the press included *Ginānjī copḍī cogaḍie vārī* (1891), *Rasālo Īmam Jāfar sādhakjo* (1902), and *Ginān granth* (1907).

46. Zawahir Moir, personal communication.

47. These schisms were a result of attempts by some dissident Khojas to question the Aga Khan's position as Imam of the community, and it resulted in court cases such as the Aga Khan Case of 1866 and the Ḥājjī Bībī Case of 1905. A Study of the Aga Khan Case, which took place before Justice Arnould of the High Court of Bombay, is presented in A.A.A. Fyzee, *Cases in the Muhammadan Law of India and Pakistan* (Oxford, 1965), 504–49.

48. Ali S. Asani, 'The *Būjh Niranjan: An Ismaili Mystical Poem* (Cambridge, Mass., 1991).

49. It was under the auspices of the Recreation Club and its successor the Ismaili Society that W. Ivanow, the celebrated scholar of Ismailism, published some of his research.

50. On the basis of scanty information it appears that Lāljī Devrāj may have played an important role in facilitating the switch from Khojkī to Gujarati within the Ismaili community of the subcontinent. This, however, has to be adequately researched before stronger conclusions can be reached.

51. Interview with Hashim Moledina, an experienced teacher of Khojkī, Karachi, January, 1982.

52. It is common even today to find non-Sindhī Ismailis who profess to have a knowledge of Sindhī, but who in fact know the Khojkī script rather than the Sindhī language.

53. See Asim Roy, *The Islamic Syncretistic Tradition in Bengal* (Princeton, NJ, 1983) and Richard Eaton, *Sufis of Bijapur 1300–1700* (Princeton, NJ, 1978).

54. Annemarie Schimmel, 'Sindhi Literature,' in J. Gonda, ed., *A History of Indian Literature* (Wiesbaden, 1974), vol. 9, part 1, p. 4.

55. Critical editions of both works, which included examinations of Khojkī manuscript texts, were presented as doctoral theses at Harvard University. The study on the *Dasa Avatāra* was submitted by G. Khakee in 1972 while that on the *Būjh Niranjan* was completed by the present author in 1984.

56. Nanji, *The Nizārī Ismāʿīlī Tradition*, p. 110.

57. G. Khakee, 'The *Dasa Avatāra* of the Satpanthi Ismailis and the

Imam Shahis of Indo-Pakistan' (Ph.D. thesis, Harvard University, 1972), pp. 479, 603, n. 2.

58. A cursory examination of the approximately 65 Khojkī manuscripts and texts in the Harvard University Library failed to produce any text that used this vowel form.

59. Khakee, 'The *Dasa Avatāra,*' p. 603, n. 2.

60. Stack, *A Grammar of the Sindhi Language,* p. 4.

61. Khakee, 'The *Dasa Avatāra,*' pp. 479, 603, n. 1.

62. Allana, *Sindhī Ṣuratkhatī,* p. 26.

63. Stack, *A Grammar of the Sindhi Language,* p. 61.

64. Khakee, 'The *Dasa Avatāra,*' p. 479.

65. Stack, *A Grammar of the Sindhi Language,* p. 4.

66. Allana, *Sindhī Ṣuratkhatī,* p. 26, note.

67. Ibid., p. 24, Allana points out that this was the reason that Khojkī was sometimes called *cāliha akharī* (forty letters). Nanji, *The Nizārī Ismāʿīlī Tradition,* documents 42 letters in the script.

68. Khojkī was used for writing not only theological terms and phrases from the Arabic language but also for writing Persian. In fact, an entire Persian text, the *Pandiyāt-i jawānmardī* was transcribed in the Khojkī script and printed in 1904 by the Khoja Printing Press (see Plate v). Ivanow remarks that since this work expressed the ideas of the Imam it was considered to be 'sacred' and therefore accorded an honour otherwise known only in the case of the Qur'an. *Pandiyāt-i Javānmardī,* Persian text ed. and trans. by W. Ivanow (Leiden, 1953), p. 3.

69. The Arabic *ṣād* (*ṣ*) was usually pronounced as *s.* In Gurmukhī, which originally had only one sibilant (*s*), a dot was placed under the character for this sound to represent the aspirated *sh* that frequently occurred in non-Punjabi words. Diringer, *The Alphabet,* p. 297.

70. It is unlikely that these modified characters were ever pronounced as the Arabic *ʿain.* Rather they were simply pronounced as the Arabic *alif.*

71. See the story in Baloch, *Sindhī Ḅolī,* 33, from al-Jāḥiz, about a Sindhī woman who pronounced the Arabic *jamal* as *zamal.*

72. This letter is not found frequently in Khojkī texts. It is quite common in MS KH 131 in the collection of the Ismailia Tariqa and Religious Education Board for Pakistan.

73. Khakee, 'The *Dasa Avatāra,*' p. 604, n. 13.

74. Ibid., p. 482.

75. In works published by Lāljī Devrāj, the letter  is always used to represent *z* or *j* but never *dy.*

76. Ibid., p. 604, n. 5. In common with other mercantile scripts, Khojkī did not originally possess signs for conjunct consonants. The introduction of these characters took place relatively recently in the script's history. The few conjunct consonants used in later Khojkī texts are derived from the Devanāgari script, i.e. [illegible] for *tr,* [illegible] for *ksh* and [illegible] for *dhr.*

77. Grierson, *Linguistic Survey*, vol. 9, Part 2, p. 437.

78. Khakee, 'The *Dasa Avatāra*,' p. 479.

79. Asani, 'The *Būjh Niranjan*', p. 77.

80. Stack, ibid., p. 7, note.

81. According to Stack's table (p. 6), the letter [illegible] represents both *ṛ* and *ṇ*.

82. G. Khakee remarks that the change of unaspirated sounds to their aspirated counterparts does not take place in all cases but no logical pattern is discernible ('The *Dasa Avatāra*,' p. 483). According to Grierson, the aspiration of the letter *b* takes place in the Kacchi/Sindhī dialect in words borrowed from Arabic and Persian. (*Linguistic Survey*, vol. 8, Part 1, p. 185).

83. It must be noted here that in most *ginān* texts, including those printed later in the Gujarati script and even in Roman transliteration, very little attention is given to accurate representation of vowel lengths.

84. Khakee, 'The *Dasa Avatāra*,' p. 604, n. 3.

7

The Khojkī Script and its Manuscript Tradition*

History tells us that until the early decades of this century, many alphabets and writing systems were current in the province of Sind. As early as the 3rd/9th and 4th/10th centuries, we have reports from Arab travellers attesting to the fact that the inhabitants of the region employed as many as 200 scripts for writing their language.[1] We do not know much about the nature of these early scripts but al-Bīrūnī, the renowned Muslim scholar and traveller of the 5th/14th century, records the names of three of them: Malwārī, Saindhava, and Ardhā-Nāgārī.[2] We can be certain that with the establishment of Muslim rule in the region and the introduction of Arabic and Persian as official languages, one or more forms of the Arabic script (the alphabet which was eventually in modern times to render all the others obsolete[3]) were added to the assortment.

That the use of multiple scripts in Sind prevailed well into the 19th century is attested by various European orientalists and travellers in the region. E. Trumpp, the German author of a well-known Sindhī grammar, noting the use of various alphabets, observes that generally the Muslim population preferred Arabic characters, loaded with 'a confusing heap of dots,' while the Hindus employed a medley of scripts known by the name Banyāṅ.[4] The

English adventurer, Sir Richard Burton, remarking on the very numerous alphabets in 'which the Sindhī tongue is written,' notes that besides 'Moslem varieties of the Semitic alphabet,' there were no less than eight scripts prevalent among the Hindus.[5] Another English scholar, George Stack, observes in his *Grammar of the Sindhi Language* that the scripts varied from one geographical region to another and that different religious and caste groups favoured distinctive script styles.[6]

Among this miscellany of alphabets, one script, Khojkī, stands out for its distinctive historical and cultural role. Khojkī or Khwājā Sindhī, as its name implies, was the 'official' script of Sind's Khoja or Nizari Ismaili community.[7] Over the course of time, use of the script also spread among the Khoja communities of Gujarat and Punjab who commonly referred to it as 'Sindhi'. Khojkī was primarily used to record the community's religious literature which was composed in Sindhī as well as a variety of other languages including Gujarati, Hindustani, Punjabi, Arabic and Persian. Since Khojkī was exclusively used by the Khojas, it served to confine the religious literature within their community, thus preventing possible persecution from those hostile to Ismaili doctrines and practices.[8] At another level, the script appears to have been influential in the development of cohesion and self-identity within the Khoja community whose members resided not only in Sind, Punjab and Gujarat, but also in East Africa (after a diaspora in the 19th and early 20th centuries). In this regard, Khojkī, like the Gurmukhī[9] and Moḍī[10] scripts of the Sikhs and Mahrattas respectively, is another example of an Indic alphabet used to enhance communal and ethnic solidarity.

The Khojkī Script and its Origins

Notwithstanding Khojkī's significant role in the Ismaili Khoja community, we know little about its origins and development.[11] Community tradition attributes the invention of the script to a 9th/15th century Ismaili preacher-saint (*dāʿī*), Pīr Ṣadr al-Dīn, an important proselytiser of Ismaili Islam in the subcontinent's western provinces. However, archaeological evidence from the ancient town of Bhambhore in Sind indicates the presence of a prototype of Khojkī in the area as early as the 2nd/8th century. This prototype has been identified as Lohāṇakī, the script of the province's Hindu Lohāṇā community.[12] Interestingly enough, according to Ismaili tradition, the Lohāṇā community was one of the groups among whom the preacher-saint Pīr Ṣadr al-Dīn actively pursued his missionary activities, bestowing the title *Khoja* on Lohāṇā converts to Ismaili Islam. Therefore, we may surmise that Khojkī is most likely a polished or more developed form of Lohāṇakī with the legendary Pīr Ṣadr al-Dīn perhaps having played a role in its evolution.[13]

Both Khojkī and Lohāṇakī belong to a group of scripts commonly known in Sind as Banyāṅ or Wāṇiko, associated primarily with mercantile communities. In its turn, Banyāṅ of Sind is associated with a larger family of Indian scripts which have been classified by Grierson under the heading 'Laṇḍā' or 'clipped' alphabets employed throughout Sind and Punjab by mercantile classes.[14] Banyāṅ, also known as *Huṭ jā akhar* (letters of the shop),[15] parallels several writing systems, in other areas of the subcontinent, associated with merchant and trading castes such as Vāṇiāī (from *vāṇīo*, shopkeeper), Ṣarrāfī (from *ṣarrāf*, banker), or Bodīā (from *bodī*, clipped or shorn) of Gujarat; Ṭāṅkrī of the lower ranges of the Himalayas; and Mahājanī (Mārwarī), the mercantile script popularized all over north India by enterprising Mārwārī traders.[16]

These mercantile scripts, which are by nature a kind of shorthand for they frequently omit all but initial vowels, are ill-suited for literary purposes. That they possess a poorly developed vowel system,[17] an imperfect set of consonants,[18] or that sometimes they represent consonants merely by ciphers, which are combinations of numbers and fractions,[19] seem not to have posed too great a hindrance for handling the demands of rudimentary accounting and limited mercantile communications such as *hunḍī*s (bills of exchange) in which almost identical phrases are constantly repeated. But these defects often proved to be great handicaps when these scripts were used for more sophisticated purposes. Not surprisingly, stories abound about the confusion caused by the misreadings of these mercantile scripts.[20]

Development of the Khojkī Script

Among this assortment of commercial scripts, a small number, including Khojkī, were actually refined and developed into vehicles of literary expression. Why did this refinement take place for some scripts and not for others? The reasons vary from one script to another, but for Khojkī, this advance was motivated by the Ismaili community's need to preserve its corpus of religious literature in a distinctive local alphabet with which adherents had the greatest familiarity and which was easy to learn. In this connection, better developed scripts such as the Devanāgarī or Perso-Arabic, which were associated with classical languages such as Sanskrit, Arabic and Persian, were probably considered alien or too sophisticated for recording Khoja religious literature which was in the vernaculars and aimed at agricultural and trading peoples.

We have very little evidence concerning the process by which Khojkī evolved from a rudimentary mercantile script of the 2nd/8th century to a more complex medium capable of handling the demands of a whole new range of expression. The study of the script is still in its infancy primarily because the majority of Khojkī manuscripts, our most important source of information about the script, still need to be systematically analysed. Nevertheless, from the limited evidence we have available, we can discern several improvements that were made to the script in an attempt to refine it. The first involved the introduction of a system of medial vowel marks called *lākanā*. Among the mercantile scripts of Sind, Khojkī seems to have been the only one to have sustained and perhaps even developed the use of this medial vowel system.[21] In addition, attempts were made to enhance the script's capacity to indicate a greater number of initial and final vowels, as well as diphthongs, signs for which were added at a rather late stage. Although these modifications did not result in a perfect set of vowels, they did render the script better suited for recording an extensive literary corpus. Incidentally, it is likely that Pīr Ṣadr al-Dīn, whom tradition credits with inventing the script, or one of his close disciples, may have been involved in introducing the *lākanā* and other refinements.[22] Table 1 illustrates the eventual organization of the script's vowel system.

The second development concerned the ability of the Khojkī script to clearly demarcate the boundaries between contiguous words so as to prevent them from coalescing into each other. Writing in mercantile scripts is, as a rule, continuous with almost no spacing between words. Consequently, adjacent words are often erroneously joined, resulting in utter confusion due to the arbitrary reconstruction of a group of letters by readers.[23] To prevent such misreadings and misinterpretations, Khojkī writing conventions were modified to include a rather simple solution to this problem: the use of colon-like punctuations to demarcate the terminations of individual words.

The third enhancement concerned the Khojkī consonant system. The script had approximately forty consonants and, therefore, was sometimes referred to as *cāliha akharī* (forty letters). In its primitive form, the Khojkī set of consonants suffered from significant defects. There were certain sounds for which the script had no characters at all (deficiency); the same sound could be represented by two or more characters (redundancy); and several sounds could be represented by the same character (ambiguity). When Khojkī was co-opted for recording Ismaili religious literature, these defects created limitations and difficulties. Gradually, over several centuries, most of these were remedied through either modification of existing characters, borrowing from the Nagari-based Gujarati script, or the creation of entirely new letters, particularly for representing Arabic characters. Table 2 illustrates the arrangement of the Khojkī consonant system as it had developed in the early 20th century.

Notwithstanding these improvements, the use of the Khojkī script in the community began to decline in the early decades of the 20th century partly as a result of the printing press. Initially, the establishment of printing presses in Bombay, such as the Ghulām-i Ḥusain Chāpākhānu and the Khoja Sindhī Printing Press, appeared to be an important impetus in promoting the use of the script by making available Khojkī literature in greater quantities. Soon, however, the considerable expenses in manufacturing printing types specifically for Khojkī, as well as the continued existence of a few flaws in the script itself (including regional variations), became serious problems in an era when literature was being widely disseminated and standardized. The Gujarati script emerged as a viable alternative so that by the 1940s printing of Khojkī books, as well as instruction in the Khojkī script, ceased except in the region of Sind, its birthplace. There, the script survived in a limited extent until the 1970s when it gave way to the Perso-Arabic alphabet, widely used in Pakistan for the Sindhī and Urdu languages.

Khojkī Manuscripts

We have discussed above the serious limitations of the Khojkī script as a system of literary expression. For the most part, these inadequacies can be explained by the script's mercantile origin and regional usage. As a commercial script, Khojkī was rather limited in its capabilities, and when it was co-opted for recording Ismaili religious literature, its limitations posed some difficulties and problems. A few of these were gradually remedied in subsequent centuries enabling Khojkī to function more efficiently as the 'official' script of the subcontinent's Ismaili community.

We do not know exactly when the practice of recording religious texts in Khojkī first began. Community tradition attributes the invention of the script to the preacher-saint Pīr Ṣadr al-Dīn. This attribution is problematic for, as we have seen, prototypes of Khojkī are associated with the script of the Lohāṇā community, dating back to the 2nd/8th century. Moreover, even if we were to assume that the *pīr* was in some manner associated with the introduction of the script in the Khoja community, that assumption does not assist us much, for the birth and death dates assigned to the *pīr* in hagiographic literature vary tremendously.[24] Matters are further complicated by the absence of any manuscripts that are earlier than the 12th/18th century; the oldest surviving Khojkī manuscript dates only to 1149/1736.[25] This dearth may be partially explained by the poor climatic conditions in the subcontinent, but religious zeal was also a factor: it seems that in the early 14th/20th century, after the publication of editions of 'standardized' *ginān* texts in printed form, a large number of manuscripts which were used to prepare these editions were buried in the ground.[26] The exact number of manuscripts involved is uncertain but believed to be approximately 3500.[27]

Nevertheless, we do have some basis to believe that a manuscript tradition in Khojkī existed prior to the 12th/18th century. Internal evidence, in the form of scribal notes, from several surviving manuscripts (including the one copied in 1736) indicates that these texts were copies made by scribes from older manuscripts.[28] It seems to have been customary to re-copy manuscripts once they began to deteriorate and disintegrate.[29] In support of a pre-12th/18th century manuscript tradition we also note that in the early years of this century, a Khojkī manuscript copied in 973/1565 was presented as evidence in a much-publicized court-case.[30] Although the present whereabouts of this manuscript are unknown, it would be reasonable to assume that the task of recording religious texts in the Khojkī script was already well under way by the 10th/16th century. In this regard, we may also note that Professor Allana is of the opinion that the script was in use among the Khojas as early as the later half of the reign of the Sumra dynasty (443–752/1051–1351).[31]

At present there are three known collections of surviving Khojkī manuscripts, which are known as *copḍā* or *pothī* in the vernacular. The first was assembled under the auspices of the Ismailia Association (now the Ismaili Tariqa and Religious Education Board) for Pakistan and housed in its library at Karachi. Containing some 250 items, this collection was organized and catalogued in the early 1970s by Zawahir Noorally, a research associate of the Association. This laudable effort resulted in an unpublished manuscript: *A Catalogue of Khojkī Manuscripts in the Library of the Ismailia Association for Pakistan.* This work, which is more of an inventory than a catalogue, provides a general idea of the type of literature in that collection. However, as a reference work, it has several drawbacks: its system of transliteration is inconsistent; the contents of each manuscript are not precisely identified (a set of 50 short *ginān*s without titles would simply be identified as '50 short *ginān*s'); location of items within the physical manuscript is not always indicated; and incipits of texts are almost never provided.

Some of the contents of the Pakistan collection were transferred several years later to the library of The Institute of Ismaili Studies in London. These were consolidated with items from other sources to create a second collection of approximately 150 manuscripts. Ms. Noorally (now Mrs Moir) embarked on the preparation of a second catalogue of Khojkī manuscripts containing much more detailed information. Unfortunately, the catalogue remains incomplete (it covers approximately one-third of the collection) and unpublished. It is also without indexes, making reference difficult.

The third collection is located at the Houghton Library in Cambridge, Massachusetts, Harvard University's depository for rare books and manuscripts. The 25 Khojkī manuscripts housed here are part of a larger collection of 120 works of Ismaili literature in Indic languages, including 45 lithographs and early printed texts in the Khojkī script. There is a published catalogue for the entire collection[32] in which the manuscripts have been systematically described and their contents analysed and indexed. Although the number of Khojkī manuscripts in this collection is small,[33] they are the only ones that are at present in the public domain and accessible for general scholarly research. Consequently, much of the discussion that follows on the specific characteristics and features of the Khojkī manuscript tradition is based on this small collection serving as a representative sample.

Provenance of Texts

The manuscripts in the collection were gathered, between 1970 and 1971, from the Ismaili communities of western India, specifically Cutch and Gujarat. All the manuscripts show signs of heavy wear and tear – a result of both their frequent use within these communities as well as the harsh climatic and other conditions under which they were stored. Among these manuscripts, 17 have notations indicating that they all originate from the region of Cutch: the majority from Kera, a couple from Bhadneshwar and one from Mundra. The rest, being unmarked, cannot be traced to a specific location with any degree of uncertainty. However, from internal evidence, we may surmise that they, too, come from a similar milieu.

Several manuscripts in the collection were kept at the community's religious centres (*jamāʿat-khānas*) where they would be frequently consulted for the various religious texts they contain. In this regard, the colophon of Ms Ism K 17 is of particular interest,[34] for it documents that the manuscript was commissioned by local religious functionaries (known as the *mukhī* and *kāmaḍīā*) for the use of their congregation. A note included on the first folio of Ms Ism K 1 declares the volume to be the property of the Bhadneshwar *jamāʿat* (congregation). Similarly, parts of Ms Ism K 22 were written at the community's headquarters (*darkhānā*), presumably in Bombay, while Ms Ism K 9 was presented by an individual for use by the *jamāʿat* of Bhadneshwar. A few works were collected from the *dargāh* (religious shrine) dedicated to the Ismaili preacher saint, Pīr Ghulām ʿAlī Shāh (d.1207/1792 or 1211/1796), at Kera.[35] Finally, some manuscripts appear to have belonged to individuals or families who, apparently, commissioned them for personal use.

As regards the locations where the manuscripts were actually written, the colophons, if they exist, are so rudimentary that they provide little or no information. Evidence concerning the origins and transmission of the actual contents of the manuscripts is also sketchy. In most cases, the scribes supply virtually no information about the source of their texts. However, it is evident, on the basis of scribal notes, that some texts were copies of other, presumably older, manuscripts.[36] On the other hand, the scribe of an early 20th century manuscript notes that his particular text, a rather long *ginān* with some prayers, was recorded during a recitation – clear evidence of an orally transmitted text being transformed into a written one.[37] At least one scribe indicates that he copied certain texts from a book published in the late 19th century by Alādīn Ghulām Ḥusayn.[38]

Binding Styles and Practices

The manuscripts exhibit two basic styles of binding with some minor variations: a traditional local style in the manner of Indian *pothā*s[39] and a foreign Western style influenced by 19th-century European book-binding practices. Generally speaking, the older manuscripts tend to use the former style while the more recent ones adopt the latter. In a few cases, we can even discern attempts to combine the two. We also note here that some manuscripts show clear evidence of having been rebound (Ms Ism K 10, Ms Ism K 22).

In the traditional *pothā* style, the untrimmed leaves of paper are collectively folded within leather covers and sewn together at the fold, without supports. As the number of leaves in a single manuscript range from 20 to over 400, the manuscripts vary in thickness from 1 cm to 7.5 cm. Usually some heavy string, such as three-ply bleached cotton, was employed for the binding. Ms Ism K 9 and Ms Ism K 20 are fine illustrations of this style. This style of binding results in two visual features characteristic of Khojkī manuscripts: a nice, round curve on the spine, especially in thicker manuscripts, with the untrimmed leaves forming a chevron.

Also typical of this style is its simple and swiftly-executed sewing pattern. The binding cord or string is sewn through the fold of the leaves and cover at an odd number of sewing stations, usually three or five. On the inside of the manuscript, at each sewing station, are placed lozenge-shaped or round leather-guards which serve to prevent the binding cord from biting into the paper. In addition, at the sewing station located at the centre of the fold, the cord may be tied into a knot. The sewing takes place in such a manner as to leave a length of the sewing cord, between 8 to 10 inches, dangling externally at the centre of the spine. This length of string, frequently knotted at the end to prevent unravelling, may have been used to secure the manuscript when it was not in use.

Usually a single piece of fine-grained calf leather, wrapped around the text and attached to it at the fold, served as a cover. Often the leather, usually reddish-brown in colour, was undecorated. Sometimes, however, the central portion of this leather cover was blind-tooled on the outside with a variety of designs, such as leaves, rosettes and grids (Ms Ism K 9 and Ms Ism K 22). In most cases, the leather cover was cut slightly larger than the paper so that the text was completely covered. Sometimes, however, as we see in Ms Ism K 4, the cover retained the same size as each page, resulting in an accentuation of the chevron of untrimmed paper. In cases where there was extra length of leather for the cover, it was often times folded over at the fore-edge rather than cut (Ms Ism K 14).

We note several variations on the basic style. For one volume (Ms Ism G2), as the thin cord was used in its entirety during the binding, an extra length of thick cord was attached to the spine. This additional length was then used to girdle the manuscript. In some manuscripts, for example Ms Ism K 4, Ms Ism K 14 and Ms Ism K 23, the sewing pattern was modified so that the cord went around the head and tail of the text instead of remaining exclusively on the spine. In such cases, it became necessary to install leather guards along the full length of the inner fold to protect against wear and tear. In smaller sized manuscripts, we find either cotton or paper guards instead of leather ones (Ms Ism G 1 and Ms Ism K 19), while some used no guards at all (Ms Ism K 3). Smaller manuscripts also tended to employ reinforced paper covers in place of the traditional leather. These paper covers were occasionally decorated. In one instance, (Ms Ism G 2), the cover, comprising of several layers of paper, was wrapped with striped cloth.

The Western style employs 19th-century European stab-sewing techniques employed for binding thin pamphlets or small pocket-size books. In Europe, these techniques were used mostly for binding material containing only a few sheets, and we find among Khojkī manuscripts the same techniques being employed, sometimes unsuccessfully, to bind fairly thick volumes. Typically, the sheets, often arranged in multiple sections, are stabbed vertically and then sewn together. The binding cords of flax or linen were then laced into laminated boards which usually served as covers. These covers would either be half-cloth (a cloth spine plus cloth tips) or quarter-cloth (simply, a cloth-spine). Occasionally, as for example in Ms Ism G 3, the covers would be full-cloth. Generally, the cloth would be of one solid colour, without any design. However, in a few instances, we find the use of striped cloth (Ms Ism G 1 and Ms Ism G 2) or of cloth, such as *ajrak*, decorated with designs traditional to the region (Ms Ism K 10). Half-cloth or quarter-cloth covers tend to have marbled paper or other decorative paper pasted on any exposed or unclothed areas. Marbled paper was also used for end sheets in some manuscripts (Ms Ism K 6 and Ms Ism K 8). Generally, the bound volume retained a flat-back spine. Manuscripts bound on this basic pattern include Ms Ism K 1, Ms Ism K 2, Ms Ism K 6 and Ms Ism K 8.

Some manuscripts also attempted to imitate other European styles. Ms Ism K 21, for example, exhibits typical 19th-century English trade binding practice in which the sewing of multiple sections took place through folds on recessed cords. This technique allowed the manuscript to open at each fold. Rounding and backing of the spine was also characteristic. Ms Ism K 10, which originally seems to have been bound in the stab-sewn pamphlet method, was rebound with another European technique – sewing on cloth tapes through the folds. Similarly, Ms Ism G 3, also bound with stabbing-and-sewing, has its cloth spine separately attached at the head and tail to the front few sections and the boards, possibly the result of impromptu repair by the owner. In Ms Ism K 11 we observe a type of variation on cleat sewing in which cuts were made into the spine folds and a lace cord sewn through.

Finally, a few manuscripts were quite eclectic in their binding, attempting to combine elements from both traditional and Western styles. Ms Ism K 15 uses a truly hybrid style. It has two sets of sewing reinforcing each other, the usual stab-sewn pattern as well as side-sewing with cords piercing through and attached to laminated boards. On the other hand, Ms Ism G 1 retains all the features of the traditional sewing system including cloth guards but uses a Western-style case covering made of hard board. Such manuscripts provide us strong evidence of traditional styles slowly being adapted to or being influenced by European styles, especially during the late 19th century.

Paper and Watermarks

The paper utilized in these manuscripts in either of local Indian origin (*desī*) or imported from Europe. While most manuscripts were written on a single type of paper, it was not uncommon to find two or more varieties being combined. The paper, which included both the laid and woven types, was usually white in colour. A single manuscript (Ms Ism K 17) uses light blue paper. The majority of the 14 watermarks are found on paper of the imported variety. These are separately identified in the individual entries of the catalogue. The watermarks suggest that most of the European paper was manufactured in the later half of the 19th century in Austria, Belgium, Germany or England. Two watermarks indicate that some of this imported paper was manufactured in Europe specifically for Indian businesses: the paper in Ms Ism K 6, Ms Ism K 8 and Ms Ism K 13, which dates to the year 1890, was made in England for Shaikh Ahmad Shaikh Dawood of Bombay, while that in Ms Ism K 2 and Ms Ism K 12 was made in Belgium for Nuzzerally Heptoolabhoy, also of Bombay, probably in 1896. Only one local brand of paper, used in Ms Ism G 2, contains a watermark. This was manufactured in Bombay, at the turn of the 20th century, under the brand name 'River Jumna' by Abdoola Saheb Abdool Rehman Hurufallah. The local paper, more common in the older manuscripts, was usually made of cotton, probably on elongated moulds. The paper was usually folded along the grain. It was customary to leave the paper untrimmed before it was bound between covers. This practice, as noted earlier, resulted in the edges of the paper forming a chevron once the manuscript was bound.

Internal Appearance and Layout

Having been written for pragmatic and practical purposes, the manuscripts generally have a plain and simple appearance. They lack any aesthetic sense in regard to the layout or appearance of their texts. Entire pages are filled with writing and contain very few illustrations or decorations of any kind. Indeed, the only significant diagrams are talismanic in nature, consisting of *taʿwīẓ* (amulets), prognostications and, in Ms Ism K 5, a drawing of *dhu'l-*

fiqār, the sword of the first Shiʿi Imam ʿAlī, and a chart listing the names of the *Panj tan-i pāk*, 'the five holy persons' of Shiʿi Islam, namely, Muḥammad, ʿAlī, Fāṭima, Ḥusayn and Ḥasan (see Plate VI). Decoration is limited to the rudimentary geometric patterns and floral designs that are occasionally used in between texts. In manuscripts bound according to traditional Indian style, the pages in the middle of the volume containing the leather guards are generally left blank. Most manuscripts are the product of two or more scribes; consequently a single manuscript may often contain examples of several different hands. Writing-styles can vary from a legible one in which letters are evenly-spaced and words separated (in Khojkī texts, usually by a colon-like sign ':') to an almost indecipherable one where letters and entire words may simply coalesce into one long line of text. In the latter case, only prior familiarity with the text ensures a correct reading by the reader.

Khojkī manuscripts very rarely demarcate the writing space for their texts. Only in Ms Ism K 19 do we find border lines being used over an extensive number of folios. In most Khojkī manuscripts, therefore, the margins are uneven and, in many cases, minimal. In these texts, generally, the amount of space between the lines of writing also varies but sometimes it is quite even, suggesting that the copyists may have used a backing of ruled paper or some other device to achieve this effect. In contrast to the Khojkī works, all three Gujarati manuscripts have clearly demarcated borders as well as ruled lines for their texts.

In almost all the manuscripts, the entire text is written in black ink. Occasionally, however, red ink was also used but never for the main text itself. Red ink is almost always restricted for use in the headings and titles of texts, for numbering verses, or for formulaic blessings and prayers. A very small number of manuscripts have a few texts written in blue ink (Ms Ism K 14) or black lead pencil (Ms Ism K 25), but these seem, for the most part, to be later additions. Inks of various colours were also used in the few illustrations such as those found in Ms Ism K 5. Frequently, to prevent ink runs and hasten the drying process, sand was lightly sprinkled on the folios. Evidence of this practice is still evident in many volumes.

Traditionally, texts begin with a typical formula of invocation, either the Sindhī '*Allāh toāhār* (*tohār*)' (meaning 'with the help of/reliance on Allah') and/or the Arabic *basmalah* customarily used to begin Islamic texts – '*Bism Allāh al-Raḥmān al-Raḥīm*' (In the name of God the Most Benificient, the Most Merciful). In the case of the *basmalah*, the phrase is invariably written in Khojkī or Gujarati, never in the Arabic script. Consequently, there are several different transliterations of this phrase, especially in Khojkī.[40] In a few instances the *basmalah* is preceded by another common Arabic invocation: '*Naʿūdhu biʾllāhi min al-shayṭān al-rajīm*' (We seek refuge in God from Satan, the accursed). This phrase, too, occurs in a greatly-distorted form in Khojkī transliteration.[41] A very small number of texts begin with the phrase typical for Shiʿi groups: '*Ya ʿAlī Madad*' (O ʿAlī, come to my help). In one instance, this phrase occurs in a slightly modified form: *Ya ʿAlī dastkhat madad* (O ʿAlī, help with the writing of this manuscript).[42] Immediately after one or more of these formulae, follows the title of the text, if it possesses one. Sometimes the title is written discretely on a separate line as a heading along with the name of the author of the composition. At other times it may be incorporated in a conventional phrase that is placed at the beginning of the work. In this phrase, the copyist states, usually in Sindhī, that he has written a particular work either with the help of God (*lakheūsī:āsare:khūdhāe:tālāeje*) or through the mediation of the Imam and the *pīr* (*lakheūsī:vasīle:shāhā:pīrje*). Less frequently, especially in older manuscripts, we find instead the phrase: '*Srī sat gur brahmā ho vācā*' (the [true] word of Srī Satgur Brahma). This phrase is followed by the title of the work and a declaration in the Gujarati language by the copyist that he has written it (*lakhiu che*).

As with the beginnings of the texts, the conclusions of texts are also marked by some conventional formulae. In a few cases, a rudimentary colophon, either in Sindhī or Gujarati, is included, stating the name of the scribe and, perhaps, the date of transcription. In the colophon, the scribe, in addition to his name, conveys his greetings (*salām*) to his readers and prays for blessings on them and their families with the Persian phrase '*khānā āvādān*' or '*khānā ābādān*'. The scribe may also seek forgiveness for any mistakes he may have committed while writing. One particularly humble copyist quite appropriately declares himself, in Cutchi, to be the abode of mistakes (*bando khatājo ghar āhe*).[43] Frequently, however, this item is missing and the copyist indicates completion by using one of the following phrases, all meaning 'completed': *tamām* (Arabic), *tamām shud* (Persian), *tamām thiyo* or *tamām thaī* (Sindhi), *tamām hūā* (Hindi-Urdu), and *tamām che* or *saṁpuraṅ* (Gujarati). In one or two manuscripts the popular phrase from the Qur'ān (2:156), '*Innā lillāhi wa innā ilayhi rājiʿūn*' (We are from God and to Him is the return), is used but, of course, in a distorted form transcribed into Khojkī.[44]

Tables of Contents

It was conventional for copyists to provide a manuscript with a table of contents. Such a table is called a *tafasīlo, tapasīlo* or *tavasīlo*.[45] It would record the location of texts in a manuscript, normally listing only titled works. Untitled works, like the short *ginān*s, would rarely be listed individually; rather they would be grouped under a single heading that would indicate their common authorship or use during certain religious festivities and ceremonies. Usually this table was placed at the end of the volume, although sometimes, as Ms Ism K 19 illustrates, it could be situated at the beginning. In manuscripts written in several sequences over a period of time, the table often occurs in the middle of the volume at the end of one or more of the earlier sequences.[46]

While the *tafasīlo* appears to be a standard feature in some texts, approximately half the manuscripts in the collection do not possess one. Even when it is found, it is not always a reliable or accurate guide to the entire contents of a manuscript. Frequently, when several copyists contributed to a manuscript, not all of them would record their texts in the manuscript's *tafasīlo*, resulting in only partial and incomplete listings. Similarly, when a manuscript was rebound, the *tafasīlo* was not revised to reflect changes in the foliation or pagination.

Dates of Recording

Well over half the manuscripts in the collection do not contain dates. Hence, the antiquity of these manuscripts can only be estimated by internal evidence such as peculiarities in script, scribal notes, or by means of binding style, paper type, etc. On the other hand, for dated manuscripts, it is important to realise that frequently dates must be used with caution, for they are not always reliable. Sometimes, a date may simply indicate when a particular text was written rather than being applicable to the entire manuscript. Therefore, manuscripts written in stages, over a long period of time, may contain several dates for each stage of writing. Ms Ism K 22, for example, is the work of several scribes over a period of 87 years. At other times, when a manuscript was a copy of an older one, the copyist would merely reproduce the date from the older one – a practice that can be quite confusing and misleading. Dates may also be unreliable in cases where manuscripts have been rebound with later, undated ones.

Dates are usually provided at the conclusion of a text, though occasionally the copyist may insert them at the beginning. Almost all dates are given in the Indian *samvat* era (the era of Vikrama beginning in 56–57 BC) commonly used in Gujarat and Sind. Only one date occurs in the Muslim *hijrī* era. Along with the year, the date includes day as well as the Indian lunar month, e.g. *1 Posh 1886 samvat.* The names of these months are invariably in their local vernacular forms. Thus the eighth month *Jeṭh* appears as *Jehitri* (Ms Ism K 20), the tenth month *Shrāvan* as *Srān* or *Sāvan* (Ms Ism K 21 and Ms Ism K 16), and the eleventh month *Bhādravo* as *Bhedarvā* (Ms Ism K 10). Sometimes, the dates will be more detailed providing information about the day of the week and the fortnight of the month in which it occurs, e.g. *Monday 11 sud Bhādarva 1971 samvat.*[47]

Scribes and Copyists

As a result of the rudimentary nature of colophons and/or their complete absence, we have very little information about the scribes who wrote these manuscripts. For over half the manuscripts in the collection we possess no information about either the identity of the copyists or their places of residence. Nevertheless, on the basis of writing styles, we can discern that while some manuscripts are the work of a single scribe, several are products of collaboration between two or more scribes. Multiple scribes collaborating on a single manuscript may or may not have known each other, for it seems after one scribe completed his specific task, any remaining blank folios were filled in with texts only much later. This practice not only accounts for the variety of handwriting styles that can often be found in a single manuscript but also, as mentioned above, the presence of several dates.

On the basis of the names that have been preserved in the manuscripts, we may surmise that most of the scribes were from Sind or Cutch. Typically, their family names terminate in the ending *āṇī* or *ānī*, as for example, Aluāṇī (Ms Ism K 9), Dhalāṇī (Ms Ism K 22), Manjīāṇī (Ms Ism K 16) and Bhimjīāṇī (Ms Ism K 10). A few names, such as Devjī (Ms Ism K 1) and Premjī (Ms Ism K 21) reveal origins from Gujarat or Kāṭhīāwāḍ. Significantly, in spite of the substantial number of Ismailis who lived in the Punjab, no names from that province are to be found. Regardless of their place of origin, all proper names have some kind of a title before them. In most cases, this consists of the word *khoja*, the title bestowed on Indian converts to Ismailism by the 9th/15th century *dāʿī* (preacher, missionary) Pīr Ṣadr al-Dīn. In some cases, the word *bhāī*, meaning 'brother,' is used either by itself[48] or in combination with the title *Khoja*.[49] Occasionally the title *Kāmaḍīā*, used to designate a religious official, also occurs before some names.[50] In the case of the copyist of Ms Ism G 3, the title *kākā* is used. This title, common among religious officials of the Imām-Shāhī splinter group, reveals, then, the copyist's affiliation with that sect.[51] In addition to titles, the names of scribes often include the word *khīāte*, meaning 'known as, named, called.' This word, which is always written between the personal and family names (e.g. Khojābhāī Harjī khīāte Kāsmāṇī), suggests that these copyists may have been known simply by their family names.

Punctuation and Orthographic Signs

One of the drawbacks of using mercantile scripts is their propensity to be misread and misinterpreted. Writing in scripts like Khojkī is, as a rule, continuous. Adjacent words are often joined erroneously, leading to alterations in the meanings of sentences. The 'mess,' as Bendrey has termed it, results in an arbitrary reconstruction of a group of letters by readers.[52] To prevent this, Khojkī adopted a surprisingly simple solution: the use of a colon-like punctuation to demarcate word boundaries. This punctuation, slightly thicker than the colon, resembles *visarga* in Devanāgari. It became conventional among scribes to faithfully insert this sign at the end of every word. Useful as the sign is to ensuring a correct reading of the text, the tendency in older Khojkī texts seems to have been to omit it.[53] Furthermore, even when it was used, the sign was often misplaced in the middle of a word, erroneously dividing it and thus causing some confusion.

In addition to the above sign, manuscripts employ other punctuation signs. One or more vertical strokes, which may or may not be preceded by colon-like dots, are used to indicate the end of a verse. Verse numbers are usually written in between two pairs of these vertical strokes (॥૧૦॥) or between two sets of dots (:૧૦:). In longer works that are divided into several parts, the number of each part may have an additional horizontal line drawn over it (:૧૦̄:). The completion of a text was also indicated by a sign – usually two long horizontal lines either on the last line or immediately below it. Under the influence of the Perso-Arabic alphabet, the superscript *shaddah* was usually placed over a doubled consonant. In a few cases, three superscript dots above the consonant also seemed to perform the same function, but this usage was quite rare.[54] Finally, the Khojkī abbreviation 𑈽 for the Arabic *Alaihi as-salām* (Peace be upon him) occurs in some texts after the names of revered religious personalities such as Prophet Muḥammad and the Shiʿi Imams.

Foliation and Pagination

Both the foliation and pagination of manuscripts tend to be erratic, with many instances of misnumbering. It appears to have been customary to number only those folios containing any significant writing. Typically, then, the centre folios, usually blank in traditionally-bound manuscripts, were left unnumbered. Several manuscripts are only partially numbered while a few are not numbered at all.[55]

The manuscripts are generally numbered according to either folio or page. As a rule, older manuscripts tend to use foliation while later ones, probably under European influence, prefer pagination. Regardless of whether a manuscript was foliated or paginated, the Khojkī/Gujarati numeral system was generally employed. In a few cases, some Arabic numerals were incorporated into this system, as in Ms Ism K 16 where the Arabic number 8 is used. There are several variations on the location of folio or page numbers. Generally these were placed at the top of the page, sometimes at the centre, and other times at the right corner. In another method, even pages were numbered at the top right corner and the odd ones at the top left (Ms Ism K 6). Folio numbers were written at the top centre of either the recto or verso side (Ms Ism K 3). Alternatively, they were placed at the top right corner of the recto or top left corner of the verso (Ms Ism K 9).

Two systems of foliation can be discerned. In some manuscripts the folios are numbered in a single sequence that includes all of them, while in others the individual texts recorded in the manuscript are separately foliated in distinct sequences. Similarly, pagination could embrace either the entire manuscript or individual texts, though the former was more common. In Ms Ism K 11 and Ms Ism K 12, the scribe paginated only those portions he seemed to have copied in one sitting, beginning a new sequence of pagination for works copied later. Rebound manuscripts are usually refoliated or repaginated, probably by the binder, but not always with great accuracy.

Conclusion

Khojkī manuscripts are of scholarly significance for the unusual genres of Islamic religious literature which they preserve. On account of the vernacular languages they employ, as well as their 'folk' and 'syncretistic' character, these genres have been generally ignored by scholars. Foremost among these are the *ginān*s, the approximately one thousand hymn-like poems, revered for centuries as 'sacred' literature by Khoja Ismaili communities. The *ginān*s are of special interest for they were the most important medium through which Ismaili missionaries propagated their ideas among Indian populations. They also illustrate the different ways in which Ismaili religious concepts and ideas were expressed within the literary and religious vocabulary of the subcontinent's regional cultures. Their general mystical and devotional tenor provides an interesting parallel to the poetry from contemporaneous *sant* and Sufi sources.

Aside from the *ginān*s of Nizari Ismailis, Khojkī manuscripts preserve several other types of literature associated with folk Islam. Included here would be various types of ritual and supplicatory prayers, songs of devotion in praise of the Prophet Muḥammad, elegies (*marṣīyā*) in Sindhi, Gujarati or Hindi lamenting the tragedies that befell the Imams of Shiʿi Islam, legends about the great Prophets, and a generous selection of amulets (*taʿwīẓ*), magical squares and formulae for exorcism generally used by Muslims for talismanic purposes. Other literature, derived from the Indian folk tradition, comprises the *Dhru Kathā*, a versified story of *Dhru*, a devotee of the Hindu deity Krishna, *Sukaṇ vāṇī*, which appears to be a collection of omens and prognostications, and folk remedies for a variety of illnesses. Interestingly, the Khojkī manuscripts also contain significant numbers of poems attributed to famous medieval North Indian poet-saints, such as Kabīr, Ravī Dās and Mirābāī, who were part of the *sant* and *bhaktī* devotional traditions.

The presence of this medley of literature in the Khojkī manuscripts throws light upon the diverse cultural and religious strands present in the Nizari Ismaili community of the subcontinent until the early 20th century when it experienced a gradual transformation of its identity.[56] As a written record reflecting a bygone era and its religious mores, the Khojkī manuscript tradition provides our only glimpse into an aspect of Khoja religious life which otherwise would have been lost.

Table 1

Khojkī Script: Vowel System (early 20th century)

(a) Initial and Independent

a	ā	i	ī	u	ū	o	e	au	ay

(b) Medial and Final
(with the Consonant )

a	ā	i	ī	u	ū	o	e	au	ay

Table 2

Khojkī Script: Consonants (early 20th century)

𑈈	k	𑈉	kh	𑈊, 𑈊, 𑈌	g	𑈊, 𑈌	gh	𑈍	ng	𑈋	nġ
𑈎	c	𑈏	ch	𑈐	j/jh	𑈑	j/jh	𑈓	ny	𑈒	dy
𑈔	ṭ	𑈕	ṭh	𑈖, 𑈖, 𑈕	ḍ	𑈖, 𑈕	ḍh	𑈙	ṇ		
𑈚	t	𑈛	th	𑈜, 𑈝	d	𑈜, 𑈝	dh	𑈞	n	𑈗	ḏ
𑈟	p	𑈠	ph	𑈡, 𑈣	b	𑈟, 𑈡, 𑈣	bh	𑈤	m	𑈢	ḅ
𑈥	y	𑈦	r	𑈧	l	𑈨	v	𑈩	s	𑈩	sh
𑈘	dr	𑈫	tr	𑈪	h	𑈖, 𑈫	ṛ/ḷ				

Notes

* This article incorporates some material from Ali S. Asani, *The Harvard Collection of Ismaili Literature in Indic Languages: A Descriptive Catalog and Finding Aid* (Cambridge, Mass., 1990), pp. 3–54.

1. G. Allana, *Sindhī Ṣuratkhatī* (Hyderabad, Pakistan, 1964) pp. 16–19, and Ibn al-Nadīm, *al-Fihrist* (Cairo, 1348/1929), pp. 27–8.

2. Abū Rayḥān al-Bīrūnī, *Kitāb al-Hind,* Eng. trans. E.C. Sachau, *Alberuni's India,* ed, A.T. Embree (New York, 1971), p. 173.

3. The British colonial authorities decided in Dec. 1852 to adopt the Arabic alphabet as the official script for Sindhi. Subsequently, a standardized version of the Arabic alphabet 'with very trifling changes or additions required for its perfect adaptation to Sindee' was developed and promulgated by the government. By 1855 the introduction of the newly-developed alphabet was fairly accomplished. Nabi Bakhsh Baloch, *Education in Sind before the British Conquest and the Educational Policies of the British Government* (Hyderabad, 1971), pp. ii-iii.

4. E. Trumpp, 'Abstract of the Society's Proceedings,' *JBBRAS,* 5 (1857), p. 685.

5. Richard Burton, *Sindh and the Races that inhabit the Valley of the Indus* (repr. ed., Karachi, 1973), pp. 152–3.

6. George Stack, *A Grammar of the Sindhi Language* (Bombay, 1849), pp. 3–8.

7. On the Nizari Ismailis of the Indian subcontinent, see the articles 'Khodja' in *SEI,* p. 256, and Abdulaziz Sachedina, 'Khojas,' in John L. Esposito, ed., *Oxford Encyclopedia of the Modern Islamic World* (Oxford, 1995), vol. 2, pp. 423–27.

8. Azim Nanji, *The Nizārī Ismāʿīlī Tradition in the Indo-Pakistan Subcontinent* (Delmar, NY, 1978), p. 9. In this respect, Khojkī may have served the same purpose as the secret languages, such as the so-called *balabailan* language, utilized by Muslim mystics to hide their most esoteric thoughts from the common people. See Ignaz Goldziher, 'Linguistisches aus der Literatur der muhammadanischen Mystik,' *Zeitschrift der Deutschen Morganländischen Gesselschaft,* 26 (1872), p. 765, and Alessandro Bausani, 'About a Curious Mystical Language,' *East and West* 4, no. 4 (1954).

9. S.S. Gandhi discusses the significance of the Gurmukhī script for the development of Sikh identity in *History of the Sikh Gurus* (New Delhi, 1978), pp. 174–5.

10. The political and cultural ascendancy of the Mahrattas in the late 18th century was also marked by the selection of Moḍī as a single, uniform script for their language, Marathi. The script was supposedly invented

by the secretary to the great Maharashtran hero, Shivājī. See B.A. Gupte, 'The Modi Character,' *Indian Antiquary*, 34 (1905), p. 28.

11. For a more detailed discussion of the origins, main features and development of the Khojkī script, see Chapter 6 of this volume.

12. G. Allana, *Sindhī Ṣuratkhatī* (rev. ed., Hyderabad, 1969), p. 20.

13. Ibid., p. 24.

14. G. Grierson, *Linguistic Survey of India* (Calcutta, 1903–28), vol. 8, pt. 1, p. 247. See also Christopher Shackle, *From Wuch to Southern Lahnda: A Century of Siraiki Studies in English* (Multan, 1984), pp. 55–9.

15. Nabi Bakhsh Baloch, *Education in Sind before the British Conquest*, p. ii, n. 2.

16. G. Grierson suggests that Laṇḍā, Ṭāṅkrī and Mahājaṇī originated in one common alphabet that was once current over the whole of north-western India; 'On the Modern Indo-Aryan Alphabets of North-Western India,' *JRAS* (1904), p. 67.

17. According to Diringer, these scripts lack signs for internal vowels and have signs for only two or three initial vowels. See D. Diringer, *The Alphabet: A Key to the History of Mankind* (3rd ed., New York, 1968), vol. 1, p. 295. Christopher Shackle and Zawahir Moir observe that the abbreviated vowel system consists of a maximum of four letters to distinguish initial and independent *a, i, e, u* (*u* also used for *o*) vowels, whether long or short. Vowels in other positions are not written at all. See their *Ismaili Hymns from South Asia: An Introduction to the Ginans* (London, 1992), p. 34.

18. In most of them a single character of the alphabet could represent two or more sounds; or, sometimes, a single sound could be represented by one or more characters. They possess only enough consonants to provide a very basic notation of the phonology of the language. There is usually only a single sibilant *s*, and the only written conjunct consonants are *tr* and *dr*. Shackle and Moir, *Ismaili Hymns*, p. 34.

19. For example, [illegible] (3/4) for the letter *n* or [illegible] (4) for letter *ch*. See J. Prinsep, 'Note on A Grammar of the Sindhi Language dedicated to Rt. Honourable Sir Robert Grant, Governor of Bombay by W.H. Whalen Esq.,' *JASB*, 6 (1837), p. 352.

20. See the examples cited in Chapter 6 above from G. Grierson, *Linguistic Survey of India,* and R. Burton, *Sindh and the Races.*

21. Stack, *A Grammar of the Sindhi Language*, p. 2, note. Stack remarks that while he had been informed that the medial vowel marks were also used with other Sindhi scripts, he had not been able to locate any corroborative examples.

22. Allana, *Sindhī Ṣuratkhatī*, p. 24, and Nabi Bakhsh Khan Baloch, *Sindhī Ḅoli jī mukhtaṣar tārīkh* (Hyderabad, 1962), pp. 114–15.

23. Diringer, *The Alphabet*, p. 291.

24. Azim Nanji notes the existence of several genealogies recording different birth and death dates for this *pīr*, including one that attributes to him a life of 225 years. He suggests the *pīr* probably lived between the second half of the 8th/14th and the beginning of the 9th/15th century. *The Nizārī Ismāʿīlī Tradition*, pp. 72–4.

25. See Zawahir Noorally [Moir], *Catalogue of Khojkī Manuscripts in the Collection of the Ismailia Association for Pakistan* (unpublished, Karachi, 1971), MS 25. This manuscript is currently in the library of The Institute of Ismaili Studies, London. It appears as the first entry in an incomplete and unpublished catalogue of the Institute's collection compiled by her in 1985.

26. Wladimir Ivanow, 'Satpanth,' *Collectanea* (Leiden, 1948), p. 40.

27. Shackle and Moir, *Ismaili Hymns*, p. 16.

28. Nanji, *The Nizārī Ismāʿīlī Tradition*, pp. 10–11.

29. During a research trip to Pakistan in 1982, I was informed of a tradition about a group of professional scribes, called *Akhund*s in the community. See Chapter 6, note 36, of this volume.

30. Nanji, *The Nizārī Ismāʿīlī Tradition*, p. 11.

31. Allana, *Sindhī Ṣuratkhatī*, p. 4.

32. See Ali S. Asani, *The Harvard Collection of Ismaili Literature in Indic Languages: A Descriptive Catalog and Finding Aid* (Boston, M.A., 1992).

33. The manuscripts date from the late 1770s to the early decades of the 20th century.

34. Manuscripts are identified here according to the sigla assigned to them in Asani, *The Harvard Collection of Ismaili Literature.*

35. For example, Ms Ism K 4, K 5, K 16, K 20.

36. See, for example, Ms Ism K 22, f. 258 v, where the scribe Khoja Jāfar Khīāte Dhalāṇī writes that he copies the text from a manuscript written by Khoja Dose Khākuāṇī. Similarly, the copyist of Ms Ism K 5 notes that he copied one item, that is the marriage prayer, *nikāḥ*, from a manuscript belonging to the Kera *jamāʿat.*

37. Ms Ism G 2, ff. 16r–47r.

38. Ms Ism K 19. Alādīn Ghulām Ḥusayn, owner of the Ghulām-i Ḥusayn Press in Bombay, was one of the first private publishers of *ginān* texts.

39. J. Platts defines a *pothā* as a 'large book, a book or a manuscript (written in long separate leaves of paper or palymyra connected by a

string through the centre).' *Dictionary of Urdū, Classical Hindi and English* (London, 1930), p. 217.

40. Some of the more frequently occurring Khojkī transliterations include: *Bhisimalāhe: rehemānrihīm; Bhasammalāhi: rehemān: rahīm; Bhisimilāhe: rehemāne: rahīme.*

41. See, for example, Ms Ism K 11 where the phrase is written in Khojkī as: *Naūz:bhilāhe: min: shetāne: laīlī: rajīm.*

42. See L Ism K 2.5.

43. P Ism K 10. Though this phrase occurs in a printed work, it was unwittingly copied from a manuscript when the printed version was being prepared.

44. In Ms Ism K 13 (f. 376) the phrase is written as: *Enā:lilāvā:enā:alehe:rājiūn.*

45. In Ms Ism K 11, this table has also been termed *firist,* probably from the Arabic and Persian *fihrist* (meaning index, summary or preface).

46. See Ms Ism K 11.

47. The Indian synodical lunar month is divided into two fortnights: the bright half (the *shud* or *sudī*) during which the moon is waxing, and the dark half (the *vad* or *vadī*) when the moon wanes. The fourteen days (*tithi*) of each of these fortnights have names commonly associated with ordinals. Before any of these names, the *shud* or *vad* is inserted according as the day in question belongs to the bright or dark half of the moon.

48. In Ism K 22 one of the scribes is called Bhāī Manjī bin Khimjīāṇī.

49. The copyist of Ms Ism K 1 is called Khoja bhāī Ladhū Devjī.

50. The scribe of Ms Ism K 25, for example, is Kāmaḍīā Alārakhiā Mūrjī.

51. According to Ivanow, a *kākā* was the headman of a small Imām-Shāhī community that had been converted from the Hindu tradition. His duty was to instruct those who were not strong in religion, to settle their disputes, and, to collect religious taxes. The head *kākā* was responsible for the distribution of income and the upkeep of shrines. In later Imām-Shāhī history, the *kākās* became an inexhaustible source of intrigue and misery to the community. W. Ivanow, 'The Sect of Imam Shah in Gujrat,' *JBBRAS,* New Series, 12 (1936), pp. 38–9.

52. As quoted in Diringer, *The Alphabet,* vol. 1, p. 291.

53. See, for example, Ms Ism K 20.

54. See Ms Ism K 20.

55. See Ms Ism K 24.

56. See Ali S. Asani, 'The Khojahs of Indo-Pakistan: The Quest for an

Islamic Identity,' *JIMMA*, 8, no. 1 (1987), pp. 31–41; Aziz Esmail, 'Satpanth Ismailism and Modern Changes Within it With Special Reference to East Africa' (Ph.D. thesis, University of Edinburgh, 1971); and Sachedina, 'Khojas,' in *The Oxford Encyclopedia of the Modern Islamic World.*

Appendix
Translations of Selected Devotional and Mystical *Ginān*s

1. Verses from the *Venti* (*Supplication*) *Rūḥānī Visāl*, attributed to Pīr Ḥasan Kabīr al-Dīn[1]

In the beginning there was God without attributes,
He who was without qualities and without form.
You are our (true) origin,
Although we have been separated from You by form.

Refrain:
This weak creature is at Your mercy;
My Lord, be kind to us; we are at Your mercy.

Countless ages have gone by
And we have continued to change form.
We have been petitioning (You) for ages;
O Lord, let us be reunited. ...(*refrain*).

Lord, in the midst of nothingness,
You gave rise to infinite astonishing acts;
In the form of the unseen, You played.
You, ancient Yogi, why this delay?
O Lord, how long can I remain like this? ...(*refrain*).

In the sixteen states (*sol thar*),[2] O Lord,
You played and played;
How can I praise this enough?
Since that very day I have been petitioning;
Lord, at least now pay heed to me. ...(*refrain*).

In the void You were in the unseen form;
Lord, You were in contemplation.
Whoever in that gathering[3] recognized You,
Him You will make return. ...(*refrain*).

Age upon age I have been waiting anxiously,
But yet the marriage (*nikāḥ*) has not taken place!
Now I am in the full bloom of youth.
O Ruler of the three worlds, preserve my honour ...(*refrain*).

Having filled my water pots (*hail*),
I have come before You, Lord.
Lord, take down my water pots,
Lest my water pots be rejected.
Forgive my sins. ...(*refrain*).

Lord, cover me with a veil (*chedo*) and watch over me,
For I have come (to you as) a sinner.
I am but a weak and humble creature.
O Ruler, it is Your honour (that is at stake)! ...(*refrain*).

For countless ages I have been waiting with hope;
O Ruler of three worlds, hear me!
The bloom of youth is upon me,
So now I will be ashamed (if You do not marry me) ...(*refrain*).

In the four ages (*yugas*), I have experienced
cycles of countless forms;
Yet my marriage has not taken place.
Lord, please marry me!
Be merciful, O Lord of miracles! ...(*refrain*).

O, Lord, how long must I remain alone?
The days pass in separation (*dūhāg*) from You;
Change my state of separation (*dūhāg*) into married
bliss (*sūhāg*).[4]
Lord of the fourteen heavens,
preserve my honour ...(*refrain*).

Mother, father, sister and relatives,
No one wants to keep me.
I have come and thrown myself on Your mercy.
Lord, my honour depends on You ... (*refrain*).

O Lord, if my honour is not protected,
Then You will have to bear the loss!
When You have a festive gathering,
Do not humiliate me (through separation) ... (*refrain*).

O Ruler, as You seat Yourself on the throne,
Then and there I will cry out for You.
From the beginning You have been holding my hand,
So how can You abandon me today? ... (*refrain*).

Lord, do not look at my misdeeds;
(I confess that) I am a sinner.
Lord cover me with a veil and watch over me:
I am only an innocent maiden ... (*refrain*).

Lord, my parents gave birth to me
(And) entrusted me to Your mercy.
Now have the decency to fulfil Your part of this trust.
O Saviour, save me ... (*refrain*).

O Lord, there are countless maidens for You;
There are thousands like me.
You are the Ineffable and the Unseen;
I am but humble dust ... (*refrain*).

O Lord, since You have taken my hand,
  uphold my honour.
O ineffable One, tell me how far our love should go.
Love me and marry me,
Even though I am sinful ... (*refrain*).

Lord, the bloom of youth is upon me;
I cannot remain alone;
It is shameful for me to look upon outside(rs).
O Lord, let the marriage ceremony be performed ... (*refrain*).

Lord, come with the marriage procession;
Do not delay (Your arrival).
Be merciful and come, O Lord,

For I am Your devoted spouse ... (*refrain*).

O Lord, speaking your name I ascend,
Ascend the *cok bazār*,[5]
Where souls from countless ages will meet,
Soul upon soul in infinite number. ... (*refrain*).

The countless souls of ages will gather.
You, come there Yourself.
As You come in, look around and search
And come to Your humble spouse ... (*refrain*).

After having walked and walked I am worn out;
I can walk no more.
Do not look upon my evil deeds.
I can live no more ... (*refrain*).

Just as a fish without water writhes in agony,
So also a wife without her husband.
Lord, bring whatever is needed for the marriage.
Delay not Your coming anymore ... (*refrain*).

O Lord, You are the Perfect One, beyond Brahma
And in indescribable form.
How can I adequately praise Your brilliance?
Your countless (heavenly) wives are
    dazzling and beautiful ... (*refrain*).

Lord, these women are heavenly;
Great and indescribable is their beauty,
(Whereas) I am but ugly and humble;
Husband, preserve mine honour. ... (*refrain*).

Lord, my attention is fixed upon You;
It is You who occupy my thoughts.
How can I capture another (like You)?
Lord, return to fulfil Your promise to me;
    do not forsake me even for a moment ... (*refrain*).

Lord, preserve my honour.
How can it be entrusted to anyone else?
On Your behalf the coconut has already been sent.
How can I gaze upon another? ... (*refrain*).

Lord, most humbly I petition You;
Hear my cries.
For the sake of my humble state, forgive me.
Lord, You are the Protector of the unprotected ...(*refrain*).

Lord, this weak creature pines for You;
Tears flow incessantly from my eyes.
You, my Lord, have many women;
Won't You try to understand my agony? ...(*refrain*).

Having pleaded and pleaded,
  how much more shall I plead?
You are the Ruler, immanent in all.
Take pity on me and meet me,
So that my honour be saved. ...(*refrain*).

Lord, do not take my sins to heart;
I am only a weak and humble woman.
I have reached the bloom of youth;
I am an innocent maiden. ...(*refrain*).

Any clothes and ornaments that may be required,
Lord, I will bring them all (for You).
I will make myself beautiful
For my Lord whom I am meeting. ...(*refrain*).

Lord, from the beginning of the beginning
  I have been petitioning (You);
Breath upon breath I contemplate.
In every nook and cranny of my being You are playing,
So that my sins flee from me. ...(*refrain*).

With the aid of Your name,
I can reach heaven.
There are so many thieves obstructing my way,
But with Your name they disappear. ...(*refrain*).

The road to heaven is full of pain,
But with Your name these pains are removed.
The one Lord is (my) true master (*sat guru*).
With the secret name He can be recognized. ...(*refrain*).

Lord, with the aid of Your name,
The great oceans give way.

Come Husband, be merciful!
I fall at Your feet. ...(*refrain*).

Lord, sobbing and sighing I plead with You.
My heart pines in longing.
O Lord, come soon,
Lest (it is too late and) the (bloom of my youth) fades away.
...(*refrain*).

Lord, the eyes of this evil age (*Kalyug*)[6] are all contrary;
They look (upon me) with evil eyes.
Lord, sometimes I make mistakes;
Then I have to begin all over. ...(*refrain*).

My Lord Yogi, be merciful;
Take me to safety.
This evil age is full of deceit and falsehood,
So rescue me soon from it. ...(*refrain*).

(My) parents and all are happy
With my marriage to You.
O Lord, come quickly and marry me;
Do not take too long. ...(*refrain*).

Lord, my youth has matured;
I am embarrassed to go out (alone).
In this evil age there is much ignorance,
In which I may become trapped. ...(*refrain*).

Lord, (for us) set up a sacred space (*chorī*);[7]
In the midst of the universe marry me.
Become manifest and marry me,
So that I can experience the bliss of marriage ...(*refrain*).

Lord, my marriage bliss lies with You,
Of which you have been in charge for countless ages.
The perfect and the imperfect, and even those
 who simply wish –
To all (of them) grant salvation. ...(*refrain*).

(But) whoever indulges in backbiting,
He will have to stay away from the Lord;
He will be surrounded by Satan
And will not acquire the true knowledge. ...(*refrain*).

Any discourse without true knowledge
Shreds (into pieces) the heart.
Lord, keep me away from such beings,
So that I can be certain of my marriage (to You). ...(*refrain*).

Listen, O believers, be virtuous,
So that you become dear to the Lord.
If you recognize Him by good deeds
    and (meditation on) the Word,
Then He will come to you. ...(*refrain*).

Abide by the true Word and the scriptures,
So that you acquire the Lord's friendship.
Believers, give the Lord a place in your hearts,
So that love (for Him) is kindled. ...(*refrain*).

Pīr Ḥasan Kabīr al-Dīn, like a woman, supplicates
And holds the hand of her Husband and Lord.
Whoever in these days of the evil age recognizes Shāh Pīr,
Will never be abandoned. ...(*refrain*).

II. Verses from *Tamakū sadhāre soh dīn* (*The Day That You Left*), attributed to Pīr Ṣadr al-Dīn[8]

Beloved, it has been long since the day you left
    (and) anxiously I wait for you.
My merciful lord and kindly master,
O my beloved, how will I spend these days without you?

My beloved gave me his word and went away from the town.
O my beloved, you gave me your word, so fulfil your love.
O my beloved, how will the day pass without you?

If only I had known about this,
    I would not have let my beloved go.
O my beloved, I would have come with you.
O my beloved, how will the day pass without you?

Beloved, when one's parents have left town,
Why, then, should the child remain (alone)?
O my beloved, how will the day pass without you?

Beloved, the agonies of the heart consume me;

Only you can soothe them.
O my beloved, how will the day pass without you?
Come and embrace me, my beloved, and look into my eyes;
In my suffering show me a little kindness.
O my beloved, how will the day pass without you?

III. *Swāmī rājo more man thī na visereji* (My Lord, the Husband, Cannot be Forgotten), attributed to Pīr Ṣadr al-Dīn[9]

My Lord, the Husband, cannot be forgotten.
Listen, O believers, (that is how) He is ever present
(in my heart).

Beloved, between You and me, there is a bond of feeling and
thought;
My Lord is immanent everywhere.

If any messenger brings a message from my Husband,
I will fall down at his feet.

(O believers), if He comes then stand up and give Him a place
to sit;
It is He who has brought salvation to you.

O believers, take a small pot (of water) and wash the feet of
the Lord;
Anoint with oil his His hair and comb it.

O believers, make a sweet dish of milk, sugar and *ghee*,
And with that feed the Sage with devotion.

O believers, prepare the bed with quilts for Him to sleep,
And very gently fan Him.

The four *satis*[10] will sing songs of good omen,
With pearls to decorate the *cok*.[11]

This *ginān* is recited by Pīr Ṣadr al-Dīn.
For my believers, there is (the promise of) heaven.

IV. Verses from *Būjh Niranjan* (*Knowledge of the Attributeless Deity*), attributed to Pīr Ṣadr al-Dīn[12]

Whenever the love kindles within the self for the Beloved,
That love will wipe out your ego.

Night and day he (the lover) is awake and cannot sleep;
Continuously his eyes weep.

It is as if the heart is set afire
With the flame which the lover himself turns into fire.

The soul feels (such cries) as if it were a bird
That it would have flown away to catch a glimpse of the Beloved.

For the love of the Beloved, I would sacrifice myself.
O (how I yearn) to go and embrace Him!

My Beloved has pierced me so with His love,
That out of separation I am groping about like a person insane.

Without the Lord, life is nothing.
For the sake of my Beloved I have cried every day.

The one who is wounded in the heart,
How can he sleep in peace?

Day and night I cannot sleep;
Every day tears flow from my eyes.

I am dying, my Beloved, because of You,
and do You not feel pity (for me)?

V. *Huṅ re piāsī tere darshan kī* (*I Thirst for a Vision of You*), attributed to Sayyid Khān[13]

I thirst for a vision (*darshan*) of You, O my Beloved!
Fulfil my heart's desire, O my Beloved!
I thirst in hope for You;
Yet, why do You not show the slightest concern for me?
I serve you with total devotion;
So why, then, Beloved, do you turn away (from me) so angrily?

Listen, my Bridegroom, pay heed to what I say.
Do not be so uncaring of me, your wife!

Grant me, my Husband, grant me what I ask,
For I suffer intensely.
Beloved, grant my heart's desire,
So I can be joyously happy.

A fish out of water, how can it survive without its beloved (water)?
For the sake of its beloved, it gives up its life.
A fish out of water is so lonely;
See how it writhes and dies (in agony)!
It writhes and convulses in vain,
While the fisherman shows no mercy.

Consider the love of the bee to be false!
For this is certainly not the way to gain the vision of the Beloved!
Consider the love of the bee to be false!
It flits from one flower to another, sipping nectar.
Such are the ways of careless and blind people, devoid of virtues,
(So self-centred) that they cannot sacrifice their lives for the Beloved.

Consider the love of the moth to be true!
For this is the way to gain the vision of the Beloved!
Consider the love of the moth to be true,
As it deliriously gives up its body.
On account of a single candle,
So many moths offer their lives!

For my Beloved, I have sacrificed everything,
For all that is dear should be offered to Him.
(Beloved) set aside this hesitation
And resolve to say something (to me).
Show mercy, O Lord, and protect me;
(O Lord), listen to my pleas!

One who wishes to be blessed with (His) vision should desire
Never to abandon the Lord for anything (or anyone) else.
The heart of one who desires to see (the Lord) becomes so attached (to Him)
That love grows day by day.
Reciting (the Lord's) name with complete concentration,
In this way, one has a vision of the Beloved.

Do not treat this destitute (female) devotee so;

If I have faults, then consider them to be virtues.
Although I may be full of sins, yet I am a (female)
devotee of yours.
Why do You not show the slightest concern for me?
If I have faults, consider them to be virtues;
(O Lord), listen to my pleas!

The one who becomes nothing[14] is called your devotee;
In this manner one pleases the Lord.
The one who becomes nothing is called your devotee,
Rising regularly (for meditation) and ever increasing in love
(for You),
Reciting the (Lord's) name with complete concentration,
Setting aside all physical (material) ties.

Stay with the Lord in complete concentration
And through (His) love experience such delights.
Stay with the Lord in complete concentration,
Loving Him intensely.
Only one who sacrifices (his) life out of love
Can have the vision of the Beloved.

I have seen nothing that matches this love!
Do whatever pleases your Lord.
One who dies the death of love
Has spent a worthy life in this world.
Perform virtuous deeds,
So that the Lord may redeem you.

Although a sinner, I am still your creature.
Remember me soon, my Lord.
Now that the Lord has remembered me,
Rejoice, rejoice my friends!
With the blessing of the Master, Mīrā Sayyid Khān says:
All difficulties and afflictions have been dispelled!

VI. Verses from *Kalām-i Mawlā* (*The Discourses of Mawlā ʿAlī*)[15]

On the Virtues of Knowledge
Knowledge has a status that
reigns supreme over all other skills;
For those whose hearts are illuminated,

recognizing God through knowledge,
All other crafts shall perish;
nothing will remain save the recognition of God.
Pay heed to this, understand it and remember it.
for this is what the Cupbearer of the fount of Paradise
(Imam ʿAlī) has decreed.

Gather in the assemblies of knowledge,
as sugar dissolves in milk.
When you dissolve in knowledge,
your heart's desire will be attained.
The mystery of '*manʿarafa*'[16] is contained in knowledge
and obtained from the perfect Spiritual Guide.
If you gather day and night in the assemblies of knowledge,
then the Guide will reveal this mystery to you.

Brothers! The assemblies of knowledge are
like the Gardens of Paradise;
If you desire to behold Paradise in this world,
then sit regularly in the assemblies of knowledge.
Paradise is the land of the pure,
so if you desire Paradise, then remain pure.
But how can you be pure without knowledge?
This is what the Cupbearer of the Fount of Paradise
(Imam ʿAlī) has decreed.

Knowledge is like a vast ocean,
without shore, without end.
It is fathomless, profound and immeasurable,
containing infinite treasures.
Those who dive into this ocean
and annihilate their own existence
Will obtain a priceless treasure,
bringing to the surface a matchless pearl.

On Prayer and Righteousness
(As) Night follows every day,
so during the day, fulfil your worldly obligations;
But come the night, sit in peace
and remember Him whose servant you are.
The people of the world say 'we must earn our livelihood;
when can we sit as God's servants?'

But Mawla ʿAlī responds: 'At the time when there is no business,
Remember your Lord in the midst of the dark night.'

God's Prophet attained the *Miʿrāj*,[17]
because all the night He meditated on the Reality (of God),
The faithful can attain that very *Miʿrāj*
by eliminating all the world's filth from their hearts.
The faithful who rise at night with steadfast concentration,
following in the footsteps of the Prophet,
Will attain the *Miʿrāj* and the vision of their Lord!

The night is exalted in status,
for while the world slumbers,
The Pīrs, Prophets and Friends [of God]
attain glory through meditation.
Even the Prophet attained *Miʿrāj* during the night,
for this is (the time) when a lover is united with the Beloved.
So if you are a true lover,
never forsake the meditation of the night.

VII. *Ū̃ncā re koṭ bahu vecana* (*A High and Lofty Fortress*), attributed to Pīr Ḥasan Kabīr al-Dīn[18]

A high and lofty fortress,
Beneath which flows a river.
I am a tiny fish adrift in the river.
O my Lord, come and rescue me.

Refrain:
I am tormented without the vision of You,
O my Beloved, O my Husband, come home!
(Although) this devotee forgot to worship You,
Yet, my Beloved, show me Your face.

I am in a (fragrant) little room of incense and sandalwood,
Whose doors are built with good deeds,
(But) closed shut with the locks of love.
O my Lord, come and open them. ...(*refrain*).

Alas, I am imprisoned in the cage of family (worldly)
attachments;
Only a few can truly understand

The agony of my body;
O Lord, come and soothe my anguish. ... (*refrain*).

Please do not be so angry;
My Lord grant me Your vision.
This is the humble plea of Pīr Ḥasan Shāh:
O my Lord, come and rescue me. ... (*refrain*).

VIII. *Ab terī mohabat lāgī* (*Stricken by Love for You*), attributed to Pīr Shams[19]

I am stricken by love for You, my Lord,
I am stricken by love for You;
My heart is pierced by love for You.
Allow our eyes to embrace, my Lord,

Refrain:
For I am stricken by love for You.

Draw open the veils and look at me face to face,
And show me your joyful face, My Lord. ... (*refrain*).

Pīr Shams thirsts for (a glimpse of) Your face;
Bless him with Your vision, My Lord. ... (*refrain*).

O Beloved, do not be so angry at me;
Allow me to accompany you, My Lord. ... (*refrain*).

Youthful frenzy does not endure for long;
Like the water of a river, it passes away, My Lord. ... (*refrain*).

Your lover will come with you;
So let there be friendship (for me) in your heart, My Lord. ... (*refrain*).

O charming, captivating and handsome Beloved, listen,
Let there be mercy (for me) in Your heart, My Lord. ... (*refrain*).

O playful, nimble, intoxicating, youthful Beloved,
Let there be love (for me) in Your heart, My Lord. ... (*refrain*).

O Beloved, I am intoxicated by Your mystery;
Passionate love has overwhelmed (my) reason, My Lord. ... (*refrain*).

When I saw Your endearing face, my heart became ecstatic.
This is what Pīr Shams has related while singing, My Lord. …
(*refrain*).

IX. *Sakhī mārī ātama nā odhār (O Friend, the Saviour of my Soul),* attributed to Pīr Ṣadr al-Dīn[20]

O Friend, the saviour of my soul,
do not go away and stay apart from me.
I have built such a beautifully decorated house for you,
come and reside in it.

O Friend, I have prepared for You a bed of incomparable beauty;
return (to rest) on this bed.
(Lying) next to the Beloved, overwhelmed by love,
I forget all of my sorrows.

O Friend, the bed-swing sways back and forth,
with (the rhythm of) my every breath.
What ecstasy is aroused in my body
when I am with the Beloved.

O Friend, to whom can I describe
the pangs of separation (*viraha*) from the Beloved?
(Perhaps if) I were to meet a wise sage
he would understand.

O Friend, the Creator of the creation
is the One who has saved me.
Pīr Ṣadr al-Dīn, grasping me by the hand,
takes me across the ocean (to salvation).

Notes

1. Translated from *Rūḥānī Visāl, Venti: Pīr Ḥasan Kabīr al-Dīn* (Karachi, 1976).

2. The reference here is to sixteen cosmological states (*sol thar*) of divine creative activity.

3. The primordial gathering of souls described in the Qur'an, 7: 172. (See Chapter 3, pp. 59–60, for a discussion of the covenant between God and humanity.)

4. For explanation of *dūhāg* and *sūhāg*, see Chapter 3 pp. 60–1.

5. An ornamented square of coloured flour in which a bride and bridegroom are seated for a short while during a number of nights before the wedding.

6. *Kalyug* is the final period in the Hindu time cycle, the age of evil.

7. Boundary of sacredness.

8. Translated from D. Velji, 72 *Gināns. Part I: Transliteration of Holy Ginans* (Nairobi, 1972), pp. 3–5.

9. Translated from *Wonderful Tradition* (Kampala, 1968), p. 20.

10. *Satis,* pious ladies.

11. See note 5 above.

12. Translated from *Būjh Niranjan* (Karachi, 1976), pp. 60–2.

13. Translated from *Ginãne Sharīf: bhag pahelo, 105 ginān*s, 1st rev. ed. (Bombay, 1978), pp. 6–10.

14. 'The one who becomes nothing' refers to the devotee who has annihilated the ego in the love of the Beloved.

15. Translated from *Kalāme Mawlā,* 8th ed. (Bombay, 1963), pp. 21–2, 34–5.

16. Reference to the saying of the Prophet Muḥammad: *'Man ʿarafa nafsahu faqad ʿarafa Rabbahu* (*He who recognizes his self, recognizes God'*).

17. The *Miʿrāj,* the heavenly ascent of the Prophet Muḥammad, is the prototype of Muslim spiritual life.

18. Translated from *Ginān-e-Sharīf: Our Wonderful Tradition* (Vancouver, 1977), pp. 89–90.

19. Ibid., pp. 9–10.

20. Translated from *Ginãne Sharīf: bhag pahelo,* p. 109.

Bibliography

Ahmad, Aziz. *Studies in Islamic Culture in the Indian Environment.* Delhi, 1964.

——*An Intellectual History of Islam in India.* Edinburgh, 1969.

Ahmed, Imtiaz. 'The Islamic Tradition in India,' in *Islam and the Modern Age,* 12, no. 1 (1981), pp. 44–62.

Ahmed, Rafiuddin. *The Bengal Muslims 1871–1906: A Quest for Identity.* Delhi, 1981.

Ali, Syed Mujtaba. The *Origin of the Khojahs and their Religious Life Today.* Bonn, 1936.

Allana, G.A. *Ginans of the Ismaili Pirs.* Vol. 1. Karachi, 1984.

Allana, G. *Sindhī Ṣuratkhatī.* Hyderabad, 1964.

Asani, Ali. *The Ismāʿīlī Ginān Literature: Its Structure and Love Symbolism.* B.A. thesis, Harvard University, 1977.

——'*Ginān,*' in Mircea Eliade, ed., *Encyclopedia of Religion.* New York, 1987.

——'The Khojahs of Indo-Pakistan: The Quest for an Islamic Identity,' *JIMMA,* 8, no. 1 (1987), pp. 31–41.

——'The Khojkī Script: A Legacy of Ismaili Islam in the Indo-Pakistan Subcontinent,' *JAOS,* 107(1987), pp. 439–49.

——'Sufi Poetry in the Folk Tradition of Indo-Pakistan,' *Religion and Literature,* 20 (1988), pp. 81–95.

———*The Harvard Collection of Ismaili Literature in Indic Languages: A Finding Aid and Descriptive Catalog.* Boston, 1992.

——'The Ismaili Gināns as Devotional Literature,' in R.S. McGregor, ed., *Devotional Literature in South Asia: Current Research, 1985–88.* Cambridge, 1991, pp. 101–12.

——'The *Ginān* Literature of the Ismailis of Indo-Pakistan: Its Origins, Characteristics and Themes,' in D. Eck and F. Mallison, ed., *Devotion Divine: Bhakti Traditions from the Regions of India.* Gröningen-Paris, 1991, pp. 1–18.

——*The Būjh Niranjan: An Ismaili Mystical Poem.* Cambridge, Mass., 1991.

——'Bridal Symbolism in Ismaili Mystical Literature of Indo-Pakistan,' in Robert Herrera, ed., *Mystics of the Book: Themes, Topics and Typologies.* New York, 1993, pp. 389–404.

——'Folk Romance in Sufi Poetry from Sind,' in A. Dallapiccola and S. Lallemant, ed., *Islam and the Indian Regions.* Stuttgart, 1993, vol. 1, pp. 229–37.

——'A Testimony of Love: The *Gīt* Tradition of the Nizari Ismailis,' in A. Giese and J.C. Bürgel, ed., *God is Beautiful and He Loves Beauty* (Festschrift in Honour of Annemarie Schimmel). Bern, etc., 1994, pp. 39–51.

——'The Bridegroom Prophet in Medieval Sindhi Poetry,' in A. Entwistle and F. Mallison, ed., *Studies in South Asian Devotional Literature: Research Papers 1989–91.* Delhi and Paris, 1994, pp. 213–25.

——and Kamal Abdel-Malik. *Celebrating Muhammad: Images of the Prophet in Popular Muslim Poetry.* Columbia, SC, 1995.

——'The Ismaili *ginān*s: Reflections on Authority and Authorship,' in Farhad Daftary, ed., *Mediaeval Isma'ili History and Thought.* Cambridge, 1996, pp. 265–80.

——'The Khojahs of South Asia: Defining a Space of Their Own,' *Cultural Dynamics,* 13 (2001), pp. 155–68.

——'Muslims in South Asia: Defining Community and the "Other",' *BRIIS,* 2 (2001), pp. 103–13.

Austin, R.J.W., 'The Sophianic Feminine Tradition in the Works of Ibn 'Arabi and Rumi,' in Leonard Lewisohn, ed., *The Heritage of Sufism.* Oxford, 1999, vol. 2 pp. 233–45.

Baloch, Nabi Bakhsh Khan. *Sindhī Ḅolī jī mukhtaṣar tārīkh.* Hyderabad, 1962.

——*Education in Sind Before the British Conquest and the Educational Policies of the British Government.* Hyderabad, 1971.

Bausani, Alessandro. 'About a Curious Mystical Language,' *East and West,* 4 (1954), pp. 234–8.

al-Bīrūnī, Abū Rayḥān. *Kitāb al-Hind.* English tr., E.C. Sachau, *Alberuni's India,* ed., A.T. Embree. New York, 1971.

Brass, Paul. 'Ethnic Groups, Symbol Manipulation and Ethnic Identity among Muslims of South Asia,' in D. Taylor and M. Yapp, ed., *Political*

Identity in South Asia. London, Dublin, 1979, pp. 35–77.

Burton, R. *Sindh and the Races that Inhabit the Valley of the Indus.* Repr. ed., Karachi, 1973.

Cole, W. Owen and P.S. Sambhi. *The Sikhs: Their Religious Beliefs and Practices.* London and Boston, 1978.

Corbin, Henry. 'Le Temps cyclique dans le Mazdéisme et dans l'Ismaélisme,' *Eranos-Jarhrbuch,* 20 (1951), pp. 149–217. English tr., 'Cyclical Time in Mazdaism and Ismailism,' in Corbin, *Cyclical Time and Ismaili Gnosis,* pp. 1–58.

——'Epiphanie Divine et naissance spirituelle dans la gnose Ismaélienne,' *Eranos-Jarhrbuch,* 23 (1954), pp. 141–249. English tr., 'Divine Epiphany and Spiritual Birth in Ismailian Gnosis,' in Corbin, *Cyclical Time and Ismaili Gnosis.* London, 1983. pp. 59–150.

——'De la gnose antique à la gnose Ismaélienne,' in *Oriente ed Occidente nel Medio Evo.* Rome, 1957, pp. 105–43. English tr., 'From the Gnosis of Antiquity to Ismaili Gnosis,' in Corbin, *Cyclical Time and Ismaili Gnosis,* pp. 151–93.

——'Herméneutique spirituelle comparée,' *Eranos-Jahrbuch,* 33 (1964), pp. 71–176.

——*Histoire de la philosophie Islamique.* Paris, 1964. English tr. Philip Sherrard, *History of Islamic Philosophy.* London, 1993.

———*Cyclical Time and Ismaili Gnosis,* tr. R. Mannheim and J.W. Morris. London, 1983.

Daftary, Farhad. *The Ismāʿīlīs: Their History and Doctrines.* Cambridge, 1990.

——*A Short History of the Ismailis.* Edinburgh, 1998.

Diringer, D. *The Alphabet, Key to the History of Mankind.* 3rd ed., New York, 1968.

Eaton, Richard. 'Sufi Folk Literature and the Expansion of Islam,' *History of Religions,* 14 (1974–5), pp. 115–27.

——*Sufis of Bijapur, 1300–1700.* Princeton, NJ, 1978.

——*The Rise of Islam and the Bengal Frontier, 1204–1760.* Berkeley and London, 1993.

Eliade, Mircea. *The Two and the One.* New York, 1965.

Encyclopedia of Religion. ed. Mircea Eliade. New York, 1987.

Encyclopedia of Islam. ed. H.A.R. Gibb et. al. New ed., Leiden and London, 1960–.

Enthoven, Reginald E. *Tribes and Castes of Bombay.* Bombay, 1922.

Ernst, Carl. *Eternal Garden: Mysticism, History and Politics at a South Asian Sufi Center.* Albany, NY, 1992.

Esmail, Aziz. 'Satpanth Ismailism and Modern Changes Within it With

Special Reference to East Africa.' Ph.D. thesis, University of Edinburgh, 1971.

——and Azim Nanji. 'The Ismāʿīlīs in History,' in S.H. Nasr, ed., *Ismāʿīlī Contributions to Islamic Culture.* Tehran, 1977, pp. 225–65.

Friedmann, Yohannan. 'Islamic Thought in Relation to the Indian Context,' *Puruṣārtha,* 9 (1986), pp. 79–91.

Fyzee, Asaf A.A. *Cases in the Muhammadan Law of India and Pakistan.* Oxford, 1965.

Gandhi, S.S. *History of the Sikh Gurus.* New Delhi, 1978.

Goldziher, Ignaz. 'Linguistisches aus der Literatur der muhammadanischen Mystik,' *Zeitschrift der Deutschen Morgenländischen Gesellschaft,* 26 (1872), pp. 764–85.

Graham, William A. *Beyond the Written Word: Oral Aspects of Scripture in the History of Religion.* Cambridge and New York, 1987.

——'Scripture,' in Mircea Eliade, ed., *Encyclopedia of Religion.* New York, 1987.

Grierson, G. *Linguistic Survey of India.* 11 vols. Calcutta, 1903–28.

——'On the Modern Indo-Aryan Alphabets of North-Western India,' *JRAS* (1904), pp. 67–73.

Grunebaum, Gustav E. von, ed. *Unity and Variety in Muslim Civilization.* Chicago, 1955.

Gupte, B.A. 'The Modi Character,' *Indian Antiquary,* 34 (1905), pp. 27–30.

al-Hamadani, Abbas H. *The Beginnings of the Ismāʿīlī Daʿwa in Northern India.* Cairo, 1956.

al-Haqq, ʿAbd. *Urdū kī ibtidāʾī nashwo numā men ṣūfiyāʾ-i kirām kā kām.* Aligarh, 1968.

Hardy, Peter. 'Modern European and Muslim Explanations of Conversion to Islam in South Asia: A Preliminary Survey of the Literature,' in Nehemia Levtizion, ed., *Conversion to Islam.* New York and London, 1979, pp. 68–99.

Hawley, J. 'Images of Gender in the Poetry of Krishna,' in Caroline Bynum et al., ed., *Gender and Religion: On the Complexity of Symbols.* Boston, 1986.

——'Author and Authority in the Bhakti Poetry of North India,' *JAS,* 47 (1988), pp. 269–90.

——and M. Juergensmeyer. *Songs of the Saints of India.* Oxford, 1988.

Hodgson, Marshall G.S. *The Order of Assassins.* The Hague, 1955.

Ibn al-Nadīm, Muḥammad. *al-Fihrist.* Cairo 1348/1929.

Ivanow, Wladimir. 'The Sect of Imam Shah in Gujrat,' *JBBRAS,* New Series,

12 (1936), pp. 19–70.
——'Khodja,' *SEI*, pp. 256–7.
——'Tombs of Some Persian Ismaili Imams,' *JBBRAS*, New Series, 14 (1938), pp. 49–62.
——'Satpanth (Indian Ismailism),' in W. Ivanow, ed., *Collectanea*, vol. 1. Leiden, 1948, pp. 1–54.
——'Shums Tabriz of Multan,' in S.M. Abdallah, ed., *Professor Muhammad Shafi Presentation Volume*. Lahore, 1955, pp. 109–18.
——'Sufism and Ismailism: The *Chirāgh-Nāma*,' *Revue Iranienne d'Anthropologie*, 3 (1959), English, pp. 13–17; Persian, pp. 53–70.
——*Ismaili Literature. A Bibliographical Survey*. Tehran, 1963.
Kassam, Tazim R. 'Syncretism on the Model of Figure-Ground: A Study of Pir Shams' Brahmā Prakāsa,' in Katherine K. Young, ed., *Hermeneutical Paths to the Sacred Worlds of India*. Atlanta, 1994, pp. 231–41.
——*Songs of Wisdom and Circles of Dance: Hymns of the Satpanth Ismā'īlī Muslim Saint, Pīr Shams*. Albany, NY, 1995.
Kellogg, S.H. *A Grammar of the Hindi Language*. 3rd ed., London, 1938.
Khakee, G. 'The Dasa Avatāra of the Satpanthi Ismailis and Imam Shahis of Indo- Pakistan.' Ph.D. thesis, Harvard University, 1972.
Khan, Dominique-Sila. *Conversions and Shifting Identities: Ramdev Pir and the Ismailis in Rajasthan*. New Delhi, 1997.
Khan, F.A. *Banbhore*. Karachi, 1976.
Krishna, Lajwanti Rama. *Panjabi Sufi Poets A.D. 1460–1900*. Repr. ed., Karachi, 1977.
Khan, Mohammad Ishaq. *Kashmir's Transition to Islam: The Role of Muslim Rishis, 15th–18th Century*. New Delhi, 1994.
Lord, Albert. *Singer of Tales*. Cambridge, Mass., 1968.
Maclean, Derryl. *Religion and Society in Arab Sind*. Leiden, 1989.
Madelung, Wilferd. 'Ismā'īliyya,' *EI2*, vol. 4, pp. 198–206.
——'Khodja,' *EI2*, vol. 5, pp. 25–7.
Mahesh, M.S. *The Historical Development of Mediaeval Hindi Prosody*. Bhagalpur, 1964.
Meeks, Wayne A. 'The Image of the Androgyne: Some Uses of a Symbol in Early Christianity,' *History of Religions* 13, no. 3 (1974), pp. 165–208.
Menant, D. 'Les Khodjas du Guzarate,' *Revue du Monde Musulman*, 10 (1910), pp. 214–32; 406–24.
Mohamed, al-Waiz Sultanali. *Wonderful Tradition: Transliteration of Holy Ginans*. Kenya, 1966.
Moir (Noorally), Zawahir. *Catalogue of Khojkī Manuscripts in the Collection*

of the Institute of Ismaili Studies. Unpublished ms., London, n.d.

Nanji, Azim. *The Nizārī Ismā'īlī Tradition in the Indo-Pakistan Subcontinent.* Delmar, NY, 1978.

——'Ismā'īlism,' in S.H. Nasr, ed., *Islamic Spirituality: Foundations.* New York, 1987, pp. 179–98, 432–3.

———'*Sharī'at* and *Ḥaqīqat*: Continuity and Synthesis in the Nizārī Ismā'īlī Muslim Tradition', in K.P. Ewing, ed., *Sharī'at and Ambiguity in South Asian Islam.* Berkeley and Los Angeles, 1988, pp. 63–76.

Nanjiani, S. *Khojā Vrttānt.* Ahmadabad, 1892.

Noorally, Zawahir. 'Ginans: Our Wonderful Tradition,' mimeographed paper. Vancouver, n.d.

——*Catalogue of Khojkī Manuscripts in the Collection of the Ismailia Association for Pakistan.* Unpublished ms., Karachi, 1971.

Orr, W.G. *A Sixteenth Century Indian Mystic.* London, 1947.

Pandiyāt-i javānmardī or 'Advices of Manliness'. Ed. and trans. by W. Ivanow. Leiden, 1953.

Pollock, Sheldon. 'India in the Vernacular Millenium: Literary Culture and Polity, 1000–1500,' paper presented at the Center for International Affairs South Asia Seminar, Harvard University, 1997.

Poonawala, Ismail K. *Biobibliography of Ismā'īlī Literature.* Malibu, Calif., 1977.

Prinsep, J. 'Note on *A Grammar of the Sindhi Language dedicated to the Rt. Honourable Sir Robert Grant, Governor of Bombay by W.H. Whalen Esq.*,' *JASB*, 6 (1837), pp. 347–54.

Qureshi, Ishtiaq H. *The Muslim Community of the Indo-Pakistan Subcontinent (610–1947).* Karachi, 1977.

Qureshi, Regula. *Sufi Music of India and Pakistan. Sound, Context and Meaning in Qawwali.* Cambridge, 1986.

Ramanujan, A.K. 'Three Hundred *Rāmāyanas*: Five Examples and Three Thoughts on Translation,' in Paula Richman, ed., *Many Rāmāyanas: The Diversity of a Narrative Tradition in South Asia.* Delhi, 1994, pp. 22–49.

Rinehart, Robin. 'The Portable Bullhe Shah: Biography, Authorship, and Categorization in the Study of Punjabi Sufi Poetry,' paper presented at the Seventh International Conference on Early Literature in New Indo-Aryan Languages, Venice, 1997.

Roy, Asim. 'The Pīr Tradition: A Case Study in Islamic Syncretism in Traditional Bengal,' in Fred Clothey, ed., *Images of Man: Religion and the Historical Process in South Asia.* Madras, 1982, pp. 112–41.

——*The Islamic Syncretistic Tradition in Bengal.* Princeton, NJ, 1983.

Sachedina, Abdulaziz. 'Khojas,' in John L. Esposito, ed., *Oxford Encyclopedia of the Modern Islamic World.* Oxford, 1995, vol. 2, pp. 423–27.

Sadik Ali, Mumtaz Ali Tajddin.'Sayyida Bibi Imam Begum,' *Hidayat* (July 1989), pp. 16–21.

Schimmel, Annemarie. 'The Influence of Sufism on Indo-Muslim Poetry,' in Joseph P. Strelka, ed., *Anagogic Qualities of Literature.* University Park, PA, 1971, pp. 181–210.

——'*Sindhi Literature*,' in J. Gonda, ed., *A History of Indian Literature.* Wiesbaden, 1974.

——*Mystical Dimensions of Islam.* Chapel Hill, NC, 1975.

——*Pain and Grace: A Study of Two Mystical Writers of Eighteenth Century Muslim India.* Leiden, 1976.

——*The Triumphal Sun: A Study of the Works of Jalāloddīn Rumi.* Rev. ed., London, 1980.

——'Reflections on Popular Muslim Poetry,' *Contributions to Asian Studies,* 17 (1982), pp. 17–26.

——*As Through a Veil: Mystical Poetry in Islam.* New York, 1982.

——*And Muhammad is His Messenger.* Chapel Hill, NC, 1985.

——*My Soul is a Woman: The Feminine in Islam.* New York, 1997.

Shackle, Christopher. *From Wuch to Southern Lahnda, A Century of Siraiki Studies in English.* Multan, 1984.

——and Zawahir Moir. *Ismaili Hymns from South Asia: An Introduction to the Ginans.* London, 1992.

Shorter Encyclopedia of Islam. ed. H.A.R. Gibb and J.H. Kramers. Leiden, 1953.

Slochower, Harry. *Mythopoesis.* Detroit, 1970.

Smith, Wilfred C. 'The Crystallization of Religious Communities in Mughul India,' in M. Minovi and I. Afshar, ed., *Yād-Nāme-ye Irānī-ye Minorsky.* Tehran, 1969, pp. 1–24.

Stack, G. *A Grammar of the Sindhi Language.* Bombay, 1849.

Stern, S.M. 'Ismāʿīlī Propaganda and Fatimid Rule in Sind,' *Islamic Culture,* 23 (1949), pp. 298–307, reprinted in S.M. Stern, *Studies in Early Ismāʿīlism.* Jerusalem and Leiden, 1983, pp. 177–88.

Trumpp, E. *Grammar of the Sindhi Language.* Leipzig, 1872.

Underhill, Evelyn. *Mysticism. A Study in the Nature and Development of Man's Spiritual Consciousness.* 12th ed., New York, 1961.

Vaudeville, Charlotte. *Kabir.* Vol. 1. Oxford, 1974.

——'Kabir and the Interior Religion,' *History of Religions,* 3 (1964), pp. 191–201.

——'Sant Mat: Santism as the Universal Path to Sanctity,' in Karine

Schomer and W.H. McLeod, ed., *The Sants: Studies in the Devotional Tradition of India.* Berkeley and Delhi, 1987, pp. 21–40.

Velji, D. 72 *Ginans. Part I: Transliteration of Holy Ginans.* Nairobi, 1972.

Wallīullāh, Shāh. *Tafhīmāt al-ilāhiyya,* ed. Ghulam Mustafa al-Qasimi. 2 vols. Hyderabad, Sind, 1967–70.

Walker, Paul E. 'Abū Ya'qūb al-Sijistānī and the Development of Ismaili Neoplatonism.' Ph.D. thesis, University of Chicago, 1974.

——*Early Philosophical Shiism: The Ismaili Neoplatonism of Abū Ya'qūb al-Sijistānī.* Cambridge, 1993.

——*Abū Ya'qūb al-Sijistānī: Intellectual Missionary.* London, 1996.

Index

Adam 59
Aga Khan III, Sir Ṣulṭān Muḥammad Shāh 1, 30
Aga Khan IV, Prince Karīm al-Ḥusaynī 2, 55, 75
Ahmad, Aziz 6
Aḥmad Shāh 86
Aiglemont (France) 3
Alamūt 14
'Alī b. Abī Ṭālib 55, 64, 71, 75, 87, 137, 138
Alādīn Ghulām Ḥusayn 132
allāh toāhār (*tohār*) 138
Allana, G.A. 41, 112, 113, 116, 122, 130
Amir Khusrau 66
Angad, Gurū 106
Anjudān (central Iran) 14
Arabic 6, 10, 16, 25, 26, 27, 30, 31, 35, 37, 38, 44, 63, 73, 75, 82, 84, 87, 101, 102, 104, 105, 108, 110, 111, 114, 115, 116, 124, 125, 127, 128, 129, 138, 142, 143
Ardhā-Nāgārī script 101, 124
Arusha (Tanzania) 13
Australia 26
avatāra (incarnation) 8, 9, 36

Bahā al-Dīn Zakāriyyā 4
Bahmanwā (al-Manṣūra) 101
Balabailān language 106
Bangladesh 3
Banyāṅ script 102 , 124
bārahmāsa genre ('twelve months') 66
bāṭin (the esoteric) 30, 56, 74
Bendrey, V.S. 105, 142
Bengal 9, 19, 30, 110
Bengali language 5, 110
Berber 16
Bhadneshwar 132
bhajans 26
bhaktas 4, 12
bhakti literature/tradition 11, 12, 26, 29, 31, 65, 73, 90, 92
Bhambhore 101
bhar joban (bloom of youth) 60
bhanitā ('signature verse') 87, 88, 89, 90, 91

Bhatias of Sind 92
al-Bīrūnī 101, 124
Bodīā script 103, 126
Bombay 3, 44, 108, 128, 132, 136
Brahma 156
brāhmins (priestly class) 11
Burma 109
Burton, Sir Richard 102, 104, 125
Burushaski 26

Canada 26, 72
cāliha akharī (forty letters) 122n, 128 *see also* Khojkī
caste system 11, 17, 18
copḍā (manuscripts) 130
caupāī metre 38, 52n
Central Asia 2, 3
Chamīalī script 104
Chishti Sufi order 8, 19, 66
chorī (sacred space) 62, 158
Corbin, Henry 8, 59
Cutch *see* Kutch
Cutchi *see* Kachchi

dā'īs 14, 16
Dakhani Urdu 110
Dakkani 19
darshan (vision) 47, 77, 161
dās, dāsī (slave) 58
da'wa (mission) 3, 14, 15
Day of *alastu* 60
Deccan 19, 110
Delhi 103
Devanāgarī alphabet/script 106, 108, 113, 114, 117
Devrāj, Lāljī 108–9
dharma (correct conduct) 11
dhikr 28, 78
Dhru Kathā 144
dīdār (vision) 57, 58, 74, 78, 79
Ḍogrī script 104
dohā metre 38
Draupadī 45
dūhāg (unmarried state) 60, 61, 154

East Africa 3, 13, 26, 44, 71, 73, 125
Eaton, Richard 19, 110
Egypt 3, 14
English 73, 74, 88
Ernst, Carl 19
Europe 26, 92

Fāṭima 2, 36, 55, 75, 93, 122, 173
Faraizi movement 30
Fatimids 8, 14

Gandhi, S.S. 106
Gangji, Ismail 41, 42
garbī (genre) 17, 38, 52n
garbo 52n, 73
Ghadīr Khumm 75
ghazal (love poem) 73
Ghulām 'Alī Shāh, Sayyid 132
Ghulām-i Ḥusain Chāpākhānu (Bombay) 108
*ginān*s 6, 10, 13, 15, 16, 17, 20, 49n; *bhanitā*s of; bride soul symbolism in 55–66; characteristics 26; and conversion 20; depiction of Quranic primordial covenant (day of *alastu*) 59–60; language and vocabulary 36–8; manuscript tradition (see also Khojkī) 42–4, 92; motifs

44–7; as oral/aural scripture 27; oral transmission 40, 42, 92–3; origins/authorship 31–5, 84, 85–94; and 'portability' 12, 36; prosody and verse forms 38–40; and Qur'an 29–31; mystical aspects 54–66 *passim*; 83; *rāgas* of 27, 58, 40, 43, 83; recitation of 40–2; 83; role in religious life 26–31, 83; spiritual marriage as a symbol in 54–5, 58
gīts (devotional songs) 71–9; characteristics 73, 82; depiction of Imam 74–7; languages 73; provenance of 72, 85; relationship to ginān tradition 72; symbol of *virahinī* in 76–8
gnosticism 8, 59, 136, 144
gopī (cow-maid) 8
Grammar of the Sindhi Language (Stack) 102, 125
granths 33, 34
Grierson, George 102, 103, 126
Gujarat, Gujarati, Gujaratis 2, 3, 15, 25, 26, 32, 33, 35, 36, 38, 39, 40, 41, 43, 44, 46, 47, 52, 55, 61, 64, 71, 73, 75, 76, 77, 78, 79, 80, 83, 97, 102, 103, 105, 106, 109, 110, 111, 112, 113, 114, 115, 116, 118, 124, 125, 126, 128, 129, 131, 134, 137, 138, 139, 140, 141, 142, 143, 144, 148, 149; script 37, 44, 109, 128
Gurmukhī script 105, 106, 110, 125
guru (spiritual preceptor) 12, 32, 47, 84, 88
Guru Granth Ṣāḥib 88

Hardy, Peter 18
Harishcandra 45, 87
Ḥasan, Imam 75
Ḥasan Kabīr al-Dīn, Pīr 33, 85, 87
Ḥasan Shāh 91
Ḥusayn, Imam 137
Hawley, John 88, 89, 92
Ḥāẓir Imām 3
Hindi 8, 66, 73
Hindu culture/civilization 5, 6, 13, 15, 16, 18, 19, 29, 30, 31, 32, 35, 36, 37, 38, 40, 45, 47, 65, 66, 76, 82, 87, 100, 101, 102, 105, 106, 124, 125, 126, 144
'Hinduism' 4
Hülegü 14
Hunza 2

Ibn 'Arabī 66
Ibn al-Nadīm 101
'id al-adha 73
'id al-fitr 73
Imam, Ismaili 8, 55, 56, 74, 78, 84; birthday of 28, 46, 72; as descendant of Prophet Muḥammad 2, 55; as depicted in *gīt* tradition 57; as interpreter of Qur'an; as spiritual guide 77; relationship of disciples to 66n, 74, 76
Imamate 64, 74
Imām-Begum, Sayyida 58, 91
Imām-Dīn 87
Imām-Shāh, Pīr 33, 34, 85, 86, 90

Imām Shāhī(s) 34, 85
India, Indians 1, 3, 5, 8, 9, 10, 11, 12, 16, 85
Indic languages/vernaculars 7, 10, 13, 31, 57
Iran 3, 14, 15, 26, 32, 36, 46, 65, 84, 91
Ismāʿīl, Imam 2
Ismaili Printing Press (Khoja Sindhi Press) 44, 109
Ismaili Tariqa and Religious Education Boards 72, 107
Ismailis *see* Nizari Ismaili tradition, Satpanth
Ithnāʿasharīs (Twelvers) 2
Ivanow, Wladimir 6, 15, 16, 17, 27, 33, 34, 42, 85, 86, 91, 107

Jaʿfar al-Ṣādiq, Imam 2
Jaisī, Muḥammad 38
jamāʿat (congregation) 58
jamāʿat-khāna (house of congregation) 25, 27, 28, 33, 41, 42, 83
Jeram, Maganlal Rugnath 13
Jinnah, Muhammad Ali 1
jnāna (knowledge) 25
Junagadh 41, 42

Kachchi 36
kāfī (*rāga* genre) 38, 73
Kahak 50
Kānipā 40
Kanji, Anaar 72
kāpāītī (spinning song) 38
Karachi 107
Kashmir 7, 106
Kassam, Tazim 6, 15, 83, 86
Kera 132
Keshwani, Pyarali 86
Khakee, Gulshan 116, 117
Khan, Dominique-Sila 7, 16, 17
Khan, M.I. 7
Khoja(s) 2, 26, 27, 33, 82–5, 92, 95n, 118n
Khoja Sindhi Printing Press 44, 108, 109
Khojkī manuscripts 129–41; binding styles and practices 133–5; collections of 107, 130–2; colophons 132, 138, 140; contents of 131; foliation and pagination of 142–3; Harvard University collection of 107, 131; internal appearance and layout of texts 136–9; paper and watermarks 136; recording of dates 140; scribes 140–1; *tafasīlo* (table of contents) 139
Khojkī script 13, 27, 92, 109, 110; and *lākanā* (medial vowel) 104, 127; its decline 128–9; inadequacies of consonant system 111, 114–16; inadequacies of orthography 111, 116–17; inadequacies of vowel system 112–14; origins 100–7, 111; parallels with Gurmukhī script 105–7; relationship to Laṇḍā alphabets 43, 102–4; representation of Arabic sounds in 108, 114–15; significance of literature in 110
Khudawadī script 104
Khuldabad 19
Krishna 8, 9, 11, 12, 65
Kutch (Cutch) 3

Laṇḍā alphabets 102–4, 105, 107; deficiencies of 42–3, 103–4
Latin (Roman) alphabet 44
League of Nations 1
Lewis, Bernard 6
Lohāṇā 101
Lohāṇākī (Lārī) script 101
Lord, Albert 93

Madelung, Wilferd 6
Mahājanī (Mārwārī) script 102
Mahrattas 43, 106, 148–9n, 125
Makhdūm-i Jahāniyān Jahāngasht (d. 1385) 9
Malwārī script 101, 124
Manichaean 8
Marathi language 106
Mārwārīs 102, 103
marṣīyā (elegies) 144
Mathnawī (Mawlānā Jalāl ad-Dīn Rūmī) 30
Mīrābāī 65, 88
Moḍī script 42, 106, 125
Moir, Zawahir 86, 92
Momnas 2
Mongols 14
Muḥammad, the prophet 2, 8, 9, 12, 28, 36, 45, 55, 66, 71, 75, 137, 142, 144
Multan (Punjab) 4, 32, 33
Multani (Siraiki) 36
Mundra 132
murīd (disciple) 56
Mūsā al-Kāẓim, Imam (Ithna ʿAshari) 6
al-Musta'lī, Imam (Bohra) 2
al-Mustanṣir, Imam-Caliph 2, 14

nafs al-ammāra (the commanding soul) 60
nafs al-muṭmaʿinna (the soul at peace) 60
Nakuru Indian Association 13
Nānak, Guru 88
Nanji, Azim 6, 15, 34, 38, 85, 92
Nar Muḥammad Shāh, Pīr/Sayyid 34, 86
Nath yogis 4, 11
Navrūz (Iranian new year) 28, 46
Navsari (Gujarat) 33
Neoplatonism 8
nikāḥ (marriage ceremony) 60
nūr (light) 25, 56, 57, 74, 75, 78, 79
Nizār, Imam 2, 14
Nizari Ismailism 1, 4, 5, 13, 14, 25, 26, 27, 31, 55, 71 *see also* Satpanth
Noorally, Zawahir (Zawahir Moir) 86, 92, 130

Oxford English Dictionary 88

pada 26, 87
Pakistan 3, 26, 44
Pandava brothers 45, 87
Pandiyāt-i Jawānmardī 34
panth (path) 50n
Persian 8, 9, 10, 15, 16, 26, 28, 30, 35, 36, 37, 39, 44, 82, 87, 91, 100, 101, 102, 105, 124, 125, 127
Perso-Arabic tradition 8, 65; writing system 104, 105, 110
pīrs 4, 5, 14, 16, 17, 26, 32, 33, 50n, 51n, 57, 65, 66, 84, 89, 90, 91, 92
pothā (manuscripts) 133
prabhātīya genre 40

Punjab, Punjabi 2, 4, 8, 12, 26, 32, 33, 36, 37, 42, 43, 64, 66, 100, 102, 105, 106, 111, 125, 126, 141
puthī literature 9

Qādirī Sufi order 86, 91
Qāsim Shāh, Imam 33
qawwālī (S. Asian Sufi devotional songs) 28, 66, 73
Qur'an 2, 25, 28, 29, 30, 46, 56, 59, 73, 74, 75, 83, 84
Qureshi, Ishtiaq Hussein 16

Rādhā 8
Ravidās 88
Recreation Club Institute 109
Religious Education Board for Pakistan 107
Renaissance 92
Rūmī, Mawlānā Jalāl al-Dīn 30, 33, 65
Rinehart, Robin 12
Risālo (Shāh 'Abdu'l Laṭif) 31
Roy, Asim 110
Royal Asiatic Society (Bombay branch) 102
Rukn al-Dīn Khurshāh, Imam 14

Sabri brothers 75
sādhanā (meditation) 11
Ṣadr al-Dīn, Pīr 30, 33, 57, 58, 85, 86, 87, 90, 91, 101, 104, 126
Sahadeva 87
Saljuqs 14
Sanskrit 11, 25, 30, 37, 84, 105, 106, 127
sant movement 4, 11, 12, 29, 92; literature/tradition 31
Ṣarrāfī script 103, 126
Sarasvatī 36
satāḍās ('heptads') 59
Satgūr Nūr, Pīr 32, 85, 87
satguru (true preceptor) 11
Satpanth (Nizari Ismaili tradition in South Asia) 2, 31, 32; conversion to 13–20; its contexts 3–13
sayyids 34, 50, 86
Sayyid Imām-Shāh 87
Schimmel, Annemarie 65
Shackle, Christopher 86, 92
Shāh 'Abdu'l Laṭif 31
Shāh Walīullāh 9
Shakti 36
Shams, Pīr 17, 33, 85, 86, 91
Shams-i Tabrīzī 33
Shamsis 2
Shiʿism Shiʿis 2, 6, 36, 47, 55, 64, 66, 71, 74, 75, 87, 137, 138, 142, 144
Shivājī 42, 106
Sikh Gurudwara Arusha (Tanzania) 13
Sikhs, Sikhism 13, 29, 75, 105, 106, 107, 110
Sind, Sindhi, Sindhis 2, 3, 8, 15, 26, 31, 32, 33, 36, 37, 38, 42, 43, 64, 66, 73, 74, 76, 100, 101, 102, 103, 104, 106, 108, 109, 110, 111, 114, 115, 116, 124, 125, 126, 127, 128, 129, 138, 140, 141, 144; 'Sindhi' as term for religious education classes 110
sī ḥarfī ('thirty letters' genre) 38
sloka (epic stanza) 38
Smith, Wilfred Cantwell 5
South Asia 3, 84

Stack, George 102, 113, 125
Sufi, Sufis 4, 8, 10, 12, 18, 19, 29, 65, 86, 91; folk poetry/literature 19, 20, 26, 65, 66, 92; orders 4, 14, 19, 32; as missionaries 18–19; *shaykhs* 12, 16
Suhrawardi (Sufi) order 4
sūhāg (marital union) 60, 61, 154
Sunni Islam 4, 14
Sūrdās 38, 88
Swahili 73

tek (*varaṇī*, refrain) 38
taʿwīl (interpretation) 56
Tāj al-Dīn, Pīr 33, 90
Taj, Kamal 72
Taj Kavi 72
takhalluṣ (pen name) 39
Ṭankrī (Tākarī) script 102

Tantric beliefs 6
taqiyya (precautionary dissimulation) 4, 10, 15
tārāb (musical tradition) 73
Tārīkh-i Imāmat (The History of the Imamat) 75
Tejpar, Aziz 13
The Institute of Ismaili Studies 107

Trumpp, Ernst 102, 104, 124
Tulsīdās 38
Turkish 3
Turko-Persian 9

Ucch (Punjab) 4, 33
Underhill, Evelyn 54
United Kingdom 3
United States 26, 73, 92
Urdu 66, 73, 75, 77, 109, 110, 114; script 44

Vaishnavite 10, 65, 111
Vāṇiāī script 102, 126
Vedas 11
vel (addendum) 39
ventīs (supplications) 47
Vimras 91
vinaya (petitionary genre) 47
viraha (love-in-separation) 8, 47, 76, 167
virahinī (yearning woman) 8, 12, 66, 76, 77, 78, 79
Vishnu 9, 12

Walker, Paul 7

ẓāhir (exoteric) 56, 30
Zanzibar 72, 73
Zoroastrian 8

Index of *Gināns*

Ab terī mahobat lāgī 40
Āe rahem rahemān 40
Allāh ek khasam subuka 87
Amar te āyo more shāhjījo 37, 45
Bāvan Boḍh 46
Bāvān Ghāṭī 45
Brahmā Gāyantri 45
Brahmā Prakāsh 46, 86
Būjh Niranjan 39, 46, 86, 91, 92, 111, 112, 113, 116, 160
Darshan dīyo morā nāth 58
Dasa Avatāra 31, 49n, 111, 112, 114, 116
Dhan dhan ājno dahaḍo 28
Hans Hanslī nī Vartā 39
Hasan Kabīr-adīn ane Kānipā no Samvād 39
Huṅ re pīasī 47, 69, 161
Kalām-i Mawlā 87, 163
Kesrī siṅh swarūp bhulāyo 39
Moman Chetāmaṇī 39, 46
Nakalank Gītā 45
Navaroznā din sohāmaṇā *28*
Putlā 45
Rūḥānī Visāl 58, 153–9
Sakhī mārī ātama nā odhār 167
Sāt swargnā kāīṁ khuliyā che dwār 28
Satgūr nā Vivā 45
Sī Ḥarfī 86
Soh Kiriya 46
Swāmī rājo more man thī na visereji 58, 64
Tamakū sadhāre soh dīn 57, 159
Ūṅcā re koṭ bahu vecana 69, 165
Ūṅch thī āyo 45